Challenging
Aphasia Therapies

Challenging Aphasia Therapies

Broadening the discourse and extending the boundaries

**edited by
Judith Felson Duchan
and Sally Byng**

Ψ Psychology Press
Taylor & Francis Group
HOVE AND NEW YORK

First published 2004 by Psychology Press
27 Church Road, Hove, East Sussex BN3 2FA

Simultaneously published in the USA and Canada
by Psychology Press
29 West 35th Street, New York, NY 10001

Psychology Press is a part of the Taylor & Francis Group

Copyright © 2004 Psychology Press

Typeset in Janson by Graphicraft Limited, Hong Kong
Printed and bound in Great Britain by TJ International Ltd, Padstow, Cornwall

The publisher makes no representation, express or implied, with regard to
the accuracy of the information contained in this book and cannot accept any
legal responsibility or liability for any errors or omissions that may be made.

British Library Cataloguing in Publication Data
A catalogue record for this book is available from the British Library

Library of Congress Cataloging-in-Publication Data
Challenging aphasia therapies: broadening the discourse and extending
the boundaries / edited by Judith Felson Duchan and Sally Byng.
    p. cm.
  ISBN 1-84169-505-X
  1. Aphasia.   2. Aphasia – Treatment.   I. Duchan, Judith F.
  II. Byng, Sally, 1956–

RC425.C485 2004
616.85′5206—dc22

                                                        2003022456

ISBN 1-84169-505-X

To Kay Glendinning, visionary and catalyst

Contents

Notes on contributors

Sally Byng is Chief Executive and Director of Research for Connect—the Communication Disability Network. She was head of the Department of Language & Communication Science at City University and Professor of Communication Disability there. She is a speech and language therapist by background and has been in research for most of her career. Her research has focused on developing, describing, and evaluating therapies for people with communication difficulties after stroke, as well as understanding the experience of living with communication disability. She has published widely on these topics, editing books, contributing chapters and articles, as well as giving presentations and teaching internationally on a regular basis.

Judith Felson Duchan is Emeritus Professor from the State University of New York at Buffalo. She has published widely in language pathology. Her particular emphases have been on autism, pragmatics, childhood language, and aphasia. She is consultant for Connect, the Communication Disability Network in London and for the Aphasia Institute in North York, Canada. Her current projects involve writing a history of intervention approaches in speech-language pathology in the US, and creating, researching, and promulgating client-centred, life-participation approaches to support those with communication disabilities and their affiliates.

Roberta J. Elman, PhD, CCC-SLP, BC/NCD, is President/CEO and Founder of the Aphasia Center of California, an independent, nonprofit organization currently providing conversational, reading/writing, caregiver, and recreational groups for more than 90 individuals with aphasia and their families in the Northern California Bay Area. Prior to beginning the Aphasia Center of California, Dr Elman was Co-Director of Rehabilitation at an outpatient medical rehabilitation center. She also served as Director of the Speech-Language Department. Dr Elman has more than 20 years of experience in the assessment and treatment of neurogenic communication disorders. She is the author of numerous professional publications and is the editor of a recently published book for Butterworth-Heinemann entitled *Group Treatment of Neurogenic Communication Disorders:*

The Expert Clinician's Approach. Dr Elman is on the steering committee of the Academy of Neurologic Communication Disorders and Sciences and serves on the ASHA subcommittee on Scope of Practice in Speech-Language Pathology. She has also recently served as associate coordinator of the ASHA Steering Committee for Special Interest Division 2: Neurophysiology and Neurogenic Speech and Language Disorders.

Audrey L. Holland, PhD, CCC, BC/NCD, is Regents' Professor of Speech and Hearing Sciences at the University of Arizona. She has served on the Advisory Council for the US National Institute on Deafness and other Communication Disorders (NIH) and is currently a member of the Secretary's Advisory Committee on Prosthetics and Special Disabilities, US Department of Veterans Affairs. She is Associate Editor of the *Journal of Communication Disorders*, and a recipient of the Honors of the American Speech, Language Hearing Association. She received the Clinical Achievement Award from the Academy of Neurologic Communication Disorders and Sciences, and the Professional Achievement Award from the Council of (US) Graduate Programs in Communication Sciences and Disorders. She has published over 140 research articles, book chapters, and reviews, has edited three books, and developed the test of functional communication called CADL (recently revised as CADL-2 with Davida Fromm and Carol Frattalli).

David Howard is a Professor in the Department of Speech at Newcastle University. Since 1972 he has been working with people with aphasia as both a therapist and a researcher, exploring how the understanding of the nature of language disorders can be used to improve and develop aphasia therapy. Over this time he has worked in rehabilitation units, at the Psychology Departments at UCL and Birkbeck, and since 1996 in Newcastle. He and his colleagues are currently investigating how intensive group and individual treatment can be combined to address both the underlying language problems and the process of self-realization as an aphasic person.

Aura Kagan is currently Programme, Research and Education Director at the Aphasia Institute (incorporating the Pat Arato Aphasia Centre)—an agency dedicated to service, awareness, education, research, and advocacy for all those affected by aphasia. She has been instrumental in the development of Supported Conversation for Adults with Aphasia™—an innovative tool for increasing communicative access to life participation. In recent years Aura Kagan has made numerous presentations and published articles describing this approach and its applications.

Sinéad Kennedy Sinéad Kennedy trained as a speech and language therapist on the Master's programme in the Department of Speech at Newcastle University. Here she experienced intensive therapy with people with aphasia at the Newcastle Aphasia Clinic, under the guidance of David

Howard and Julie Morris. She is currently working as a Speech and Language Therapist in child and adolescent psychiatry in her native Dublin. Her current focus is the introduction of a speech and language therapy service to a high support unit for adolescents with emotional and behavioural difficulties.

Jon Lyon is the Director of Living with Aphasia, Inc., a non-profit agency dedicated to addressing the long-term needs of people confronting aphasia. He spends his professional time working directly with such individuals in everyday contexts to make their lives more productive, rewarding, and of choice. He has published numerous articles and book chapters on methods dealing with such intervention. He is the author of *Coping with Aphasia*, an in-depth chronology of facts and suggestions for minimizing the enduring effects of aphasia, and returning purpose and direction to daily life.

Julie Morris co-ordinates the Newcastle Aphasia Clinic at the University, a facility funded by the Tavistock Trust for Aphasia as a research project. The project examines the efficacy of intensive speech and language therapy for adults with aphasia. Julie completed her thesis in the Department of Psychology at York University with Sue Franklin and Andy Ellis. The work examined therapy with clients with auditory processing disorders. This remains an area of interest for her, along with other aspects of language processing in aphasia and exploring the therapy we use. She has held a variety of clinical and research posts and enjoys the challenge of attempting to combine clinical work with measuring efficacy of our intervention.

Claire Penn trained at the University of the Witwatersrand in South Africa. Soon thereafter she won a British Council Scholarship and spent some time in England (at Cambridge and Reading) developing her interests in linguistics and aphasia. On her return to South Africa, she taught at Wits University and gained her PhD on syntactic and pragmatic approaches to aphasia. She continued in this line of research, publishing on aspects of assessment and therapy in adult and child language and on sign language. Dr Penn is currently based in the United States at Case Western Reserve University. Throughout her career Dr Penn has always kept active in aphasia therapy, being the founder member of the Stroke Aid Society in South Africa and co-author of the book *Stroke: Caring and Coping*. She has been involved in advocacy groups and in the development of a national stroke consensus document. In addition to her university position (where she holds an endowed Chair) she has a private practice and acts as a consultant for a rehabilitation hospital.

Carole Pound is Director of Therapy and Education at Connect—the Communication Disability Network. Connect is a new national charity offering therapy, education, and training underpinned by research. Connect has developed from the work of the City Dysphasic Group at City

University, a therapy and support centre for people affected by long-term aphasia, where Carole was centre director for a number of years. Prior to this she worked as a speech and language therapist in acute and neuro-rehabilitation settings. Carole has co-written a range of publications about aphasia including *The Aphasia Handbook* and *Beyond Aphasia—therapies for living with communication disability.* She is co-editor of the *Aphasia Therapy File.*

Amy E. Ramage is an Adjunct Assistant Professor at San Diego State University and is the coordinator of the Aphasia Clinic there. She has worked as a speech-language pathologist in hospital and rehabilitation settings as well as in pre-schools and schools. She received her PhD from the University of Arizona where she was actively involved in the Aphasia Research Project, both as a clinician and a researcher. Her independent research has focused on understanding language breakdown in aphasia by exploring how normal people break down and adapt to breakdowns in language processing under stressed conditions. Her work is designed to develop a model of adaptation to processing impairments in aphasia and apply it to the development of new treatment paradigms.

Martha Taylor Sarno is Professor of Rehabilitation Medicine at the New York University School of Medicine and Director of the Speech-Language Pathology Department at the Rusk Institute of Rehabilitation Medicine. Professor Sarno has been dedicated to the study and treatment of acquired aphasia for several decades and has received many honours and awards in acknowledgement of her contributions to our understanding of the challenges of living with aphasia, ethical–moral issues, functional communication, and patient and family advocacy and education. In 1982 she was awarded a Doctor of Medicine *honoris causa* by the University of Göteborg, Sweden. She has edited several textbooks and is widely published in journals, book chapters, monographs, and publications intended for the patient and family. She is currently participating in a team working with the Hastings Center for Bioethics in a study of the ethical–moral issues encountered by the families of patients with aphasia secondary to head injury. Professor Sarno founded the National Aphasia Association, was a founding member of the Academy of Aphasia, and is Board Certified in Neurologic Communication Disorders.

Nina Simmons-Mackie is Professor of Communication Sciences and Disorders at Southeastern Louisiana University. She has worked for over 20 years as a speech-language pathologist in hospitals, home health, and outpatient services. She has served as a rehabilitation programme manager, speech pathology department director, clinical researcher, and university teacher. She obtained a PhD from Louisiana State University. She has received the Honors of the Louisiana Speech-Language-Hearing Association, and the Clinical Achievement Award of the ASHA Foundation and is a Fellow of the American Speech-Language-Hearing Association. Throughout her career she has focused on acquired adult communication disorders, particularly aphasia. Currently, her key areas of interest include aphasia therapy interactions, conversation in aphasia and related disorders, social models of management, and applications of qualitative research.

Introduction

This book is a challenge to established practices in aphasia therapy. Because it does not take the commonplace for granted, it serves to broaden the discourse and extend the boundaries of thinking about therapy. The authors challenge professionals to:

1   include considerations of moral and ethical responsibility in their practices;
2   focus on engagement in life as well as on amelioration of language impairments;
3   promote ways to identify relevant directions for therapy;
4   engage in reflexive thinking on how clinicians' identities influence their therapy choices;
5   engage in reflective thinking on issues such as power relationships in therapy, the impact of limited resources, and benefits and blindfolds created by clinical models.

The themes in this book were first raised at a conference in 2001 in the UK. The conference marked the opening in London of Connect, the Communication Disability Network. The authors, each of whom presented papers at this launch conference, argue here that the best therapies are conducted in a reflective environment wherein all are involved in the process of service delivery, including those with aphasia. Growing out of the authors' personal reflections, the chapters raise important issues for speech language therapists/pathologists and their clients with aphasia. Below is a chapter-by-chapter taste of the specific treats in store for readers.

Chapter 1. Challenging aphasia therapies
Sally Byng and Judith Felson Duchan
As editors, we introduce the book by highlighting what we take to be some of the challenging themes—ones that many of the authors touch upon. There are nine such themes:

1   Combining the personal and the professional
2   Challenging the tacit assumption of cure

3   Addressing time, resource, and system barriers to quality therapy
4   Providing enough time to attain personal change
5   Understanding that aphasia is more than a language impairment
6   Dealing with power relations during therapy
7   Recognizing misplaced therapies and identifying misguided therapists
8   Combining therapy, philosophy, and tools
9   Making room for reflective practices

In Chapter 1 we talk about the different challenges associated with these themes, and invite readers to reflect on their own practices as they engage in imaginary dialogues with the authors.

Chapter 2. Aphasia therapies: Historical perspectives and moral imperatives
Martha Taylor Sarno
The scale of the challenges being set out in this book is made plain right from the start by Martha Taylor Sarno, who reminds us that the enterprise of aphasia therapy relates to the "moral worth of humanness". She pulls no punches—providers of therapy are "members of a moral community seeking to empower and restore individuals to a meaningful life experience". And the challenge doesn't end there. She situates therapy as an ethical responsibility. Human freedom is at stake for people who have difficulty communicating. The moral imperatives for therapists that this stance implies are awesome but real. What is just as awesome, but in a different way, is that Martha Taylor Sarno has been upholding the moral and ethical challenges of aphasia therapy for over 50 years, publishing her first paper in 1951, through times when her perspective was not recognized or possibly even valued. But that has not made a difference to her view, and she has remained constant to her theme.

Her chapter takes a historical perspective on the thinking behind aphasia therapies. She confronts the tensions that exist between two approaches: the better researched and resourced approaches that focus on remedying the impairment, and approaches that address the role that society, the self, and social stigma play in making the processes of learning to live with aphasia even harder.

This author reveals the impact of the current culture and practice of health care in the United States on services to people with aphasia and contrasts that with the complexity of the process of learning to live with aphasia. She identifies the core of learning to live with aphasia as being about "transition and transformation". How can that be achieved in a very few prescribed sessions of therapy? She sounds an alarming note of caution: the current healthcare environment in the US may be permanently damaging the possibility of rendering care that is both relevant and responsible.

Chapter 3. Dare to be different: The person and the practice
Carole Pound
The challenges continue in Carole Pound's chapter, where she reveals the personal barriers she has faced on her journey both as a therapist and as

someone learning to live with disability. She provides a powerful and absorbing insider's perspective on the complexities of the "recovery" process—the conflicting, sometimes opposing and confusing factors that influence the process of adapting to a new life. She draws convincing parallels between learning to live with pain and the issues that people learning to live with aphasia are grappling with.

Her insider's perspective of both the therapist's mindset and the preoccupations of the "patient" enable us to see how conflicts can arise in the recovery and treatment process which might become barriers to the re-engagement with everyday life for people new to disability. The fact that these conflicts may not be articulated and may exist through tradition and familiarity underlines the value of reflective practice. Carole challenges the power dynamics underlying much rehabilitation practice, underscored by both the media and long-held perceptions of disability.

The chapter ends with a brief description of some tools for the therapist's toolbox which can enable therapy practice to facilitate a more positive perspective on disability, enable people to see and take up new directions, to take more control over their new lives, and to identify small changes that can have bigger impacts. The author provides insights on why the process of aphasia therapy can be so puzzling for the therapist too: the chapter should empower therapists to cope with the contradictions, anxieties, and ups and downs that they often face in partnering people who are learning to cope with unanticipated difference.

Chapter 4. Evolving treatment methods for coping with aphasia approaches that make a difference in everyday life
Jon Lyon
Dealing with the everyday, the substance of life, is a major theme in Jon Lyon's chapter. He begins with a reflection, in keeping with many of the chapters in this book, on the progression of the directions his therapies have taken during the course of his professional life. And he ends with a description of the life-discipline that he is applying to develop and enhance his own quality of life—using lessons learned from people with aphasia. In between, Jon Lyon challenges the traditions of aphasia therapy. He conceives of therapy as addressing "broken life systems". This enables him to convey a practical, problem-solving way in to focused, holistic therapy. He illustrates the provision of targeted activities that have wide implications, involving a variety of players in the aphasic person's life and with the person with aphasia playing an instrumental role in the implementation of his or her own therapy.

In this chapter one of the many challenges that Jon Lyon poses to the therapy community is to question concepts of coping currently being used. He suggests that coping is often portrayed as a long drawn out process, requiring many stages. Jon, in keeping with his focus on practical problem solving, views coping as dealing with the immediacy of the moment, with flexibility in dealing with life as both it and the person with aphasia change.

In the context of recognizing that for someone with aphasia life will never be the same again, Jon Lyon emphasizes the value of enabling the person with aphasia to address changes to key personal relationships.

Chapter 5. Context, culture, and conversation
Claire Penn

Claire Penn's introspection into the therapy journey is brave. In this chapter she describes both the journey she has taken as a therapist, leaving us with vivid accounts of the milestones that shook and shaped her perspective on the role of aphasia therapist, and the journey of one particular woman with aphasia, Valerie Rosenberg, with whom she worked. The two voices that come through in the chapter, Claire Penn's and Mrs Rosenberg's, convey the collaborative nature of the process of therapy, a collaboration that rarely comes across in published accounts of therapy. The direction and focus of therapy seems more usually to be determined by the therapist rather than by a genuinely joint endeavour.

We describe the introspection as brave because Claire Penn lays open to inspection not only the therapy but also the companionship and support that she offered to Mrs Rosenberg and gained from her. In the prevailing positivist tradition of writing about therapy, few authors would risk describing this holistic approach to providing a service to someone learning to live life with aphasia. However Claire Penn was led in what she provided largely by the explicitly expressed needs of Mrs Rosenberg, which, significantly, resulted in the breadth of issues that they addressed together. She ends by offering some perspectives on the characteristics required of an aphasia therapist, memorably exhorting therapists to realize both that "perkiness is not next to godliness" and, more soberly, that therapists need to "accept ambiguity, uncertainty, and change, for after all that is what life is".

Chapter 6. Just kidding! Humour and therapy for aphasia
Nina Simmons-Mackie

Nina Simmons-Mackie is serious about being funny. Her chapter concerns how to "do" humour in therapy and she provides a rich catalogue of tools for the therapist to use in "doing humour" in therapy. She illustrates vividly how therapy is so much more than task or activity. Therapy also relies heavily on the dynamics between therapist and person with aphasia. Humour, as Nina conveys, is a wonderfully rich vehicle for these dynamics. If tasks and activities are the "engine" of therapy, then we learn that humour can be the critical oil that keeps the engine turning. But more than that it can be powerful as a therapeutic tool in its own right, reaching the parts that other therapies cannot reach.

Instead of seeing humour as an optional extra to the serious business of communication work, we see that humour in and of itself can effect critical change. Many therapists might regard the ability to use humour therapeut-ically as being dependent on the personality of the therapist. Intriguingly,

Nina Simmons-Mackie provides us with a range of techniques to use, which could be learned and adopted by any therapist. Therapists might find the concept of developing a "humour assessment" both liberating and a welcome change from the usual routine of assessment construction!

A theme running throughout the chapter is of the inappropriate use of professionalism, which she dubs "terminal professionalism". We challenge any therapist who reads this chapter to resist trying out some of the wealth of ideas within it.

Chapter 7. Learning from Roger Ross: A clinical journey
Audrey L. Holland and Amy E. Ramage

The impact that a person with aphasia can have on both the therapy and the therapist comes through strongly in Audrey Holland and Amy Ramage's chapter. Here Audrey describes the therapy that she undertook with Roger Ross, who appears as a charismatic and powerful man. Roger Ross's skills in self-diagnosis, identifying what he needed in therapy and campaigning for and developing long-term support systems for people with aphasia, demonstrate the importance of sharing power in the therapy relationship. Audrey's preparedness to listen, to respond, and to share the role of developing the content of therapy with Roger Ross enables them to engage together in effective therapy.

These authors, by example, ask clinicians to attend to how the person with aphasia perceives his or her difficulties, and what will help the person to address those difficulties. Those perceptions can enable the therapist to short-circuit the more traditional process of professionally led formal assessment. Careful listening and space given for the person with aphasia to explore can lead to conclusions about what to address in a more creative way. The matching of the therapist's ingenuity, and preparedness to try something unfamiliar, in response to the aphasic person's insights can lead to innovative and effective therapy. The real meaning of therapeutic partnership and "patient-centredness" (a much misused phrase) comes across vividly in this chapter. The philosophy underlying Audrey Holland's therapy is clear—that of maximizing the strengths of the person with aphasia. She and her co-author illustrate in this chapter how her principle governs her way of proceeding in her work with people with aphasia.

Chapter 8. Group treatment and jazz: Some lessons learned
Roberta J. Elman

The theme of mutual engagement in therapy with the person with aphasia is also central in Roberta Elman's chapter. It is evident in a number of issues she covers. She is frank in looking back over her career as a therapist, wishing that she had, on occasion, worked differently. She remembers feeling compelled to do highly structured therapies when she felt much more inclined to listen to people and engage with them where they were, in what mattered to them.

The theme of her chapter, likening the process of undertaking therapy for aphasia to the process of musical improvisation, provides a helpful image for therapists thinking about how to "do" therapy. The process of therapy as she describes it is very liberated. She says that it may not even feel as if therapy is being done, particularly in group therapy, the medium that she uses predominantly in her work. Therapists let the group take its own direction. This means that the therapist must trust people to develop the therapy in the way that is most useful for them. Roberta challenges therapists to think about whose needs *really* determine the course of therapy: those of the therapist (and perhaps the organizations and systems within which they work) or those of the person with aphasia.

Chapter 9. The value of therapy: What counts?
Julie Morris, David Howard, and Sinead Kennedy
Challenges to what we perceive to be success or improvement in therapy are offered in the chapter by Julie Morris, David Howard, and Sinead Kennedy, raising issues about "what we value in change". They describe the work that they undertook with an individual, in a setting where they could provide therapy on both a one-to-one and a group basis. What will be striking for many readers is that this therapy began when the person, Lawrence, had lived with aphasia for 7 years. The authors begin the chapter by describing the nature of the impairments that Lawrence featured, and then relate it to the therapy that they designed. As in the case of Roger Ross in Chapter 7, the areas that the therapy addressed were shaped not just by test results, but also by the perceptions of both Lawrence and his wife about the priorities they faced in communication. In keeping with the current emphasis on implementing evidence-based practice, the techniques they tried were generated largely from ideas culled from the research literature on effective methods of tackling specific impairments.

These authors evaluate the effects of the therapy in a range of ways, by reviewing Lawrence's "performance" on measures of his impairment, but also by taking seriously his perspectives (and those of his wife) on his therapy. It was clearly important to Lawrence that he was gaining control over the situation in relation to his communication, and that his perspectives on the therapy and how he was engaging with it were acknowledged. As is so familiar to many therapists, measures of the changes to Lawrence's "performance" showed little change, while his perceptions suggest that he has gained considerably from the therapy.

Chapter 10. Consumers' views of what makes therapy worthwhile
Aura Kagan and Judith Felson Duchan
The ownership of expertise about aphasia is at the heart of Aura Kagan and Judy Duchan's chapter. Who has the right to identify and describe the changes that therapy has made to someone with aphasia? The range of frameworks that are currently used to evaluate aphasia therapies and the

methodologies for gaining user (or consumer) evaluation of therapies are reviewed. Aura and Judy make the case that the dimensions of change as defined by people living with aphasia are different from those defined by others, especially healthcare professionals, who focus more narrowly on dimensions of impairment or service delivery.

Their chapter describes a process that they undertook with aphasia "veterans"—people who have long experience of living with aphasia—to reveal the critical dimensions of change as they perceived them, and in so doing they identify a methodology that could be repeated in any clinical context. As has become familiar in outputs from the Aphasia Institute in Toronto, they propose a highly practical, engaging, and relevant resource to act as a communication ramp in enabling people to reflect on what matters to them about how their lives have changed, and what those changes are. These perceptions about relevant dimensions of change also have implications for the content of therapy. If people perceive the important dimensions of change as relating to participation in life, how they feel, and how the world treats them, then these must also be key areas to address in therapies.

The chapter demonstrates that the challenge of authentic inclusion in consultation, for people whose disability is in the very medium of consultation, not only can, but also must, be met. In doing so we change the traditional power relations of therapy—people with aphasia as the consultants and advisors, not therapists—offering new revelations to enable improvements in practice.

1 Challenging aphasia therapies

Sally Byng and Judith Felson Duchan

This is a book of challenging musings by speech-language therapists/pathologists who work with individuals who are living with aphasia. The authors, international authorities in the field of aphasia therapies, explore their thoughts about how people with aphasia live with their communication disabilities and how they learn new ways of communicating. The authors also explore how they, themselves, have learned about doing therapy through the process of engaging in it.

While those writing these chapters have published widely, here they are departing from what they are accustomed to. The usual mode in journals and books in the field of speech-language therapy/pathology is to write objectively about impairments, tasks, and client progress. In this book, the authors become introspective, and focus on their own experiences as clinicians and on their relationships with their clients. They ruminate about learning processes—both their own and their clients. And in doing so they reveal some of the conundrums arising from working in the field of aphasia therapy.

The book is intended for speech-language therapists/pathologists and students in English-speaking countries who work with people living with aphasia. It may also be of interest to researchers and practitioners in therapy-based professions, e.g., psychology, psychotherapy, and occupational therapy. The writing is reflective and personal, and includes particular examples and issues that have given the authors pause.

Our authors have challenged their ways of doing "business as usual" in different ways. Some have taken a long hard look at their own identity as therapists and examined some of the principles and ethics underpinning their perspectives on therapy (Martha Taylor Sarno, Carole Pound, Jon Lyon, and Claire Penn). Others have reflected on the nature and process of therapy, sometimes using different media (music and humour) to provide a fresh perspective on interaction in therapy (Nina Simmons-Mackie, Roberta Elman, Julie Morris, David Howard, and Sinead Kennedy). And still others have offered some examples of practices in providing therapy or getting feedback on outcomes, which reflect their views of the relationship between the therapist and the person with aphasia (Carole Pound, Audrey Holland, Amy Ramage, Aura Kagan, and Judy Duchan).

A number of themes emerge from the writings in this book. Here we will give you a peek at a few, others we leave for you to discover on your own as you read these challenging chapters.

COMBINING THE PERSONAL WITH THE PROFESSIONAL

Perhaps one of the most obvious features of this book is the sense of the personal journeys that the contributors have undertaken in their development as therapy practitioners. What is clear is that being an aphasia therapist requires a willingness to be open to personal change, to face personally difficult issues, and to be prepared to think about and learn from one's personal experiences. Therapists must also be prepared meet the challenges that come from interacting with others, their clients, who are facing major life changes. Taking on such concerns requires not only the skill to support others but also the ability to reflect on one's own life issues, and a willingness to be open to challenges and questions.

Several of the authors provide examples of how to integrate the personal with the professional. They do this in different ways. Martha Taylor Sarno, when reflecting on what it means to be a person and a therapist, asks that we be aware of our own feelings of vulnerability and that we examine our personal assumptions about the relevance of our therapy approaches. Carole Pound follows suit by plumbing her own experiences as a patient. Carole also draws lessons for the disability movement as she outlines some parallels between her personal and professional experiences.

Claire Penn and Nina Simmons-Mackie offer other takes on how to relate the personal and professional. Claire considers how her former teachers facilitated her search for a personal way of doing therapy, and Nina sees humour as a way for professionals to become more accessible personally to their clients.

Reading these authors' personal accounts reveals their rich potential for developing insights for aphasia therapies. Until now there has been little attention given to the personal side of therapy in the literature on aphasia. We do not seem to think about the impact that working with people with aphasia can have on how and who we are. Nor do we look directly at who we are for our impact on our clients. The contributions in this book demonstrate how creative and liberating it can be for therapists to examine their personal histories to discover how best to conduct themselves in their therapies.

CHALLENGING THE TACIT ASSUMPTION OF CURE

There is another area of reflection running through the chapters in this book. It has to do with the fact that therapists cannot offer a cure for aphasia. Now this may not feel like a very novel observation, but a number of the contributors hint, directly and indirectly, that therapists might not recognize this fact. How much does the way we practise actually suggest, covertly, to people with aphasia that we think they can get back to where they were before their stroke? By taking them through steps to help them "get better" are we giving them the false assumption that the steps will eventuate in cure?

Even if we were to be explicit about the long-term and chronic nature of aphasia, we must still contend with the stories conveyed in the media and other venues of popular culture that promise what Carole Pound has described as "restitution stories", in which the person with the disability conquers the problem and returns to his or her former life.

What are people living with aphasia to make of the fact that we think we can help them to get so far, but no farther? This worry is poignantly expressed by Valerie Rosenberg, who is quoted by Claire Penn as asking questions such as "Is this permanent or what?" in reference to her aphasia, and wondering "What happened with my bargain with God?".

What support are we giving our clients to deal with the impact of not being able to be who they were again? Martha Taylor Sarno addresses this need for support explicitly as an ethical issue. If therapists provide therapy for only a part of the impact of aphasia, and knowingly do not provide support for other aspects of the impact, particularly if those impacts affect functioning in life, is that practice ethical? Claire Penn's description of her client who committed suicide, despite having made what Claire judged to be an excellent recovery, demonstrates the importance of this issue. And Carole Pound offers some suggestions for how to become involved in supporting people to "live with aphasia". She recommends "doing therapy differently" with a focus on the social and everyday life aspects of the disability.

Julie Morris, David Howard, and Sinead Kennedy raise issues about the differences in therapy in the acute stages and therapy delivered several years post-onset. What must it be like for someone who has lived for 7 years with an impairment, and the disability that stems from it, to return to therapy? What is someone looking for and anticipating will happen at this stage? How do ideas of therapy cures change with time?

ADDRESSING TIME, RESOURCE, AND SYSTEM BARRIERS TO QUALITY THERAPY

Jon Lyon and Martha Taylor Sarno raise a further, related issue: the use of resources. How much does providing therapy for aphasia cost? Jon Lyon tells us the cost of his course of intervention with Patty, and broadly what was achieved for the expenditure. He effectively raises the question—what do other therapies achieve for people with aphasia, in life terms, at what cost? This is a bald question, but one that, we suspect, is not met directly enough by people providing services.

We bemoan the lack of available resources. Martha Taylor Sarno and Jon Lyon bring this problem home as they describe the virtually negligible support for aphasia therapy in the current US healthcare system. But we do not see evidence that service providers have thought through what that means for the priorities in providing therapy, nor researchers asking what that means for the priorities in research.

How, for example, do therapists negotiate with people with aphasia what service they could deliver in, say, 20 sessions? If a therapy would need much more than 20 sessions, yet that is all that is realistically available, is it ethical to embark on it, when it is unclear whether the remaining time needed to have an impact on someone's life will be funded? And do we make that evident to people at the outset? These are crucial questions facing all therapies.

Much of the literature suggests that for therapy to address the impairment effectively, many sessions are required. When therapists realize they do not have this option, do they give up and not even start therapy because they know they do not have the resource required at the outset? Jon Lyon offers an interesting solution to this vexing problem. He suggests that we could do a lot more to empower our clients to manage their own therapy, after which point they won't need a therapist! Martha Taylor Sarno provides another direction for solving the resource problem. She invites clinicians to examine how to use existing resources such as adult education and access to other community-based resources to support those with aphasia.

In their chapter, Julie Morris, David Howard, and Sinead Kennedy add yet another issue to the concern about resources. A common assumption made by therapists and those with aphasia has been that with more resources, the desired improvement would be obtainable. This was not the case for their client, Lawrence. Even after their intensive 162 hours of language therapy, Lawrence did not improve dramatically on the quantitative measures used, but he and his wife felt that significant gains had been made—both in the use of a specific strategy to support communication and in his confidence. This leads to questions about how much and what type of therapy is required to increase confidence, which seems to have been an important by-product of the therapy for Lawrence.

PROVIDING ENOUGH TIME TO ATTAIN PERSONAL CHANGE

It does not take much imagination to see that becoming aphasic represents a major life event, for anyone. Nor does it take much imagination to realize that recovering from losing your ability to talk and learning to live a new way of life cannot be achieved overnight, or even in a few months, as is brought home in Claire Penn's story of Valerie Rosenberg's phases of therapy, and in Carole Pound's description of the phases of living with a disability.

It is clear from Valerie's own words and Claire Penn's description of the therapy process that people learning to live with aphasia must go through a significant period of personal development and skills acquisition. Essentially that is what rehabilitation involves—learning new skills and adapting your identity—regardless of the disabling condition you are experiencing.

Why is it that we have had such difficulty getting across this obvious message about the importance of long-term rehabilitation, especially to third-party payers? Could it be because of the undue focus on sophisticated neurolinguistics, on the complexity of the impairment, on the creation of a scientific mystique around aphasia, that Martha Taylor Sarno draws attention to? Have we obfuscated many of the other real issues where people need support in our efforts to gain scientific credibility? And in so doing, have we prevented the people who make decisions about healthcare spending from understanding the significance of aphasia in people's lives, and what it takes to provide people with the support they need to make their journeys back to life again?

Aura Kagan and Judy Duchan talk about these issues in relation to how aphasia therapies have been evaluated. These authors review the various approaches to measuring therapy outcomes and conclude that even those outcomes that are consumer-based do not probe deeply enough into the dimensions of success that are in the minds of those with aphasia. The authors identify various things that have blocked professionals from obtaining authentic client-based evaluation of their therapies, and then offer some solutions to these professional barriers.

UNDERSTANDING THAT APHASIA IS MORE THAN A LANGUAGE IMPAIRMENT

Aphasia is a life-changing event. All of the chapters in this book attest to that. The authors treat recovery as a complex process and provide examples of their attempts to address multiple issues that arise for people. What they reinforce is that planning a programme of therapy for someone with aphasia needs to comprise an imaginative, broad-based range of opportunities. Those opportunities should have to do with language and communication, identity and lifestyle, involving not just the person with aphasia, but those with whom they live. None of the chapters takes into account only one of these facets of therapy. How the balance of those components is negotiated is complex. It is what Jon Lyon calls a "systems" approach.

The invisible nature of aphasia is, according to Martha Taylor Sarno, a large part of the difficulty in coping with it. For example, a commonly occurring aspect of aphasia is psychological depression and isolation, which has to do with the general experiences related to suffering and depression—something that is not obvious to those who see the problem strictly in terms of language impairment. Carole Pound asks that we see aphasia therapy as including the everyday aspect of the disability, and how to cope. She offers a number of examples of how support at this level is needed to meet therapy relevant for clients with aphasia—suggestions that go beyond working with language impairment.

Claire's Penn's "pragmatic, wholistic" therapy involves a set of strategies to meet her clients' life challenges. Early in her client's therapy, Claire developed with Valerie Rosenberg a set of verbal mediators, strategies, hints, what Claire calls "one-liners" to guide Valerie in organizing, remembering, conversing, and coping as she engaged in everyday life activities. (Helpful strategy guides like this are also a feature of Audrey Holland's work with Roger Ross.) Later, in their course of therapy that Claire calls "taking stock", she and Valerie worked on setting directions for the future.

When Jon Lyon describes his client with aphasia as experiencing a "loss of intimacy", as someone whose life has been thinned out because of her confinement, he is seeing aphasia as much more than a language impairment. And when Nina Simmons-Mackie makes an appeal for including humour in the scope of communication and communication disability, she is seeing language and communication as ranging beyond words and sentences into a wonderful new realm of the comical.

DEALING WITH POWER RELATIONS DURING THERAPY

What the chapters in this book also reveal is that it is not sufficient only to think about the topics that therapy addresses—one must also consider the role that the therapist plays and how therapy is conducted. Nina Simmons-Mackie, Aura Kagan, Judy Duchan, and Carole Pound all draw attention to the power that the therapist wields. The impact of the relationship on the outcome of therapy is also described by Roberta Elman, Audrey Holland, and Carole Pound. All argue strongly for client-directed approaches rather than clinician-dominated ones. Carole Pound, for example, describes the authoritarian clinician who assumes all of the responsibility for therapy direction and content. She makes a strong appeal for clinicians to give up their power and allow their clients to identify their own problems and the course of therapy.

When analyzing the dynamics of humour in a therapy session Nina Simmons-Mackie makes the startling discovery that therapists are the ones who usually crack the jokes and the ones who have the option of whether or not to laugh. She found it to be the notable exception when a client initiated humour or failed to respond to something funny said or done by the clinician. She takes these as signs of the power of the therapist over the client.

Roger Ross, the person Audrey Holland and Amy Ramage introduce us to, was interested in directing his own therapy groups and in controlling his own therapies. This raises another issue of client power—does client power ever need to be challenged? We would suggest, as do Carole Pound, Audrey Holland and Amy Ramage that clinicians who empower their clients need also to know when *not* to go with the clients' preferences. Roger Ross's disdain for coffee and cake groups should not be presumed to be the opinion of other people with aphasia.

Aura Kagan and Judy Duchan offer a method for giving those receiving therapy the means to evaluate their own progress. The structured interviews, using methods of supported conversation, offered the people they talked with a way not only of evaluating the success and failures of their own therapies, but also of discussing aspects of therapy that they would recommend to others with aphasia.

RECOGNIZING MISPLACED THERAPIES AND IDENTIFYING MISGUIDED THERAPISTS

Our authors are not only adventuresome in exploring new areas of therapy, they are also willing to take the risk of criticizing their own past therapies and those of others. Mistakes in the choice and execution of therapies are described by:

- Martha Taylor Sarno when she talks about the minimal attention in the past to psychosocial aspects of aphasia;
- Nina Simmons-Mackie in her examples of humour that is either misplaced or offensive;
- Jon Lyon when he talks about "restoration therapies" that have a single focus on changing a small part of an impairment;
- Audrey Holland and Amy Ramage who give an example of a therapist who lacks self-doubt, assuming she knew better than her aphasia client about whether there is such a word as "pert";
- Roger Ross, Audrey's client, who was able to describe/diagnose his difficulties (e.g., "I have no sound patterns in my head") more succinctly and transparently than his clinicians might have done (e.g., "difficulty in accessing the phonological lexicon");
- Roberta Elman who remembers with embarrassment and regret her early therapies composed of drills, which she used to consider the important work, to the neglect of conversation, which she then considered to be fluff;
- Carole Pound, who remembers a time when she was searching for a therapy grail, and ignoring the everyday aspects of disability;
- Carole Pound, again, who remembers her own stories being hijacked and misinterpreted by medical professionals;
- Aura Kagan and Judy Duchan who critique evaluation done without consumer consultation.

COMBINING THERAPY, PHILOSOPHY, AND TOOLS

Each of the authors in this volume addresses issues about the doing of therapy. It becomes obvious, when probing their attitudes, that their therapies are underpinned by powerful philosophies about the nature, content, and ethics of change for people living with aphasia. These philosophies find their expression in the specific therapies and tools used.

In Martha Taylor Sarno's chapter she traces the functional philosophy of clinical practice in aphasia to frameworks used in rehabilitation medicine. She also presents a moral perspective for deciding among aphasia therapies, and from this perspective advocates for aphasia to be treated as a community issue, and as an issue that does not fit with a traditional view of aphasia as a medical problem.

Carole Pound also offers a philosophical rendering of aphasia therapy. She regards therapy as an organic, ever-changing, lived experience that involves collaboration and negotiated reflection between therapist and client. Her non-authoritarian, complex view of the nature of therapy leads her to prefer some sorts of therapies and clinical tools over others. She favours therapies such as doing poetry, countering the restitution narrative, and training partners to converse with those who have aphasia. She warns against using therapies that are based on impossible dreams and those that treat the person with a disability as a patient rather than a person.

Jon Lyon advocates therapies that impact on daily living (having substance), ones that are long-term (sustainable), and ones that are cost-effective. He acknowledges the conflict between long-term and cost-effective values, and designs therapies that empower those with aphasia to manage their own therapies.

Jon Lyon's therapies stem from a model that he and his colleagues in America have called a "life participation approach" to aphasia. The model, a version of which is presented in Jon's article, leads to various therapies that he describes in relation to his client Patty. These include slowing up interactions, using key words, arranging for his client to volunteer, working with Patty to assume more household responsibilities, and the use of interactive drawing. Jon used these methods as tools to enhance connections between his client and her family members. The philosophy of the therapy was a life-participation one. His philosophy led him to analyze his client's social interactions in terms of barriers and facilitators. The analysis then led him to the selection of therapy tools for removing barriers and facilitating family interactions and activities.

Claire Penn also regards the purpose of therapy as life-empowering. She calls it "humanistic" because it is not prepackaged, she calls it "pragmatic" because it is sensitive to everyday life contexts and needs, and she calls it "conversational" because it focuses on social communication, rather than on fixing someone's language impairment. Her hope for therapies is that they allow the person to transcend their aphasia identities—a hope that regards aphasia as much more than a language problem, and regards people with aphasia as more than their disability.

Funny therapy, that which incorporates and values humour, is not your usual take on what clinical activities and interactions look like. Nina Simmons-Mackie, by focusing on humour that accompanies therapy, widens the view of what counts as language and communication and challenges usual notions of what constitutes therapy. Her philosophy, drawn from conversation analysis among other places, views humour as a necessary and positive interactional genre. In so doing, she challenges the ordinary boundaries of professionalism (as serious business) and invites clinicians to have fun as they interact with their clients.

Roberta Elman worries about the success and validity of therapies that are carried out in a drill format, presenting material as content to be memorized. She argues convincingly that "making language", like improvising in music, needs to be seen as a creative process, and one that is controlled by the language or music maker, not the music teacher or therapist. She also, by personal example, encourages clinicians to take risks and break new therapy ground. She describes a stage in her thinking when doing group therapy didn't fit her notion of therapy, and how breaking out of that restriction was liberating for her.

Maximizing strengths is the philosophical principle that guided Audrey Holland's therapy with her client Roger Ross. She and Amy Ramage, her co-author, advocate taking risks by doing therapy that might seem foolish. Their "fools rush in" approach involved trying unproven methods—an especially brazen suggestion at this time when healthcare professionals need to justify what they are doing by citing evidence-based research. Noteworthy in this chapter are the vivid descriptions of the particular therapy tools selected (e.g., autocueing, provision of homework, and use of crib sheets), that both meet her client's needs and are consistent with the clinician's own philosophy of therapy.

One of the several philosophical imports of the chapter written by Julie Morris, David Howard, and Sinead Kennedy has to do with the usefulness of therapy evaluations that do not mesh with the client's sensibility about therapy progress. They offer an example from their client, who felt he had made considerable progress in reading—progress that was not revealed by the objective tests. They conclude that tests don't tell the whole story, nor do evaluation measures based on client feedback. They see evaluation measures as tools that should change depending on the questions being asked and by whom.

A second philosophical issue that they raise has to do with the way group therapy is regarded. In a philosophical frame that treats aphasia as a language impairment, clients see individualized therapy as a better means to their goal of improving their language. Groups in this philosophical frame are good for practising language skills learned in individual therapy. Experiences of group therapy seem to be regarded by clients more favourably (as described by Roberta Elman and Carole Pound) when they are explicitly working within a different philosophical frame, a frame of reference regarding aphasia as more socially based. In this frame, issues related to the challenges of living with aphasia, coping with disability, and the disabling barriers imposed by others may be more easily and satisfyingly addressed in a group problem-solving setting than in an individual session. The key is to match the frame to the changing needs, priorities, and perceptions of the person with aphasia. This may involve challenging their perceptions, attitudes, and interactions.

As you may have noticed, this introductory chapter is replete with questions and issues raised–questions without answers. This is in keeping with a book about challenges and reflections. We feel the need to enter a period of challenging questions that lead us to a mood of introspection rather than one of finding quick solutions or easy answers. In this period of worldwide re-evaluation of healthcare resources and allocation, it behoves us to tread carefully and talk to one another about our perception of priorities and need. Our authors, who would generally be regarded as the ones to go to for the answers, are here raising the important questions. They have begun a dialogue that we invite others to join, in various forums—practice, research, education, and collaboration with service users.

MAKING ROOM FOR REFLECTIVE PRACTICES

The challenges raised by our authors lead to a strong call for therapists to engage in both reflexive and reflective practices. Reflexive practices have to do with considering the personal aspects of doing therapy. Reflective practices relate to how therapy is going in general. Much is written about both the reflexive and reflective practitioner in occupational therapy, social work, and in other areas of the health professions. But there is little attention given to this in the field of speech and language pathology/therapy. This is not to say that therapists are oblivious to how things are going for themselves or their clients, but rather that their reflections are seldom shared or talked about in the literature. Nor are they built into the course of everyday practice. Such activity, because it is so unfamiliar, is likely to be considered self-indulgent or even pompous.

Our authors give readers of this volume a model for both reflexive and reflective practices. They show, by example, the value of (1) examining their personal histories and values for insights into their current decision-making practices; (2) examining how aphasia therapists in America got to where they are today; (3) evaluating the medical model and its inherent notion of cure; (4) being supervised by seasoned therapists; and (5) engaging clients in reflection about the relevance of their therapies. The authors do not all draw the same conclusions from their musings. Rather, they represent a rainbow of practices, offering yet another challenge to the reader, who can examine different approaches from the point of view of those who advocate for them.

This book is a response to our felt need to create a venue within which aphasia therapists could think and reflect alone and with others about what they are thinking and doing as they carry out their therapies. The authors show how they have changed what they do as a result of spending time thinking about what they have done. They demonstrate, by example, how personal and professional reflection has provided them with a broader understanding of their therapies and has made them more open to change. We thank them for their courage, and hope that their examples motivate others to think and talk about the challenging issues they raise.

2 Aphasia therapies: Historical perspectives and moral imperatives

Martha Taylor Sarno

It is both an honour and a pleasure to contribute the keynote paper to this publication, marking the launch of "Connect", the Communication Disability Network, for this is a truly significant occasion in the history of aphasiology. It is an important occasion especially for those of us who are part of that history, because of our commitment to the well-being of those with aphasia and their families.

My comments will contain many biases. None will be right or wrong, correct or inaccurate. They simply reflect a perspective which has evolved over a long career that has spanned major revisions in the social and healthcare landscape, revisions that have also shaped the nature of aphasiology. Furthermore, while my experience has been limited to the US, I believe that, except for the details of differences in individual national policies and legislation, I will be discussing issues that are true in all western medicine.

Communication disorders have been the consequence of injury and disease for as long as *homo sapiens* have had language, and the number of people with aphasia has increased. This increase is due to the greater number of survivors and longer life span, combined with modern-day technological advances, as well as to an increase in the incidence of motor vehicle accidents. Each year in the UK there are approximately 20,000 new cases of aphasia (Parr, Byng, Gilpin, & Ireland, 1997), and about 100,000 new cases in the United States (Damasio, 1992). In 1990 the National Institutes of Health estimated that there was a population of one and a half million Americans living with aphasia (National Institutes of Health, 1990). The figures are particularly impressive when one considers that in the United States the aphasia population is larger than the combined populations of individuals with multiple sclerosis, muscular dystrophy, cerebral palsy, and Parkinson's disease, conditions that have historically had the benefit of well-funded research and services, while aphasia has not.

Before the First World War, the aphasia literature contained only a few reports of systematic attempts to "treat" people with aphasia (Broadbent, 1879; Mills, 1904). During and after the war, however, several aphasia rehabilitation programmes were developed, especially in Germany (Franz, 1924; Goldstein, 1942; Isserlin, 1929) but also in other parts of Europe (Poppelreuter,

1915), the United States (Franz, 1924; Frazier & Ingham, 1920; Nielsen, 1936), and the UK (Butfield & Zangwill, 1946; Head, 1926). These programmes were designed for military personnel with aphasia secondary to head injuries, which were usually gunshot wounds, incurred in combat. The efficacy of these programmes, one of which followed 90–100 patients for as long as 10 years, was well documented (Goldstein, 1942, 1948). They inspired several landmark studies between the two world wars (Butfield & Zangwill, 1946; Weisenberg & McBride, 1935).

During the Second World War specially designed hospital-based programmes for war veterans were established in the United States (Backus, 1945; Granich, 1947; Sheehan, 1946; Wepman, 1951), Germany (Goldstein, 1942, 1948), and Russia (Luria, 1948). All of these programmes reported effective treatment of aphasia secondary to gunshot wounds. A renewed interest in aphasia therapy emerged after the Second World War, extending its scope to include the civilian population, which until then had been ignored. Of course, unlike the young war veterans who had sustained head trauma, civilians tended to be middle-aged or older-aged and had aphasia secondary to strokes. Their potential for improvement, with or without intervention, was considered poor beyond the first few days and weeks of spontaneous, natural recovery.

This notion of the limited potential for recovery was underlined by the fact that, in that period of history, the word "stroke" still carried the highly charged meaning "stricken by God". The stroke "condition" was so highly stigmatized that in 1951 quotation marks surrounded the word "stroke" in a book on the topic written by a leading aphasiologist (Wepman, 1951). Most health professionals referred to the event as an apoplexy, a cerebrovascular accident, or apoplectic attack. Until the term "stroke" was used in the media to report the condition in public figures such as Sir Winston Churchill, President Dwight Eisenhower, and Ambassador Joseph Kennedy, the term was unacceptable. Strokes were then viewed as a natural and necessary stage of the ageing process. The patient could generally count on an "at home", intergenerational, extended family to meet daily needs. After the Second World War, social and demographic changes shaped the conditions that facilitated the introduction of aphasia *rehabilitation* for civilians who had had strokes, as an integral component of the healthcare system. The population explosion created a greater need for services and the dramatic increase in the size and prosperity of the middle class played a major role in these changes. The demand for these services was also increased by the fact that more people became aware of their existence and availability, through the expanding media revolution.

Given these realities, it was inevitable that the field of speech-language pathology experienced significant growth in the post-war period. This growth was enhanced by the fact that a new board-certified specialty of medicine was being established in the United States, at that time called "physical medicine and rehabilitation", designed primarily to deal with the problems of chronic disabling disorders like stroke. All of these factors played a part in changing societal attitudes towards stroke and aphasia as well as towards ageing, chronic disease, and human potential. The possibility of improving the function of disabled individuals and thereby eliminating, or at least reducing, their handicaps became a goal. The disability movement was about to begin.

Aphasia rehabilitation is indebted to the field of rehabilitation medicine for its philosophical foundation and its contemporary adoption of a functional perspective for assessment, treatment goals, and outcomes. This medical specialty introduced the notion of measuring a physically disabled individual's independence in the conduct of the activities of daily living, with a functional frame of reference. This functional frame became the hallmark of the specialty of rehabilitation medicine. Furthermore, it was rehabilitation medicine that first conceived of the then radical idea that intervention for the disabled requires a team of health professionals, and more to the point, that the team should include a speech-language pathologist. Today we take for granted both the value of a functional frame of reference and the collective expertise of a team of health professionals as fundamental to good care.

I had the good fortune to have been the first speech-language pathologist who served as a member of a rehabilitation medicine team and therefore I had the opportunity to develop the first aphasia rehabilitation programme associated with the specialty of rehabilitation medicine. But it would be 30 years before the concept of functional communication would be of interest to speech-language pathology.

In the 1950s there were virtually no aphasia rehabilitation services and only 1600 speech-language pathologist members of the American Speech Language and Hearing Association in the United States. There are now more than 100,000 members, many of whom provide aphasia rehabilitation services. Services are available in all types of facilities from nursing homes and private practices to specialized, often hospital-based, formal aphasia programmes.

Since the establishment, over half a century ago, of dedicated programmes for civilians with aphasia, we have experienced the introduction of and exponential increase in the availability of not only treatment services but also dedicated textbooks, journals, university courses, teaching aids, and software for computer-assisted therapy. Support services and informational materials are available for patients and caregivers. Professionals meet and exchange information at meetings of the Academy of Aphasia, the Clinical Aphasiology Conference, the International Aphasia Rehabilitation Congress, the British Aphasiology Society, and the Dutch Aphasia Association, to name but a few of the international bodies with a focus on aphasia. Furthermore, aphasia advocacy organizations now exist in many of the developed nations of the world.

In spite of the noted scope of improvements, there is yet to develop an adequate realistic and relevant intervention model that goes beyond a functional model. In fact, it may be that the contemporary context of activity, in the current high-tech, materialistic environment, has given rise to unrealistic expectations and an underestimation or neglect of the interpersonal, social impact of aphasia on the person and family.

Only those who experience aphasia know the full meaning of its effects on all aspects of life, especially the many "webs" in our lives, the interpersonal relationships that preserve and connect us to our world. Such webs depend almost entirely on our ability to communicate. Aphasia not only disconnects the person from the community but invariably alters the person's identity and sense of self. It is not at all surprising that the most often studied and reported psychological sequela of aphasia is depression (Sarno, 1986, 1993, 1997).

We have learned from personal accounts that feelings of devastation, alienation, vulnerability, powerlessness, and a loss of personhood are pervasive (Newborn, 1997; Raskin, 1992; Wulf, 1979). One person described the experience as "Aphasia delivers a crippling blow to that part which our culture proclaims to make man a thinking, bright human being: the communicative arts" (Wulf, 1979, p. 36). Many feel that they do not count any more (Parr & Byng, 2000). Except in a very mild form, aphasia produces a profoundly altered life. Clinicians know, all too well, that the psychosocial consequences of aphasia persist for a very long period of time, often indefinitely. But in-depth studies using the methodologies of the social sciences, designed to identify and assess the nature of personal suffering in aphasia, have been limited (Parr & Byng, 2000). Biomedical interpretations of illness have been criticized for leaving the experience of suffering out of assessments of disease (Cassell, 1991; Kleinman, 1995).

It seems self-evident that a condition that strikes at the very heart of personhood, our ability to communicate, calls for an intervention model that accounts for everything we know about humans: personality, human nature, emotional imperatives, adjustment factors, compensatory behaviours, and all the other attributes of our species. A psychosocial model with focus on the long term is required, taking into account the temporal factors which make aphasia an ever-changing condition with different issues and influences at different points in the recovery and adjustment continuum. The model needs to be based on the idea that living with aphasia is a process of transition and transformation. This incorporates the idea of an evolving self, with ample opportunities for facilitating a transition from one life to another as the self is reconstructed. The model must embrace the idea that aphasia recovery is a dynamic, adaptive process that is constantly moving towards enhancing interpersonal, functional communication. To this end it should not be burdened with the constraints of artificially structured therapeutic contexts requiring static responses. Such contexts cannot replace an authentic functional experience.

That is not to say that the simulated, role-playing activities often used in treatment serve no purpose at all when played out in the unnatural clinical environment, but they cannot equal the real-life experience. These techniques, when ultimately attempted in a real situation, may serve to improve a lack of confidence or a sense of failure and hopelessness. But the person with aphasia must also have an opportunity to deal with the grief that comes with loss, feelings of powerlessness, and the many barriers people confront when living with aphasia.

Of course, the intervention model must also incorporate some traditional aphasia treatment which stresses addressing the impairment, but this should not be allowed to dominate the focus of the person/therapist relationship, for it ignores some of the most important needs. In fact, one might argue that such an approach may serve to highlight the impairment rather than the value of the individual as a person, member of a family, and a larger community. This is not to undervalue the quantity, intensity, and superb quality of work in linguistics and aphasia which has dominated the aphasiology literature in recent decades. This work, however, has been accorded a high priority while interest and funding in the psychosocial dimensions of aphasia have been almost non-existent. Experience in the clinical management of people with aphasia argues for a need for change of emphasis in the allocation of resources and funding (see Chapter 4 by Jon Lyon for more on this issue).

In the past decade, a welcome break from traditional aphasia therapy models has emerged in a small number of alternative approaches perhaps best represented in the work of Kagan (1995, 1998), Lyon (1992, 1995, 1996, 1997), Simmons-Mackie (1993, 1998, 2000), Simmons-Mackie and Damico (1996, 1997, 1999), Elman (1998, 1999), Holland (1991), and Pound, Parr, Lindsay, and Woolf (2000). Many of these nontraditional approaches include communication partners as fundamental to implementation. All are based on a social, interactive, view of aphasia rehabilitation. Their objective is to help restructure the person's identity and sense of self, thereby enhancing the possibility of social experience and interaction. In these approaches, the person with aphasia is viewed as a part of a personal environment that is embedded in a larger communal/societal context.

These creative contributions, which were designed to facilitate the most natural and accessible communicative skills, have enriched our inventory of techniques that facilitate the most natural, accessible communicative skills possible with an emphasis on conversation as an interactive experience. A new emphasis on the effectiveness of group treatment has also added to a focus on aphasia as a social loss (Elman & Bernstein, 1999; Fawcus, 1992; Kearns, 1986; Pound et al., 2000). By facilitating conversation these techniques contribute to a person's identity and sense of self.

No model of intervention would be complete or faithful to the realities of aphasia without a component that accounts for the role of society. Society's ignorance and lack of awareness of aphasia has been seriously aggravated by the lack of visibility of aphasia (Parr et al., 1997; Sarno, 1986). We almost instinctively accommodate disabled individuals who use wheelchairs, crutches, guide dogs, or other aids that help to make the world more accessible. The deaf are immediately identified when they use manual signs. By contrast someone with aphasia cannot facilitate social interaction by informing a stranger in a public place that aphasia is causing the communication difficulty, since hardly anyone knows the term.

The invisibility of aphasia is a tremendous disadvantage in the public environment; it interferes with the accommodation of the individual, and reduces the probability that the public can learn about aphasia by random exposure to the people who have it. Therefore, without some proactive initiatives to change society's understanding of and response to aphasia, the continuing lack of public awareness clearly increases the social isolation of those living with aphasia. Of equal concern is the prevailing public perception that those who have impaired communication are either retarded or mentally disturbed. Society's intolerance of differentness and its perpetuation of the stigmatization of the communication-disabled has also contributed significantly to the difficulty of effectively educating the public.

One of the greatest barriers to the development and provision of relevant and effective services in the history of aphasia rehabilitation has emerged in the past decade (Davis, 2000; Frattali, 2000). Meaningful intervention has become increasingly challenged and far more difficult to deliver in the face of the drastic restructuring that has taken place in healthcare delivery, particularly in the United States. The scenario is not universal across regions, cultures, or nations, but we have clearly entered an entirely new era of health care, one that is driven by economic realities.

In the United States we are now engaged in practising aphasia rehabilitation under the dictates of what is referred to as "managed care"—a term that refers to financial arrangements which have been designed to control rising health costs. There are many types of third-party payers including private insurers, employer-related private insurance, state and federal insurance. As a consequence, healthcare providers are no longer able to provide either the type, frequency, or duration of services that in their judgement are appropriate to the particular individual needs of the person with aphasia.

Variations in service provision across the US are extreme, and depend on the type of facility. Guidelines are often unclear and require seemingly endless communication between provider and insurer for verification and authorization before services are delivered. In general, insurers are less restrictive in the reimbursement of assessments than treatment. If treatment is reimbursed it is more likely to be reimbursed while a patient is hospitalized than later as an outpatient. In other words, insurers are highly unlikely to reimburse individuals with aphasia for individual treatment sessions, and many will only cover individual therapy and not group therapy. People with aphasia are rarely, if ever, reimbursed for psychological or social support— what has been called "maintenance". As a consequence, unless a person with aphasia is showing objective, documentable, evidence of communication improvement, insurers generally deny reimbursement for continued intervention. Third-party reimbursement practices are particularly restrictive for outpatients in rehabilitation centres and hospitals. Furthermore, in the US the new Prospective Payment System (PPS), which ties reimbursement to diagnostic category, places significant limits on the number of days that a disabled individual will be able to remain in an inpatient rehabilitation facility, further impairing the experience of people with stroke and aphasia.

The drastic changes that have taken place in the delivery of services to people with aphasia in the United States have inhibited clinical practices in ways that may have a permanent effect on our ability to render care that is relevant and responsible. At this time the average length of stay in the United States for a stroke patient in an acute hospital is 5 days rather than the 2-week average stay of only a decade ago. The current acute hospital stay is so short that there has been a marked increase in the establishment of new home healthcare and skilled nursing facilities (Frattali, 2000). In the current environment, those fortunate enough to be referred to a rehabilitation hospital will remain there for an average of 19 days, rather than the average rehabilitation inpatient stay that, not long ago, exceeded 3 months. Once discharged, insurance coverage for outpatient rehabilitation services averages from four to ten sessions rather than the 6 to 9 months provided only a decade ago. In addition to the devastating reductions in covered rehabilitation services, fewer patients are being referred for rehabilitation services on discharge from the acute hospital. At the present time there is little evidence that the managed care situation will improve for those with aphasia or other chronic conditions.

Our mandate is clear. The current healthcare environment requires a re-evaluation of the roles of people providing rehabilitation services to people with aphasia, and what we can achieve with them, and an exploration of alternative means for providing services. The existing issues and barriers challenge our most creative and inspired thinking if we are to restructure the context of aphasia rehabilitation.

Among the most compelling issues that need to be addressed are:

- limited access to rehabilitation services stemming from economic realities;
- adherence to a medical model of recovery and rehabilitation;
- the perception of aphasia rehabilitation as almost exclusively a process of repairing language;
- an uninformed and intolerant society which has stigmatized the condition;
- the lack of specialized facilities that provide opportunities for social interaction and peer support as a component of a comprehensive treatment, education, and research programme.

Many of the issues we face stem from aphasiology's persistence in adhering to a medical model which focuses our attention on pathology rather than handicap or disability. When pathology is the priority of concern, the goal is for a return to a pre-aphasia state, a goal that is not only unrealistic but counterproductive if it remains an intervention target (see Chapter 4 by Jon Lyon for further discussion of this assumption). The medical model has also helped to foster the idea that the long-term issues of living with aphasia can best be solved in a healthcare environment. Yet most of the world of medicine has abandoned long-term quality of life concerns as it increases its dependence on technologically based procedures and practices, in our cure-oriented western society. This has served to further "medicalize" the management of patients beyond the acute stage.

The adoption of a social model for aphasia rehabilitation in the post acute phase is long overdue and has already been addressed by some aphasiologists. However, the abandonment of a medical model calls for a major shift in the underlying bases of the training of aphasia clinicians. If we adopt a social model, the academic curriculum will need to incorporate a far greater emphasis on the social sciences, sociology, and psychology than it does at the moment. It will perhaps even include some supervised clinical practice in counselling. A social model calls for a revision of intervention practices away from the traditional focus on static, non-interactive techniques intended to repair the language deficits manifest in aphasia, to approaches that acknowledge the social, interactive basis of human relationships. A high-priority therapeutic goal is living with aphasia in the context of family and community. Insisting on maintaining relevance to real-life activity in all intervention techniques helps to ensure that the purpose is viewed as primarily psychosocial. Unfortunately, many therapists see the social model as relevant only as the patient is preparing for the termination of treatment.

A model that provides a useful perspective of aphasia rehabilitation, called the "psychosocial transition model" focuses on long-term outcomes and social support and the shifting of attention towards issues of self-definition and social role identity (Glass & Maddox, 1992). These authors refer to the concept of a "life space" representing the totality of interaction for each individual. The psychosocial transition model calls attention to the importance of a temporal dimension in the coping process—that is, it acknowledges that many different phases of adaptation take place at different points in the recovery continuum, beginning with the sudden changes brought on by aphasia, the immediate alteration of life space, and adaptation, which includes a sense of mastery despite deficits.

Models in which the primary focus is on repairing the impaired language in aphasia run the risk of overlooking and, in fact, undermining the importance of the conversational interaction that dominates our relationships and, therefore, the meaningfulness of our lives. By providing alternative means of interaction through access to social activity, and a focus on communicative strategies or other activities, those with aphasia are helped to redefine themselves and resume a role in the family and community.

There is an urgent need to make aphasia a more "visible" disability and develop a social environment in which people with aphasia are not marginalized or devalued because they may not have returned to gainful employment. In the current climate, the challenge to change society's view of aphasia will require a systematic and aggressive programme of public education at all levels. All avenues of education need to be utilized.

A broad-spectrum initiative that reaches out at the local, regional, and national level is needed, such as media exposure, public service announcements, lectures for public attendance in the community, exposure to personal accounts of individuals with aphasia and their caregivers, videos and films designed to educate the public about life with aphasia. All need to be systematically utilized to promote understanding and engagement in the public sphere. Aphasia associations around the world are involved in speaking for the aphasia community through public education. But it will take a more organized approach to make a difference. This will require funding, which is at present not generally available to those who could initiate and contribute to such a programme. This initiative can only be realized in a community of individuals who appreciate the socially disabling nature of the condition and the significant part that an enlightened society can play in remedying an unacceptable situation—by helping to create and/or foster the social networks that people with aphasia need if they are to be members of a society/community and the opportunities they need for work, whether paid or volunteer. An educated public will insist on social policy changes that enhance the possibilities of people with aphasia being accepted as members of the community, thereby bringing greater visibility to the disability.

We should also utilize community resources that are already in place but have not yet been used in the service of the aphasia community. Adult education, volunteer programmes, senior citizen groups, and academic programmes could be accessed for the benefit of people with aphasia in ways not yet explored. Utilizing community resources also helps to further public education concerning aphasia, and transfers the effort from medical environment to the community. Civic groups and family foundations can be solicited to fund such programmes.

Little has been said in the aphasia literature about the necessity for or creative possibilities of accommodating people with aphasia within the community. Our dependence on telecommunication networks for everything from purchasing groceries, gifts, and airline tickets online; the corresponding need to respond to elaborate menus on voice-message systems requiring speedy and accurate auditory comprehension; and the present-day need to utilize numerical response language when interfacing with telephone message systems—all these are totally unforgiving to the individual with aphasia. We have a responsibility and an obligation to develop initiatives that will address the potential for providing accommodations for those with aphasia to access our everyday information systems, albeit through unorthodox means. As with other disabilities, people with aphasia should also have access to aides who act as surrogate communicators.

"Connect", the Communication Disability Network, both as a concept and a reality, represents an extraordinary effort to develop a model centre for aphasia unique in the history of aphasia rehabilitation. The Connect initiative reflects our very best thinking and understanding of the impact of aphasia on the person, family, and community. Its existence highlights the need to consider the long-term effects of aphasia in psychosocial domains requiring long-term, sometimes lifetime support, with education and social opportunity. As part of an ongoing effort with plans for expansion to other regions of the UK, the scheme incorporates a community-centred approach to the larger UK aphasia community which should have a significant effect on the ways in which aphasia intervention and professional training evolve in programmes, new and old, around the world. The Connect programme will become the benchmark for clinical aphasiology practice.

I have always been impressed with the richness and meaningfulness that the experience of working in aphasia rehabilitation has brought to my own personal and professional growth and fulfilment. It has highlighted my respect for individual differences and the value and vulnerability of our humanness. The experience continues to introduce a fresh understanding of what it is to be a person (Jennings, 2001) and reaffirms the complexity and breadth of our communicative interactions.

What I have said in this chapter suggests the need for a somewhat different course of development in aphasia rehabilitation, which will need thoughtful, supportive engagement by clinical aphasiologists if we are to make a difference. Our efforts must be ever mindful of the transitional nature of aphasia, which varies and changes in response to the time under consideration—that is, the temporal layers that characterize life with aphasia which vary in their evolution from person to person. I believe that each of us has a unique relationship to our communication behaviour—each comprising a universe of its own. The effective aphasia therapist is one who negotiates the means to enter that universe with the person experiencing aphasia.

Much has been said recently about quality of life and the person with aphasia. Quality of life may tell us something about the experience, but not the "moral worth of humanness, or it may tell us something about *becoming (more fully) human*, but never about the value of *being human*" (Jennings, 1999, p. 103). The literature contains virtually nothing about the compelling ethical-moral issues that are inherent in a discussion about people with aphasia, who are perceived as lacking in value or personhood. Human communication is a foundation for human freedom, for human agency and the ability to act voluntarily (Horner-Catt, 1999). Those who work with the communication-disabled are members of a moral community seeking to empower and restore individuals to a meaningful life experience. We have a duty and an ethical responsibility to sustain each individual's personhood as much as possible by maintaining, sustaining, and creating relationships, connections, and commitments with the person.

> It is one thing to give care and protection out of a sense of pity, or charity, or professional duty, or even love; it is another to maintain

relationship and connection with the other for as long as possible out of a sense of the moral importance of that connection per se.

(Jennings, 2001)

I am grateful to Jennings (1993, 2001) who reminds us of our universal vulnerability and frailty and the need to keep before us the moral imperative of connecting with persons with aphasia, whose status and moral personhood has been traumatized by medical events beyond their control. They suffer a private injustice to which we have a moral obligation to respond, with our best efforts to restore their membership in the human community.

ACKNOWLEDGEMENT

Preparation of this chapter was supported in part by a grant to the author from the Jacob & Valeria Langeloth Foundation.

REFERENCES

Backus, O. (1945). Rehabilitation of aphasic war veterans. *Journal of Speech Disorders, 10*, 149–153.

Broadbent, D. (1879). A case of peculiar affection of speech, with commentary. *Brain, 1*, 484–503.

Butfield, E., & Zangwill, O. L. (1946). Reeducation in aphasia: A review of 70 cases. *Journal of Neurology, Neurosurgery and Psychiatry, 9*(2), 75–79.

Cassell, E. J. (1991). Recognizing suffering. *Hastings Center Report, 21*, 24–31. New York: Briarcliff Manor.

Damasio, A. (1992). Aphasia. *New England Journal of Medicine, 326*(8), 531–539.

Davis, G. A. (2000). *Aphasiology: Disorders and practice*. Boston, MA: Allyn & Bacon.

Elman, R., & Bernstein, E. (1999). The efficacy of group communication treatment in adults with chronic aphasia. *Journal of Speech-Language Research, 42*, 411–419.

Elman, R. J. (1998). Memories of the plateau: Health-care changes provide an opportunity to redefine aphasia treatment and discharge. *Aphasiology, 12*, 227–231.

Elman, R. J. (1999). Introduction to group treatment of neurogenic communication disorders. In R. Elman (Ed.), *Group treatment of neurogenic communication disorders: The expert clinician's approach*. Boston: Butterworth-Heinemann.

Fawcus, M. (1992). Group work with the aphasia adult. In M. Fawcus (Ed.), *Group encounters in speech and language therapy*. Leicester, UK: Far Communications, Kibworth Publishers.

Franz, S. (1924). Studies in re-education: The aphasics. *Journal of Comparative Psychology, 4*, 349–429.

Frattali, C. (2000). Health care restructuring and its focus on functional outcomes. In L. Worrall (Ed.), *Neurogenic communication disorders: A functional approach*. New York: Thieme.

Frazier, C., & Ingham, S. (1920). A review of the effects of gunshot wounds of the head. *Archives of Neurology and Psychiatry, 3*, 17–40.

Glass, T. A., & Maddox, G. (1992). The quality and quantity of social support: Stroke recovery as psychosocial transition. *Social Science Medicine, 34*(11), 1249–1269.

Goldstein, K. (1942). *After-effects of brain injuries in war: Their evaluation and treatment.* New York: Grune & Stratton.

Goldstein, K. (1948). *Language and language disturbances.* New York: Grune & Stratton.

Granich, L. (1947). *Aphasia: A guide to retraining.* New York: Grune & Stratton.

Head, H. (1926). *Aphasia and kindred disorders of speech* (Vols 1 & 2). London: Cambridge University Press.

Holland, A. (1991). Pragmatic aspects of interventions in aphasia. *Journal of Neurolinguistics, 6*, 197–211.

Horner-Catt, J. (1999). *The language of clinical ethics.* Paper presented at the Academy of Neurologic Communication Disorders & Sciences, San Francisco, CA.

Isserlin, M. (1929). Die pathologische Physiologie der Sprache. Ergebnisse der Psyiologie. *Biologischene Chemie und Experimentellen Pharmakologie, 29*, 129.

Jennings, B. (1993). Healing the self: The moral meaning of relationships in rehabilitation. *American Journal of Physical Medicine and Rehabilitation, 72*, 401–404.

Jennings, B. (1999). A life greater than the sum of its sensations: Ethics, dementia, and the quality of life. *Journal of Mental Health and Aging, 5*, 95–106.

Jennings, B. (2001, February). *The ordeal of reminding: Traumatic brain injury and the encumbered self.* Paper presented at the Hastings Center and Disability Ethics Center Meeting, Rehabilitation Institute of Chicago.

Kagan, A. (1995). Revealing the competence of aphasic adults through conversation: A challenge to health professionals. *Topics in Stroke Rehabilitation, 2*(1), 15–28.

Kagan, A. (1998). Supported conversation for adults with aphasia: Methods and resources for training conversation partners. [Clinical forum.] *Aphasiology, 12*(9), 816–830.

Kearns, K. (1986). Group therapy in aphasia: Theoretical and practical considerations. In R. Chapey (Ed.), *Language intervention strategies in adult aphasia* (2nd Edn). Baltimore: Williams & Wilkins.

Kleinman, A. (1995). *Writing at the margin: Discourse between anthropology and medicine.* Berkeley, CA: University of California Press.

Luria, A. R. (1948). *Rehabilitation of brain functioning after war traumas.* Moscow: Academy of Sciences Press.

Lyon, J. G. (1992). Communication use and participation in life for adults with aphasia in natural settings: The scope of the problem. *American Journal of Speech-Language Pathology, 1*, 7–14.

Lyon, J. G. (1995). Drawing: Its value as a communication aid for adults with aphasia. *Aphasiology, 9*, 33–50.

Lyon, J. G. (1996). Optimizing communication and participation in life for aphasic adults and their primary caregivers in natural settings: A use model for treatment. In G. L. Wallace (Ed.), *Adult aphasia rehabilitation.* Boston: Butterworth-Heinemann.

Lyon, J. G. (1997). *Coping with aphasia.* San Diego, CA: Singular Publishing Group.

Mills, C. (1904). Treatment of aphasia by training. *Journal of American Medical Association, 43*, 1940–1949.

National Institutes of Health (NIH) (1990). *US Department of Public Health Services. NIH Publication 91, 391.* Washington, DC: US Department of Health and Human Services.

Newborn, B. (1997). *Return to Ithaca: A woman's triumph over the disabilities of a severe stroke.* Rockport, MA: Element Books.

Nielsen, J. (1936). *Agnosia, apraxia, aphasia: Their value in cerebral localization.* New York: Hoeber.

Parr, S., Byng, S., Gilpin, S., & Ireland, C. (1997). *Talking about aphasia.* Buckingham, UK: Open University Press.

Parr, S. P., & Byng, S. (2000). Perspectives and priorities: Accessing user views in functional communication assessment. In L. Worrall & C. Frattali (Eds.), *Neurogenic disorders: A functional approach.* New York: Thieme.

Poppelreuter, W. (1915). Ueber psychische ausfall serscheinungen nach hirnverletzungen. *Munchener Medizinische Wochenschrift, 62,* 489–491.

Pound, C., Parr, S., Lindsay, J., & Woolf, C. (2000). *Beyond aphasia: Therapies for living with communication disability.* Oxford, UK: Speechmark Publishing Limited.

Raskin, A. H. (1992). The words I lost. *The New York Times,* 19 September, p. 19.

Sarno, M. T. (1986). *The silent minority: The patient with aphasia.* Hemphill Lecture, Rehabilitation Institute of Chicago.

Sarno, M. T. (1993). Aphasia rehabilitation: Psychosocial and ethical considerations. *Aphasiology, 7,* 321–334.

Sarno, M. T. (1997). Quality of life in aphasia in the first year post stroke. *Aphasiology, 11,* 665–679.

Sheehan, V. (1946). Rehabilitation of aphasics in an army hospital. *Journal of Speech and Hearing Disorders, 11,* 149–157.

Simmons-Mackie, N. (1993). *Management of aphasia: Towards a social model.* Workshop presented at the Julie McGee Lambeth Conference, Denton, TX.

Simmons-Mackie, N. (1998). A solution to the discharge dilemma in aphasia: Social approaches to aphasia management. [Clinical forum.] *Aphasiology, 12,* 231–239.

Simmons-Mackie, N. (2000). Social approaches to the management of aphasia. In L. Worrall & C. Frattelli (Eds.), *Neurogenic disorders: A functional approach.* New York: Thieme.

Simmons-Mackie, N., & Damico, J. (1996). Accounting for handicaps in aphasia: Communicative assessment from an authentic social perspective. *Disability and Rehabilitation, 18,* 540–549.

Simmons-Mackie, N., & Damico, J. (1997). Reformulating the definition of compensatory strategies in aphasia. *Aphasiology, 11,* 761–781.

Simmons-Mackie, N., & Damico, J. (1999). Social role negotiation in aphasia therapy: Competence, incompetence and conflict. In D. Kovarsky, J. Duchan, & M. Maxwell (Eds.), *Constructing (in)competence: Disabling evaluations in clinical and social interaction,* Mahwah, NJ: Lawrence Erlbaum Associates Inc.

Weisenburg, T., & McBride, K. (1935). *Aphasia: A clinical and psychological study.* New York: Commonwealth Fund.

Wepman, J. (1951). *Recovery from aphasia.* New York: Ronald Press.

Wulf, H. (1979). *Aphasia: My world alone.* Detroit, MI: Wayne State University Press.

3 Dare to be different: The person and the practice

Carole Pound

Neurology is largely a veterinary business—it deals almost exclusively with what can be measured and tested; hardly at all with the inner experience, the inner structure, the subjectivity of the subject. It prides itself on managing to exclude these, on being wholly objective science, on being wholly concerned (like physics) with the public, the visible, the demonstrable. No personal terms are allowed in neurology . . . we do not have any "neurology" of identity.

(Sacks, 1991, p. 189)

In *A Leg to Stand On* (1991) Oliver Sacks gives a masterly account of his experience as doctor turned patient. My aim in this chapter is to describe my own account of being both a therapist and patient—these separate but mysteriously converging paths. I am attempting to put into words a strangely elusive reality, because I am convinced that the very inability to articulate the contradictions of disability and identity within rehabilitation is perhaps the force that drives professionals and patients to the safe haven of science and objectivity. The resulting silence allows little place for dialogue and negotiation, thereby reinforcing the powerful voice of medicine to which Sacks alludes.

Besides the reliance on objectivity, is a reliance on the notion of cure. The Siren's song of restitution or cure has many seductive properties to both patient and practitioner, luring us to the promise of return to health, wholeness, and therefore re-engagement with the life that we knew. The recognition that one or both parties, clinician and patient, work from this false promise of cure can be easily suppressed. The alternative path, that of learning to live with disability, value difference, and engage with a changed identity, is a longer, more uncertain journey. This second path is beset with problems of articulating inner experience, making connections between impairments and identities, and, as therapists, listening to painful struggles of others—struggles that we may lack the strength to hear or the power to cure. However, my hope is that by retracing some of my own faltering steps as patient and practitioner I might enable therapists to enter into more explicit dialogue with themselves, their colleagues, and their clients about some of the navigation points in learning to live with difference.

In this chapter, then, I will attempt to explore the complex interrelationship of therapy, disability, and change. In particular I will discuss the importance of identity and expertise in living with a disability. In doing so I will draw on ideas from disability studies and from narrative approaches to illness. In an unusual departure from my more comfortable approach to talking about therapy I will also draw heavily on my personal experience of facing and learning to live with sudden acquired disability. I will try to relate how personal experiences of and reflections on participating in therapy as patient, therapist, and bewildered traveller have shaped many aspects of the therapy service that my colleagues and I aspire to offer in the organization in which we work—Connect, the Communication Disability Network. I will end with examples of some of the principles and processes that underpin our culture and practice at Connect. I offer these ideas in the hope that they will provide discussion points for those of us who struggle daily to understand the tantalizing paradoxes of the "neurology of identity".

THE CONTEXT

Now for my personal interaction with disability. This is not an easy story to write about. How much should I expose of my personal thoughts, struggles, beliefs, to an audience with whom I interact as a "professional" not a "patient"? Many therapists I know work long and hard to "hear the story" of the clients they work with, so an inside experience is unlikely to surprise or offend you—but this is my story and I *am* struggling to interact with you simultaneously as Carole the speech and language therapist and Carole the "patient", the person on the other side of the rehabilitation divide. Two selves so clearly related yet so carefully circumscribed and kept distinct. It puzzles me now how little I reflected on the unnatural disengagement of these two protagonists. Clearly as therapists we need to acknowledge and maintain professional boundaries. But how much does the distancing of therapist aims, action, and experience from client aims, actions, and experience interfere with our mutual understanding of and communication about ourselves as we interact in therapy?

So what happened to cause me to experience chronic disability first-hand and to want to become a therapist? Thoughts of therapy and disability could not have been further from my mind as I graduated from university and set off hopefully to life as a tennis coach in the south of France. I looked forward to suntans, glamour, freedom, quite apart from fine wine and passionate liaisons on the Cote d'Azur. How ironic that just 2 days before the spinal injury that left my right arm an immobile shadow of its former self, I was attending a coaching course where we were made to experience incoordination and incompetence by trying to play left-handed.

As a consequence of catapulting from my moped into a wall, I lost my supermodel looks (though not my imagination), my arm stopped working, and the severed nerves introduced me to nerve pain, my daily companion since that time. My tennis coaching career over, and my interest in rehabilitation stimulated, several years later I happily settled on a different career as a speech and language therapist.

Why am I telling you this? I sense a nagging need to justify my apparent "off piste" narrative of "personal tragedy". My professional voice warning me not to expose too much of my self, not to risk your perceptions as a—a what; "tragic victim", unprofessional self-discloser, "poorly adjusted" disabled person, a person who courageously got her life back together, superwoman? Perhaps this streak of self-consciousness illustrates nothing more than my personal fears. Or perhaps my well-formed worry fantasies represent an internalization of those well-recognized responses to disability within western civilization, responses that focus on loss, tragedy, and separateness.

PATHWAYS THROUGH THERAPY

My early career as a patient was dominated by pain, confusion, and a determined quest to "get better". This meant a focused pursuit of the best surgery, the best physiotherapy, and even the best prosthetic device which might offer some kind of bizarre dysfunctional movement to a patently nonfunctioning arm. Time with therapists was precious—not just because it gave access to skills and expertise that would surely improve movement, but because it provided a rare circumscribed space to talk about an impairment, pain, which dominated my life but which I neither understood nor felt able to talk about to others in my everyday life. A hidden disability that had no name worthy of it—"pain", such a bland, reductionist term with no association to the surreal and utterly pervasive sensory, affective, and emotional experience I was living with.

Only recently have I made more explicit connections between pain and aphasia. Both seem steeped in mystery, myth, and paradox, the intense physical and psychic reality of both and yet the way their intangible nature defies vocabulary, description, and meaningful conversation. Physiologically the reality is located at the point of lesion, yet psychologically it has a new and far more invasive geography, reverberating through one's whole self and sense of self—the hidden, invisible nature of pain and aphasia, and their propensity for being misunderstood by others. For example, others easily interpret the difficulty of dealing with pain as psychological weakness, and the difficulty of controlling language as intellectual incompetence. And finally there is a parallel between the sense of expectation and ultimate disappointment experienced by those who live with pain and aphasia, that modern medicine can promise so much yet deliver so little.

The illusion of medical omnipotence was fostered in my case by early experiences of rerouting nerves and muscles in my arm. I will be forever grateful for those miraculous interventions. Perhaps these small miracles equate with the subtle but reassuring shifts in communication that well-directed language therapy can deliver. But, these changes not withstanding, I would also strongly agree with Wendell (1996, p. 137) who warns, "Knowledge of how to live with the suffering and limitation it cannot cure remains on the margins of medicine and medicine's cognitive and social authority helps to perpetuate cultural ignorance about disability and incurable illness."

UNDERSTANDING THE NATURE OF RECOVERY

Understanding the nature of a complex impairment took many years of asking questions, scouring medical books, and keeping an eye out for medical advances in the management of brachial plexus lesions and chronic pain. One of the most confusing aspects of these early years of being disabled was the concept of "coping" and adjustment. By this time I was fully engaged in my speech and language therapy training, and discovering amongst other things the psychology of grieving and the language of rehabilitation. If I personally was still keen to pursue more medical interventions and still experiencing wild mood swings, had I really reached a stage of acknowledgement and acceptance of my own "loss"? If not, was I secretly signing up to the club of "pathological" grievers—those tragic figures who were stuck in a dark, Dantesque, and hope-free limbo of anger and depression? To the external world I may have played a rather convincing part of "coping well", but my body and mind frequently screamed a different and silent story.

Other sources of confusion were the frequent appearances of newspaper articles and television programmes where the latest techniques in nerve regeneration experiments were proudly paraded by medical experts. Encouragement to pursue miracle cures and read up on bionic arms were not in short supply. This direction came not only from well-meaning family and friends but via regular television, radio, and newspaper accounts. The story in the UK of PC Olds, a policeman crippled by a criminal's bullet 20 years ago and bravely trying to walk again with electric implants, captured the nation's interest. As did his "understandable" suicide when the miracle did not materialize. Advances in science and technology give well-publicized hope to many spinally injured people today and continue simultaneously to reinforce the omnipotence of science and, implicitly, the inability of the human spirit to cope with living differently. This open, public discussion of hope and cure was, for me, in complete contrast to the powerful and solitary debate that raged in my head and in my emotions as I incompetently managed the real "adjustment" process. Role models within rehabilitation and the media were those who worked hard and battled to overcome the odds, not those who struggled with anger, challenged the power of medicine, demonstrated pride and confidence in self-management techniques.

Initially, as a therapist, I felt largely untroubled by these contradictions. My job was to help patients understand their condition, improve their speech and language as much as neurological damage allowed, and somehow support them to "come to terms" with their changed lives (which of course I could only glimpse from my therapy rooms in the hospital or rehabilitation unit). It was troubling that rehabilitation rarely spanned a period adequate to reach anything approaching the end point on these pathways. Looking back, I cringe at some of my clumsy attempts to speed realistic adjustments to limitations on the part of patients and families. I also, retrospectively, question decisions about the timing and allocation of time to different parts of the rehabilitation process. How little option I gave clients in how they divided their precious therapy time, and how unclear I was in setting out the different components of therapy. For example, it was not difficult for me to listen to language errors and tales of determination. But to listen to the repeated stories of chaos and confusion and to develop therapeutic interventions appropriate to learning to live with difference—these offered therapeutic challenges of a quite different dimension. Rare newspaper reports and television programmes about language impairment may have raised my therapist hackles, as they wildly misrepresented the reality and possibilities of therapy, but I saw them as isolated irritations, rather than as an extension of the medicalization of disability that each of my work settings supported. I felt, as a therapist, very comfortable within the culture of rehabilitation, and for many years, in spite of my own experiences of disability, quite unable to challenge hard-won roles, expertise, and status as a therapist.

NEW APPROACHES TO DISABILITY

It was therefore a rude awakening to me as a therapist to discover writings from the disability movement in the early 1990s. Redefining disability and the primary source of disability as located in the social environment led to convincing challenges to the supremacy of medical and philanthropic models of disability. These disabled people quite justifiably were challenging my power and status in the "disability industry" and articulating stories of oppression and exclusion. This was not what I heard in media reports, or indeed from many clients and relatives new to a life of disability. Yet such themes and alternative stories had a startling clarity and connection with some of my experiences as a disabled person and as carer of a family member with a long-term disability. Hearing alternative stories of living with disability was both a revelation and liberation to me as a disabled person.

As a therapist, there was a different but also welcome engagement with a new perspective on disability. Barriers in terms of attitudes, access to information, and accessible communication environments did indeed seem a critical part of learning to live with disability for people with aphasia. Instead of simplistic concepts of "coming to terms" and adjustment, these new disability discourses spoke of personal and social struggles. Personal and political accounts of disability led naturally, in some cases, to a genuine celebration of difference, a sense of unabashed affirmation which I noticed reverberated with the voices of some people with disabilities who came through our rehabilitation services—people who were variously described as "poorly adjusted", "lacking in insight", or "exceptional" in the way they had "accepted" their illness.

But as a therapist, reading this material also produced a profound discomfort. As I explored the literature further I felt discomfort at the angry voice of the oppressed and dispossessed (disabled people) railing against their powerful oppressor (the non-disabled rehabilitation workers). No one can deny the reality of the power divide between therapist and patient (see, for example, French, 1994; Oliver, 1996) but relocating the source of disablement as within the social and medical environment is a stern challenge to a therapist's hard-won status and accoutrements of power.

Having analyzed and conquered my initial defensiveness, I evaluated the "social model of disability" literature with a more measured eye. Some key concerns remained. Amongst them was a worry that some of these commentators were employing directness and simplicity for political expediency, to swing the pendulum of power to the other extreme. Spinally injured wheelchair users, with their energy and language intact, may indeed be able to participate on equal terms in an environment adapted for wheelchair users. But how do people with language and cognitive disabilities gain equal access to work, meetings, positions of power? And how can environments be modified to allow equal participation for people with impairments such as pain and fatigue? Other than some feminist discussions of the sociology of the impaired body (Morris, 1996), the disconnection between impairment and disability seemed radically oversimplified. Nevertheless, there was something fresh, raw, and appealing about these disability discourses, and at last a dialogue about difference that went beyond the focus on loss and adjustment.

DEVELOPING NEW IDENTITIES: CONTROL, TRANSCENDENCE, AND SOMETHING IN BETWEEN

It is not uncommon for people within the disability movement to talk about acquiring disability as the best thing that ever happened to them. This is a challenging concept for non-disabled people. But it also challenges many people struggling to live with chronic illness and disability. How many disabled people, if offered a cure for their disability, would take it without hesitation? This is not to negate the ease with which many people with disabilities identify clear gains and positive development of aspects of their identity intricately bound up with their experience of disability. But re-construing one's sense of self and self-identity to incorporate the physical, emotional, and lifestyle changes associated with a new state of (disabled) being is not an easy transition.

Whilst the social model of disability extols the virtues of the positive disabled identity, an affirmation of what it is to be disabled (Swain & French, 2000), it is less explicit about how such a state might be achieved. This is particularly the case for those whose communication, lifestyle, and person-hood has taken a battering from the impact of stroke. These individuals are grappling with profound changes without language and within a culture that regards and treats disability as personal tragedy.

From my own experience I can identify some clear milestones in develop-ing a more positive disabled identity. This was a long and rocky road, and only the glorious tool of hindsight allows me to see some coherent themes emerging. The themes have to do with my perception of lack of support, of groping in the dark. Gaining some sense of control over my condition came through accessing a body of information on my condition, not just from doctors but from frequent "checking out" interactions with therapists. Check-ing out why I was experiencing this or that twinge, checking out my inter-pretation of new information with someone better versed in neurophysiology, trying out my still hesitant ability to articulate bodily and psychological experiences of my disability with a knowing listener, seeking reassurance that my latest self-management technique was sensible and valid. This was another reason why the time and space with therapists felt so precious to me. I supported this by reading and re-reading academic reports in the books and journals of medical libraries, or case notes and letters written about my condition. Perhaps this skilling up meant that over time I was able to read media reports of scientific advances with interest but also with a more measured and more critical eye.

Another form of control and mastery came from the increasing knowledge that I could live with the unpredictability and uncertainty of my condition. This might be dependent in part on pacing myself or using techniques to help me sleep. But it was also about replacing the fear and foreboding of how I would handle a future problematic situation with the reality of getting through the bad days in a rather ordinary and everyday way. Living with something that never leaves you can easily lead to being absorbed by your condition. The high-tech dramas of surgery, hospital appointments, and new treatments take on a status and significance that more mundane every-day strategies lack. Taking it easy, having a hot bath, swigging a gin and tonic may seem little match for more costly high-profile medical interven-tions administered by scientific experts, but to date it is these everyday supports that offer most significant forms of relief, even if they do remain both transitory and incomplete.

Another turning point was learning that pleasure and pain are neither mutually exclusive, nor in mortal combat with one another. I came to realize that expending energy on having fun and living life was rather more important than preserving all one's energy and motivation for doing therapy and chasing dreams of cure. I was able to get lost in the flow. I was able to reach some kind of transcendence through concentration and engagement in activity. This was not the tangible cure or change I had hoped for. However its therapeutic power to remove me from absorption in illness offered a magical escape from a focus on pain, difficulty, and disablement. I would compare this sense of losing consciousness of pain and the self in engagement in the moment as akin to Lyon's discussion of the person with aphasia losing consciousness of their aphasia in the "flow" of engagement with conversation or other pleasurable activity (Lyon et al. 1997; see also Csikzentimihalyi, 1990).

Techniques in self-management are widely acknowledged as powerful methods of taking control for people living with chronic illness and disability. In many intractable conditions such as arthritis and pain management there is now sound evidence that such techniques are the key contributor to change in one's sense of well-being (e.g., Barlow, Williams, & Wright, 1999; Lorig, Mazonson, & Holman, 1993). But while the acknowledgement of patient expertise and self-management techniques rightly form the cornerstone of government initiatives to shift power from the professional to the patient (Department of Health, 2001) we should not be naive in considering the hurdles for both professionals and patients in locating and valuing expertise. For me, another key milestone in acknowledging my strength and experience as a disabled person was the recognition that through my experience I had acquired an expertise that my doctors and therapists lacked, and that I really could make a contribution. However for many years the uncertainty with which I experienced each day was no match for the clarity and certainty of the medical perspective, and consequently I afforded my growing expertise little value or status.

It is interesting now to reflect on how telling one's story to others—to patients, to therapists, to medical students—can be a moment of affirmation or diminishment depending on the dynamics of the situation. So being prodded and poked in front of medical students, having one's story hijacked and reinterpreted by the medical expert (as on the occasion where an eminent consultant instructed his visitors how "these people often feel utterly hopeless"), can merely serve to reinforce the knowledge and power of the expert doctor/therapist (and the utter hopelessness of the patient!).

An opportunity to contribute a genuine lived experience is different. On several occasions I was encouraged by medical practitioners who involved me through thoughtful listening and careful questioning. In many cases also, an explicit statement from the therapist or doctor that they cannot really be close to your everyday experience was an important inroad to sharing some understanding of my condition. This quite simple technique endowed *me* with power and offered me an avenue for exploring different ways forward with a respected partner in my therapy.

Finally, this development of a sense of expertise and control seemed located in the process of recognizing true expertise in other people who live productively, thoughtfully, and expertly with their own disabilities. In the early days after my accident I failed totally to recognize this expertise, believing all the answers must surely lie with the people in white coats and uniforms. No one with "patient" status approached the expert role for me—how could they, when they hadn't been able to "overcome" whatever disability they had? Yet perhaps it was exactly that wider view on expertise, knowledge, and its integration with real life (outside the hospital ward) that might have accelerated my increasing confidence in my coping techniques.

THE DYNAMICS OF THERAPY

Do these themes have any resonances for people with aphasia struggling to construct a more robust disabled identity? I believe a range of similar themes and transitions emerge from interviews with people living with aphasia (Parr, Byng, Gilpin, & Ireland, 1997; Simpson & Pound, 2001). Here, I will focus on just a few of the changes and challenges to my practice as an aphasia therapist resulting from these insights on power, control, and expertise.

1   Frequently and explicitly acknowledge the person's expertise in their condition. In some ways this is the experiential competence parallel of the "I know you know" catchphrase of the Aphasia Institute in Toronto, where conversation partners are trained to explicitly acknowledge the aphasic person's communicative competence (see, for example, Kagan, 1998).
2   Appreciate the skills involved in, and the value and impact of authentic, responsive listening. This may be a part of group or individual therapy or it may be the tool of an in-depth interview. Whilst many clients may not give this particular experience of therapy the same status as direct exercises on language, speech, or writing, it is likely to be equally or more beneficial. Be sure to record some of the content and process of this listening "therapy" to provide the clients' thoughts and reflections back to them with the same tangibility as is achieved with language, speech, or writing exercises.
3   Think about how to provide access to opportunities for people to tell their own stories and hear the stories of others (Barrow, 2000; Pound, 1999). Many people dismiss groups and sharing of experiences as ineffectual because they lack the focus and clarity of one-to-one exercises. The challenge of sharing stories of expertise is to provide a context that pays attention to structure, clarity, and process. This means, as with any good therapy, giving careful thought to the therapeutic aims of the group, and to the preparation of environment, materials, and resources

which will allow these aims to be met. What environmental conditions are required? How will story telling and listening be supported, clarified, and recorded? What skills does the group facilitator require to support the process of focused group-work? How will individuals in the group be communicatively supported? What are the opportunities outside the therapy room for sharing experiences and expertise?

4   Allow your therapist expertise to interact with but not overpower the expertise of the person living with aphasia. Offer experiences and insights but do not make assumptions that they fit this particular individual. Offer theoretical and academic insights but make them sufficiently accessible so that people can challenge them. Share your own views but be aware that these always risk being received as more important than the views of "patients".

5   Be genuinely prepared to change your view on an issue in response to the views of service users. This does not mean that service users' views should go unchallenged. Provide a context and a culture where your views can also be genuinely challenged.

NARRATIVES OF ILLNESS AND DISABILITY

Listening to, bearing witness to, and interacting with the stories and expertise of the patient or wounded storyteller, is one of the therapeutic principles of narrative-based practice (Greenhalgh & Hurwitz, 1998). This rapidly growing literature is likely to offer an easier, less challenging approach to redistributing power and expertise than the politics of disability. Narratives of illness (Frank, 1995; Kleinman, 1988) provide a framework for listening to the stories of patients and practitioners in order to better understand and navigate the experience of illness.

Arthur Frank (1995) describes the person suddenly confronted with illness or disability as the "wounded storyteller". It is through telling stories, recounting illness narratives, and integrating these into life narratives that a person might best navigate the biographical discontinuity, the disorientating storm, that sudden illness whips up.

Frank identifies three overarching narratives—chaos, restitution, and quest—which together underscore the plot and storylines of living with chronic disability. The chaos narrative tells of the body being swept away with no sense of control or possibility of return to order. Events lack sequence or causality, and the person is buffeted by confusion and experiences beyond their control. The restitution narrative uses the storyline of "Yesterday I was healthy, today I'm sick, but tomorrow I'll be healthy again". As in television commercials about the restorative function of a particular medication, this storyline has both a sense of predictability ("tomorrow I'll be healthy again and back to normal") and a faith in some external agent (doctor, medication, therapist) bringing about the restoration to health. In this way the restitution narrative allows for the self to be dissociated from the body ("I'm fine but my body needs fixing") and for the expertise of others to be the critical agent of change. Within the quest narrative, illness is viewed as a journey in which the traveller seeks alternative ways of understanding and being ill. The teller of quest stories accepts the challenge of illness and seeks to use it in some way. Illness becomes an opening for a new way of living and the teller reclaims a sense of agency that is absent for the authors of tales of chaos and restitution.

Whilst Frank does not suggest that people who acquire chronic disabilities pass neatly through these different narratives in a linear progression to the nirvana of "acceptance" it is tempting to equate the dominating themes to phases of illness biography. The chaos and confusion of the early days where all is lost and in turmoil. The determination and motivation to recover, typically through the expertise of doctors and therapists as restitution narratives predominate. And finally, for some, the peace or new direction of the quest narrative, where life again has a purpose as does the disability/ illness one is living with.

COMPETING NARRATIVES AND SIMULTANEOUS NARRATIVES

Reflecting on my own illness navigation, I can remember vividly the chaos of the early months and years as all seemed lost—career, confidence, future hopes and dreams. As the twitch of some movement returned there was a shift to the "work hard, get more surgery, get another degree of elbow flexion" perspective. The focus of getting more recovery, more movement, more hope from biomedical interventions was a strong and seductive songsheet to sing from. The fact that this narrative interacted minimally (if at all) with my everyday life—I still could not brush my teeth, comb my hair, have any relief from the routine of pain or the sense that my life was not whole—did nothing to lessen its grasp. The messages around me also nurtured this narrative—not just the reports of bionic arms and medical discoveries, but also inevitably the thrust of my speech therapy training, where the individual model of disability reigned supreme.

Reflecting back on my therapy practice at this time, I feel the powerful grip of restitution. Entry through the gates of Disability World as a customer or provider seemed to set up a chain reaction of cosseting and protection through the (hopefully shortlived) storm of chaos. But then, moving deeper inside this new world, the cementing of patient and practitioner in the complicity of restitution would be an exhilarating, mysterious ride together. The requests I most heard were to "make my speech better" and "restore me to normal" not to "help me lead a new life as a disabled person". How much were these messages filtered through my own illness and practitioner narrative? How much were they the consequence of a lack of imagination on the part of patient and therapist? How much were they mediated by the default vocabulary of a person exploring a new world without access to that new world's language? But even when I tried my best to navigate a new story with a patient, I wonder how much faith I had that a rewarding new direction could be found? My training and ideas for therapy were driven largely by a focus on changing the impairment, not supporting the journey, and I lacked confidence in my skills to travel new and uncertain roads.

THE SEDUCTION OF THE RESTITUTION NARRATIVE

What were the turning points for me in escaping the grip of restitution? As both patient and practitioner it was the realization that living with disability did not mean having to be strong and "courageous" all the time—the discovery that admitting to feeling crap was not a signal that I had failed to adjust. I finally realized that I could still hope for improved pain relief without expending disproportionate energy pursuing dreams of cure. Unlike the powerful public narratives of restitution where direct, emotive language underscores the heroic battles and courageous struggles of superheroes, it was the realization that my everyday struggles were, like those of many others, full of monotony, but also of uncertainty and unpredictability. Surviving those everyday struggles is perhaps just as "superhuman", but is not recognized as such.

I suspect that many other practitioners feel, as I do, the stomach turning cringe of failure when a client eagerly tells of a newspaper or television report about the latest cure for brains. Those clients, who seem to be moving forward with their life, taking control and integrating their past and new disabled self, are suddenly catapulted into new expectations of restored function by the latest stem cell research, or media neuroscience. The seduction of a new cure can feel so at odds with the matter of getting on with your life as a disabled person. The imposition of the importance of cure, and the implication that a person cannot be whole or good enough without a cure is in direct conflict with the self-respect of people with disabilities (Wendell, 1996).

Perhaps this is exactly the tension it is easy to feel when working on improving someone's language ability while simultaneously working with them to learn to live with their ongoing limitations. How easy it is to urge a client to strive for more words, longer sentences, greater accuracy of word production. Careful selection of personally relevant vocabulary items and stimuli can support both client and therapist in linking this work to real life and collaboratively pursuing a "better life" with more words. But what is real life in the context of living with stroke and aphasia? Is a return to life as a whole and confident person contingent upon access to words or access to, for example, feelings of self-esteem, fun, and life opportunities as a person who lives with part of their language system missing? How do therapist and client reconcile lack of full linguistic recovery with being comfortable and satisfied with a new "whole" identity as a person with aphasia? What explicit attention should therapist and client pay to promoting that more elusive goal of improving life without improving language?

A significant realization in my therapist career, as in my patient career, was understanding that wanting a cure and learning to live with disability can and frequently do exist as fickle but close neighbours. The therapies described below, in particular the "access to information" in the health issues group, are a few examples of therapies that I believe can explicitly work to create a natural coexistence for competing narratives. Clear and repeated access to information presented in a non-sensationalized manner, with space for discussion and reference to self, can be a powerful tool in effective self-management.

DOING THERAPY DIFFERENTLY: WHAT DOES THIS MEAN IN PRACTICE?

Daring to be different in practice, for me, then has entailed a rethinking and reconceptualization of the scope and focus of therapy. It has also entailed learning to live with the paradoxes and contradictions of therapy in a way that reflects the paradoxes and contradictions of learning to live with disability. Below I itemize some of the key factors of change in my practice as a result of these insights. I do not propose these as a prescription for success but more as speculative reference points about how to change tack in therapy to be consistent with a resource-constrained and evidence-focused world.

1 Attend to attitudes and assumptions within therapy and life which impact on the development of new identities—identities that integrate and do not apologize for aphasia:
   - Acknowledgement of the full impact of context and culture on the content of therapy and how clients perceive it.
   - Acknowledgement of the way narratives, particularly of restitution, imbue the context and content of therapy as well as the external world in western society.
   - Acknowledgement of the roles that power and status play on the undertaking of and engagement with therapy.
   - Attention to the time and conditions that allow for therapeutic and social context to be a part of therapy—for example, what frameworks and resources go into focused group therapy?
   - Discovery of the conditions and opportunities external to the "therapy room" work that can support engagement in activity and life in a way that does not reinforce incompetence or further disempower.

For example, people with aphasia can take part in teaching (e.g., training others to be conversation partners). In this case therapeutic attention should be given to the process of preparation, feedback, and highlighting the specific usefulness of the person with aphasia's experience. This allows for a foregrounding of control rather than tokenistic use of clients in training exercises.

- Exploitation of fun and creativity as a tool and focus of therapy. Therapy is a serious business but laughter and lightness and a freeing from a focus on doom and damage can be a prime facilitator of learning and moving on (see Chapter 6 by Nina Simmons-Mackie).

2 Reflection on the role of the therapist and on how to make use of therapeutic skills as a resource for support and expertise in relation to the person with aphasia:

- Act as a reference point—for clarifying and revisiting information, advice, and research, and working with the person to locate themselves within this knowledge.
- Act as a guide—to show people what is (and is not) available and where sources of help can be found.
- Act as an advocate—giving people with aphasia and others the tools to access services, complain about service gaps, expect flexible and multifaceted support opportunities.
- Act as an interpreter—clearly translating for people the benefits and advantages of more "oblique" therapy experiences, for example, sharing stories with peers, participating in group-work, practising both skills and new identities in a carefully supported way.
- Create the conditions that allow for more than a "patient–therapist" relationship. Boundaries are important but enabling someone to feel like a person as opposed to a patient, and modelling person-to-person (not therapist-to-patient) interaction is a powerful tool for supporting re-engagement with non-patient life and roles.
- Balance confidence and focus based on therapist expertise with respectful listening and exploration of therapist naiveté—i.e., work at the opportunities for integrating and valuing the integration of therapist and client experience.
- Be confident in spending time with other key players in the rehabilitation process—this may mean training sessions with other rehabilitation staff and supporters, direct interventions with relatives and friends, or opportunities for greater reflection on practitioner narratives and the way they interact or clash with the core narratives of clients and relatives.
- Be a skilled conversation partner (Simmons-Mackie & Kagan, 1999) and also a skilled narrative partner (Pound, 1999).

Does this list imply that administrative, listening, and more generic skills should replace or have priority over the technical skills of language and communication therapy? Most definitely not. I still greatly value the technical knowledge and expertise that my physiotherapists shared with me. I have no doubt that, were I to become aphasic, I would seek the best aphasia therapist possible to help improve my language skills. But in retrospect I also realize that this form of expertise alone did not move me forward. I valued the careful listening of therapists and non-therapists, and the challenge to view things differently that came from people who lived with disabilities themselves. Ultimately it was these people with their entirely different knowledge and understanding of the world of the "other" that helped me to realize that my greatest steps in rehabilitation happened outside the therapy room.

Listening to clients discussing their likes and dislikes of individual therapy, it is often difficult to find features that relate to more technical aspects of language exercises. More often they highlight time, space, and a listening relationship as the features of therapy they most value. It is this intense and rather intimate relationship that acts as a rock in a time of stormy chaos. It is this holding ground that becomes the first real reference point to a clearer direction and more hopeful future. That is not to undervalue the technical skills of the therapist, but it is also not to make light of the benefits of listening, respect, and mutual engagement. Fortunately these skills are not the privileged domain of speech and language therapists, opening up the potential of more creative, long-term options of support and therapeutic sustenance from a wider range of people.

DOING THERAPY DIFFERENTLY: IDEAS FOR ACTIVITIES

While conditions and a clear framework for delivering therapy are important, focused therapeutic activities also offer valuable footholds for the travelling therapist. A fear that either the activity or the conditions may be applied in a recipe-book fashion make me reluctant to describe therapeutic activities that might support some of this work. Yet the activities and exercises are often the most tangible point of therapy for clients and therapists alike. I offer the following not so much as tried and tested therapies but as a way of introducing opportunities to explore some of the paradoxes of therapy with clients, relatives, and peers.

Poetry: Reconstruing identity and recognizing power

"Cebrelating difference" is the way Chris Ireland, Connect's poet in residence, describes her aphasia poetry (Ireland & Pound, 2004). With so much attention to language errors as a source of deficit within both therapy and everyday life, this is no mean achievement. Far from wanting her "errors" to be corrected, Chris works and plays with her aphasia language to entertain, challenge, and move her audiences. This type of approach has a more powerful voice within disability arts culture where people with disabilities celebrate their difference and diversity in poetry, song, dance, imagery, and other forms of performance and creativity. This affirmative sense of identity (Swain & French, 2000) is a direct challenge to the personal tragedy interpretations of disability which often constrain and confuse newly disabled people. Somers (1994) and Thomas (1999) talk about the way people with disabilities frequently become trapped by these dominant stories and have few options for creating more confident stories of self and disability, "People construct identities (however multiple and changing) by locating themselves or being located within the repertoire of emplotted stories" (Somers, 1994, p. 613). Within healthcare settings and rehabilitation services, people learning to live with stroke frequently only have access to others' stories of chaos and restitution, risking perpetuation of more of the same.

Within the poetry workshops that Chris leads, participants (with and without aphasia) are encouraged to explore their own aphasia world, to have fun with language and to share experiences and stories of disability. Examples of some of the reactions to My Asphasia Word (see Figure 3.1) include a comment from a relative of a person with severe aphasia that "a curtain has been lifted—it's given me insight into the mind of a person with aphasia". Other reactions and points of discussion include the acknowledgement from people with aphasia about the violation of their world by others, the struggle to reclaim a new life, and the positive sense of being reborn (Khosa, 2004).

Through the model of aphasia as something powerful and through claiming difference as something creative, the poetry workshops give people an opportunity to associate with a positive, dignified way of living with disability. Not everyone may share Chris's "cebrelation" of difference. But not all of us share the same reactions to and opinions about Shakespeare and Chaucer either—other great storytellers who use their language in creative and novel ways. Reactions to poetry are not right or wrong, in the way that grammatical constructions can be accurate or inaccurate. They are just different.

Health issues: Responding to restitution

The "health issues group" at Connect was set up in response to people's need to know more about stroke, aphasia, and the huge body of research that tends to be either presented as a miracle cure by the media or explained in what is often jargonized gobbledygook on the internet and in research papers. The group is also a direct response to the powerful and pervasive role of the restitution narrative in modern western society. Unaddressed, this narrative can frequently seem to batter a clinician's best attempts to move someone on from a narrow focus on therapy and "getting better" to a life with a disability. The group therefore aimed to give people with aphasia access to a more rounded representation of research and information about stroke and health

ASPH/ASIA

MY ^   WORD

My BRAIN is bigger than

My WORDS

Maybe loud cymbols in LIFE

My WORD is bigger than

My BRAIN

Maybe viel visions insight

My BLUE is bluer than

My WORLD

Maybe reflect crazy mirrors

In the PINK more roseier than

My WAYS

Maybe childlife we lost

Figure 3.1 My Asphasia Word.

issues. By providing people with access to meaningful information and the opportunity to discuss its relevance to their condition, the group aimed to help people develop a realistic view on healthcare choices and, where appropriate, find ways of accessing further information or treatment.

In the RAW more rawer than

The OTHERS

Maybe body–mind–soul merge in pain

SPIRALLING down

Hues – rhythm – tingling than

DEEPER – DEEPER – DEEPER

DEEP at the END

Analytical VIPERS

INVADE MY SPACE

MAYBE – MY WAYS – MY WORLD

MY WORD

APHASIA

MY   ^   WORD !!!!

Chris Ireland, 1999

Figure 3.1 (Cont'd)

The group covered discussion about stem cell research, latest developments in clot-busting drugs, and an exploration of the benefits of alternative therapies in chronic disability. Because of issues arising around poor access to information, several sessions became dedicated to developing a GP toolkit, which would help individuals be proactive and assertive in accessing meaningful information from their doctors. Inevitably, another important part of the process was allowing group members the opportunities to tell and listen to narratives of illness that people had accrued over their careers as users of healthcare services.

Training conversation partners: Recognizing expertise

A frequent tale from people who live with aphasia is of being disengaged from life, excluded from involvement, or allowed in, but only on the periphery, as a "charity case". Because aphasia as a condition has become the professional domain of speech therapists, neurologists, neurolinguists, cognitive neuropsychologists etc., the people who live with aphasia are often not "allowed" to be expert in their own condition. The experience of being assessed and "done to", firmly perpetuates the entrapment within patienthood and inequality.

One way of actively involving people with aphasia and explicitly acknowledging their expertise is to engage them as trainers in education and awareness-raising initiatives. By this I do not mean being wheeled out to exhibit some weird and wonderful disorder of language, but as storytellers and people with powerful experiences to recount. To have some control over the content and delivery of the teaching, roles need to be negotiated and training aims agreed. Time needs to be spent on the initial explanation, the process of giving feedback, and the post training debrief.

The training conversation partners programme at Connect is largely based around the ideas of Aura Kagan and Jon Lyon, and focuses attention on the notion of competence. Kagan (1995, 1998) critically identifies the role of conversation in maintaining emotional and social well-being. Without participation in conversation and opportunities to reveal their inherent competence, people with aphasia risk becoming trapped in the negative spiral of reduced opportunity, social participation, and maintenance of self-worth. Teaching non-aphasic individuals to develop their own conversation-partner skills and acknowledge the (often masked) competence of the person with aphasia thus represents a source of power and control rather than passivity and patienthood. With conversation ramps, time, and assertiveness training, people with aphasia can both engage in conversation and actively provide feedback to trainees that they are too fast, too woolly, or too patronizing. As commentators throughout the training, they not only talk about but also demonstrate their expertise in their condition. In addition to making a contribution, people with aphasia acquire a status and power that validates their expertise and hopefully engages them in enjoyable conversations as a byproduct of the training.

It ain't what you do it's the way that you do it

In summary, each of the above, as with any group activity, offers the opportunity for discussion, sharing stories, expressing opinions. These ideas for therapy are nothing new or earth-shattering. But with attention to the issues of process and context expressed above, the groups offer a means of explicitly tackling themes of identity and expertise, access to information and control, and social engagement. By not apologizing for aphasia but acknowledging the desire to minimize its effects they can offer a more rounded approach to the complexity of learning to live with disability.

CONCLUSION

In summary, I have used my personal experience as patient and practitioner to discuss why reaching some state of "acceptance" or coming to terms with chronic disability is such a long and often lonely path. Not only is one battling the condition, but also the media, the views of friends and family, and even the friendly fire of the therapists and doctors. People with disabilities themselves may also be difficult to associate with, being a part of the "otherness" from which the newly disabled person is striving to distance themselves.

Register (1987) calls acceptance: "ability to regard the illness as your normal state of being" (p. 31). This could mean learning to identify with a new body, communication style, and social role. Wendell feels that for her,

> this had many advantages: I stopped expecting to recover and postponing my life until I was well . . . I changed my projects and my working life to accommodate my physical limitations, and, perhaps most important, I began to identify with other people with disabilities and to learn from them.
>
> (Wendell, 1996, p. 177)

Learning to live with disability and difference is full of interesting paradoxes—the desire to get on with your life, but the seduction of pathways to therapy and cure, the desire to be ordinary, but the inescapable facts of difference, the apparent enormity of the potential of therapy yet its insignificance in the grander scheme of life. Perhaps we need to be more mindful of these paradoxes as we listen to the hopes and aspirations of our clients. As travelling companions possibly our most precious gift is to be familiar with and unfazed by these contradictions. This is the positive alternative to the distanced healer described by Montaigne who "paints seas, rocks and harbours while sitting at his table and sails his model of a ship in perfect safety. Throw him into the real thing and he does not know where to begin" (Montaigne, Essays 3.13., quoted in Sacks, 1991).

REFERENCES

Barlow, J., Williams, B., & Wright, C. (1999). Instilling the strength to fight the pain and get on with life: Learning to become an arthritis self manager. *Health Education Research, 14*(4), 533–544.

Barrow, R. (2000). Hearing the story: A narrative perspective on aphasia therapy. *Bulletin of the Royal College of Speech & Language Therapists, 576*, 8–10.

Csikzentimihalyi, M. (1990). *Flow: The psychology of optimal experience.* New York: HarperCollins.

Department of Health (2001). *The expert patient: A new approach to chronic disease management for the 21st century.* London, UK: Department of Health, http://www.doh.gov.uk/cmo/ep-report.pdf

Frank, A. (1995). *The wounded storyteller.* Chicago: University of Chicago Press.

French, S. (1994). *On equal terms: Working with disabled people.* London: Heinemann Butterworth.

Greenhalgh, T., & Hurwitz, B. (1998). *Narrative-based medicine.* London: BMJ Books.

Ireland, C., & Pound, C. (2004). Cebrelating poetry and aphasia—Celebrating difference and diversity. In S. Parr, J. Duchan, & C. Pound (Eds.), *Aphasia inside out.* Buckingham, UK: Open University Press.

Kagan, A. (1995). Revealing the competence of aphasic adults through conversation: A challenge to health professionals. *Topics in Stroke Rehabilitation, 2*(1), 15–28.

Kagan, A. (1998). Supported conversation for adults with aphasia: Methods and resources for training conversation partners. *Aphasiology, 12*, 816–830.

Khosa, J. (2004). Still life of a chameleon: Aphasia and its impact on identity. In S. Parr, J. Duchan, & C. Pound (Eds.), *Aphasia inside out.* Buckingham, UK: Open University Press.

Kleinman, A. (1988). *The illness narratives: Suffering, healing and the human condition.* New York: Basic Books HarperCollins.

Lorig, K., Mazonson, P., & Holman, H. (1993). Evidence suggests that health education for self management in patients with chronic arthritis has sustained health benefits while reducing health costs. *Arthritis and Rheumatism, 36*(4), 439–446.

Lyon, J., Cariski, D., Keisler, L., Rosenbek, J., Levine R., Kumpula, J. et al. (1997). Communication partners: Enhancing participation in life and communication for adults with aphasia in natural settings. *Aphasiology, 11*, 693–708.

Morris, J. (Ed.) (1996). *Encounters with strangers.* London: Women's Press.

Oliver, M. (1996). *Understanding disability: From theory to practice.* London: Macmillan.

Parr, S., Byng, S., Gilpin, S., & Ireland, C. (1997). *Talking about aphasia.* Buckingham, UK: Open University Press.

Pound, C. (1999). *Learning to listen and helping to tell.* Speech & Language Therapy in Practice Conference, Rotterdam: The Netherlands.

Register, C. (1987). *Living with chronic illness: Days of patience and passion.* New York: Batam.

Sacks, O. (1991). *A leg to stand on.* London: Picador.

Simmons-Mackie, N. (2004). Just kidding: Humour and therapy for aphasia. In J. Duchan & S. Byng (Eds.), *Challenging aphasia therapies* (pp. 101–117). Hove, UK: Psychology Press.

Simmons-Mackie, N., & Kagan, A. (1999). Communication strategies used by "good" vs "poor" speaking partners of individuals with aphasia. *Aphasiology, 13*, 807–820.

Simpson, S., & Pound, C. (2001). *Learning to live with aphasia and disability: Stories of self identity*. Paper presented at the Royal College of Speech and Language Therapists Conference, Birmingham, UK.

Somers, M. (1994). The narrative construction of identity: A relational and network approach. *Theory and Society, 23,* 605–649.

Swain, J., & French, S. (2000). Towards an affirmation model of disability. *Disability & Society, 15,* 569–582.

Thomas, C. (1999). *Female forms: Experiencing and understanding disability.* Buckingham, UK: Open University Press.

Wendell, S. (1996). *The rejected body.* New York: Routledge.

4 Evolving treatment methods for coping with aphasia approaches that make a difference in everyday life

Jon Lyon

This chapter presents a therapeutic gestalt. The journey it chronicles, though, is linear in time. It highlights what I have learned as a clinician and clinical researcher over thirty-some years of treating people confronting aphasia and stroke. It attempts, as well, to speak to key lessons learned along the way from survivors, not just as clients, but as friends.

The two key lessons learned are too extensive to detail in full here — but then, you needn't see every slide of a friend's trip down the Amazon to glean the sense of its watery, lush green context or to capture its beginning, middle, or end. In fact, the intent and focus of this chapter rest more with where the journey led rather than understanding every step en route. Accordingly, it starts with an overview of the trip's conclusion, followed by a brief case example of key theoretic parts in those lessons learned. It next places these theoretic constructs into a visual model and addresses their management. It concludes with a metaphor for treatment that derives from my schooling over these many years from affected parties.

MY JOURNEY'S LANDMARKS

Before turning to the journey's end, let me highlight a few landmarks that surround it and, in retrospect, seem as if they guided its progression. They are reflected in the title of this chapter, in the phrase, "that make a difference in everyday life".

Making a difference in everyday life

In my view, there are three treatment outcomes that define whether aphasia interventions make an appreciable difference in daily life: substance, sustenance, and cost. Each is important to the growth and longevity of aphasia treatment in today's often curtailed healthcare systems.

Substance

First, treatments must yield substantial benefits to the process of living daily life—that is, outcomes must be life-altering. Their ends must qualify as "life-essential". Furthermore, these gains need to extend beyond the person with aphasia; they must assist and benefit others, those whose daily routines will never be the same because they are confronting the constancy and permanency of aphasia's enduring disability. This means we must either: (a) repair or augment *language and communication* sufficiently in the person having aphasia so that chosen life processes resume for key affected parties, or (b) augment chronically altered *life systems* of such individuals, stemming from disrupted communication, so that value and importance return to daily life.

To date, speech-language pathologists (SLPs) have devoted the bulk of their therapeutic efforts to part of the first treatment option: clinical repair of language and communication in the person having aphasia. Ensuring that such gains appreciably impact on the living of daily life for key affected parties (Pound, Parr, Lindsay, & Woolf, 2000), or managing aphasia's enduring long-term life disability, have only begun to emerge as viable undertakings (Byng, Pound, & Parr, 2000; LPAA, 2000). These two issues, however, are essential and integral to finally yield life-altering outcomes. Treatment of communication outside preferred life contexts can only yield such ends if that treatment of communication notably enhances the living of all of life. When life systems and functions are only minimally compensated through traditional emphases on language/communication restoration, as is typically the case with moderate to severe chronic communication breakdown, then active and chosen re-involvement in life must play a more central role in long-term management plans.

Sustenance

A second defining treatment outcome is that realized gains be sustainable. Benefits to living life must continue after treatment's end. As well, whatever gains accrued must transfer to and benefit other novel and/or untreated daily activities. To achieve the latter, interventions must extend beyond functionality in circumscribed life arenas of communication, such as expression of basic needs, answering a phone, or chatting with a friend. As espoused by a life participation approach to aphasia (LPAA, 2000), they must affect broader life venues, and must enhance attitudes and feelings, social connections with others, and participation in chosen daily routines.

Cost

Third, treatment outcomes must justify their effort and cost. Besides enhancing the act of living life, they must satisfy basic payer and consumer requisites.

As noted in an earlier text (Lyon, 2000), such requisites are neither mutual nor shared among healthcare "players". Payers seek minimal expense while ensuring stable health, basic return of function, and prolonged wellness. Consumers desire maximal care for optimal return of lost function and emotional well-being, and social inclusion at minimal personal expense. For us, the providers, this means we must somehow devise interventions, that yield greater functionality and inclusion at less expense.

To some extent, this cost has been addressed in healthcare systems that attempt to restrict service delivery to offerings that shift treatment away from repair of the communicative impairment (basic language skills) and towards its disability (communicative use in daily life). Although this tack may conform better to payer demands, it is questionable whether it has provided improved consumer satisfaction. To achieve the latter and keep payers at bay, it would appear that we may need to do more to "pass on" management responsibilities directly to consumers. We must hone skills that empower them to manage their own therapies, outcomes, and destinies more completely. To accomplish this, our treatment role needs to shift from attempting to "fix" (using direct "hands on" attempts at repairing communicative systems) to advising (consulting in ways of circumventing barriers in life when even somewhat repaired communication does not readily overcome those barriers). Even when our treatments of the language/communication impairment are optimal, they seldom "restore" function to its prior, non-injury levels. Thus, seldom is there no need to address the disabling features to daily life. We must begin that process from the outset of injury rather than as an afterthought. Initially, this intervention involves better counselling about the totality of injury and how, in a time-based manner, the consequences of injury (both acute and chronic) might be addressed.

As advisors, we must do more to find cost-effective ways that permit consumers to return intermittently to us for "life-adjustments", especially as long as they demonstrate the ability and motivation to work independently. Over time post-onset, and as they become more aware, able, and responsible for themselves and their altered lives, it only stands to reason that they will know better what is most missing and still sought in life. Given changing performance levels, we must be able to advise and guide them, primarily through consultation, in how to proceed towards other life-altering ends. It is towards these ends that we must continue to strive if aphasia treatment is to gain the prestige and availability it so desires.

THE JOURNEY'S CONCLUSION

Paul Ehrlich, Professor of Biological Sciences at Stanford University, and known in America for his 1960s book, *The Population Bomb*, recently completed another noteworthy text: *Human Natures* (Ehrlich, 2000).

In this era of scientific specification about genetics, particularly the mapping of the human genome, Ehrlich's book suggests that environmental influences in the living of life are actually more significant in determining our basic human natures than our genes. Note that Ehrlich refers to our "natures", not nature. He contends that there is no single human nature, but rather that we are a blend of many natures. He argues that no pre-ordained genetic code will unveil a magical map that explains the totality of our behaviour or make-up, and he believes our secrets rest in a complex interplay between heredity and environment. Ehrlich writes:

> . . . the notion that we are slaves to our genes is combined with reliance on the idea that all problems can be solved by dissecting them into ever smaller components—the sort of *reductionist approach* that has been successful in much of science but *is sometimes totally unscientific*. It's like the idea that knowing the color of every microscopic dot that makes up a picture of your mother can explain why you love her. *Scientific problems have to be approached at the appropriate level of organization if there is to be a hope of solving them.*
>
> (Ehrlich, 2000, p. 4)

So, too, Ehrlich's metaphor holds true for fashioning effective treatments for people confronting aphasia. We cannot hope to resolve their dilemmas without first addressing them at their proper level of organization. Certainly, at times, we need to dissect the whole in order to create an effective management plan, but each individually designed and directed "surgery" can only work if it remains embedded in the broader schema of each person's initial framework. When we stray from this tenet, we risk getting lost in counting coloured dots instead of supporting what is possible for an individual, and, likely, most beneficial within that constellation.

Strangely enough, as alluded to by Ehrlich, we are often told that it is "for the sake of science" that we must study, categorize, and conclude from every "dot" in order truly to capture the image's whole. But no matter how scientifically inspired or how well we examine each pixel in a particular photo, we will never, through that means alone, learn "why" we love that face. Those answers rest at an entirely different organizational level.

Ehrlich's principle accentuates the significance of my journey's conclusion, where my therapeutic forays have led me over the past three decades. Table 4.1 details my prime treatment phases over this interim, as well as some associative references. With each phase, you will find a brief description of what was done, where, why, what worked and didn't, and what prompted the next cycle of exploration.

Briefly encapsulated, my professional journey began with speech/language restoration in the person having aphasia (Phase 1: Mid 1960s to late 1970s). From there, it moved towards a novel system of augmenting communication when verbal expression was severely restricted in the injured

Table 4.1 My professional journey

WHEN WHERE REFS	WHY FOR WHOM	WHAT HOW MUCH	WHAT WORKED	WHAT DIDN'T WORK	CONCLUSION WHAT'S NEXT?
(when) • Mid 1960s to late 1970s (where) • University and hospital clinics	(why) • To restore language and communication (for whom) • Person with aphasia	(what) • Schuellian-based language stimulation; Bruce Porch's treatment along "the fulcrum of the curve" (how much) • 100s of hour sessions. . . . until clinical gains ceased/ "plateaued" (whatever that means) or affected person "able" or "willing" to participate	for most: • Instilled hope at a time of personal and emotional despair • Legitimized one's changed personage by immediately showing that an absence of words was *not* an absence of mind • Reinforced comm. use with its current form and content; got client "moving forward" by focusing on return rather than dwelling on loss • Some gradual gains in lang/comm for some: • Moderate gain in lang/comm • Enough to jump-start adaptive ways to learn to "live with" functional differences	• Many "treated" lang/comm. forms/ strategies didn't "transfer to" or "work in" real life • Nor did treatment deal with life processes or systems once permanency of injury was known	(conclusion) • Therapy was more palliative than curative; targeted only the impairment (WHO, 1980) of language • Overall, though, outcome better than credited in today's healthcare system • Emanated from a medical model, where efficacy hinged solely on proven clinical return to impaired lang/communication • Didn't assess, nor attempt to, its psychological merit to patient and family • (Viewed as antithetical "hand-holding") however, in retrospect,

(when)
- Late 1970s to late 1980s

(where)
- Hospital clinics

(references)
- Lyon & Sims, 1989
- Lyon, 1995a,b

(why)
- To enhance comm. interactions in daily life for adults who were verbally restricted

(for whom)
- Person with aphasia

(what)
- PACE-like; communicative use broadened to accept "interpretable" content instead of linguistic accuracy
- Began probing drawing's potential: the ability to draw recognizable objects, actions, simple and multi-stage concepts for comm. purposes

(how much)
- The latter couple of months of treatment, when verbal restoration had proven to be minimal

- Those with moderate-severe Broca's communicate better with drawing than without
- Drawing often helpful in accessing inner thought and establishing a means of interacting/turn-taking that otherwise was not there through speech, writing, gesture, or comm. boards
- Success depended on skill, ease, and comfort of use with the normal interactant

- People with aphasia do not draw normally, nor should one expect them to; drawings are often unrecognizable to naive interactant
- Most users unable to draw comm. on command
- Not an automatic dyadic "choice" in real life
- Latency or readiness commonly associated with its use
- Success has more to do with how it's presented and used, than the often interpreted "refusal" to try it as a comm. aid

for a few:
- Big improvement in lang/communication; able to return to self-determined lifestyles

a primary and significant offering and effect

(what's next)
- Notable void was in addressing the effective use of communication in daily life

(conclusion)
- Drawing is "another comm. door" (a medium through which to interact); when appropriate, it is more advantageous than not
- Best used interactively, not as an isolated "taught" compensatory skill

(what's next)
- Even when advantageous, dyads used it sparingly in real life; lack of use had as much to do with their comfort and patience, as well as, meaningful activities "to talk about"

Table 4.1 (Cont'd)

WHEN WHERE REFS	WHY FOR WHOM	WHAT HOW MUCH	WHAT WORKED	WHAT DIDN'T WORK	CONCLUSION WHAT'S NEXT?
(when) • Late 1980s to mid 1990s (where) • Hospital clinics and real life settings (references) • Lyon, 1996 • Lyon, et al., 1997 • Lyon, 1997	(why) • To enhance involvement and participation in real life in order to counterbalance lacking self-confidence/pride; besides building image/esteem, critical in creating reasons to want to comm. (for whom) • 5–6 months following end of traditional tx	(what) • Pairing adult with aphasia with a novel community volunteer, teaching them how to interact easily and effectively, and then using this friendship to foster participation in chosen activities in real life (Communication Partners) (how much) • Person with aphasia, community volunteer and significant other(s)	• Activities of choice in real life • Bolstered desire/ ability of person with aphasia to self-initiate, -determine and -regulate participation • With purpose cause outside him/herself rather than being treated as a person unable to talk, viewed as a person • Provided reason "to be"; created "flow"; sustainable following tx's end	• Didn't readily change other "forms" and "operations" of daily life, either for affected adult or those closely/ intimately a part of those life processes • Didn't "halt" the common, and insidious separation and isolation of people within prime relationships, i.e., a loss/erosion of personal intimacy	(conclusion) • An effective intermediate and practical step towards establishing self-value in one's changed status in life • Didn't adequately address eroding personal aspects of life within key relationships (what's next) • More attention needed in achieving ways of keeping affected parties "together" communicatively and personally

| (when)
 • Mid 1990s to late 1990s

 (where)
 • Real life settings

 (references)
 • Lyon, 1999b | (why)
 • To enhance interpersonal communication in real life
 • Keep involved parties more "connected" in negotiating and conducting "the basics" of daily life

 (for whom)
 • 2–6 sessions following end of traditional tx | (what)
 • Focused on value and role of communication in daily life, more than "its form" and the "need" to exchange content
 • Instructing, modelling and coaching couples in ways to stay connected communicatively (interactional comm. therapy), rather than solely conveying content (transactional comm. therapy)
 • Dependent on refinement of a DIFFERENT set of comm. skills
 • More about shared style, comfort and pleasure in the act of communicating than extracting every morsel of meaning

 (how much)
 • Person with aphasia and significant others in daily life | • Understood by interactants intellectually, and "endorsed" strongly when modelled
 • More complex to incorporate; process more difficult than it appears
 • Can, though, with ongoing commitment of ALL interactants, work to become an aid to daily interactions | • Not used as often or as freely as desirable; hard for normal adult "tempo" (give and take) at first; tendency to focus too much on content and not enough on manner and camaraderie of interaction
 • Hard, as well, to rid non-aphasic interactant of personal biases about the nature of the problem and how best to circumvent them; feels foreign...as one would expect in that this has never been a part of their prior interaction | (conclusion)
 • A valuable "step" in helping to establish and keep personal ties stronger between "key" affected parties

 (what's next)
 • "Sooner" as a treatment focus rather than later; vital component in addressing joint wellness of within framework for the conducting of daily life in its changed forms |

Table 4.1 (Cont'd)

WHEN WHERE REFS	WHY FOR WHOM	WHAT HOW MUCH	WHAT WORKED	WHAT DIDN'T WORK	CONCLUSION WHAT'S NEXT?
(when) • Mid 1990s to late 1990s (where) • Real life settings (references) • Lyon, 1999b; Lyon, 2000	(why) • To restore familiarity, form and "fun" to daily routines by attempting to re-establish pre-injury ratios of free and obligated time in chosen daily activities (for whom) • Months/years following the end of traditional tx	(what) • Asked affected parties to detail time spent prior to injury and currently in free and obligated activities; using prior-to-injury ratio as referent, began working with each person on ways to move current values towards earlier values; not the same activities as before, but generally more obligated time for people with aphasia and more free time for significant others/all persons whose daily life is continually impacted by the absence of the uninjured self of the person with aphasia	• Enhanced overall daily quality to all affected parties; tended to give more responsibility and purpose in life to the person with aphasia, while "freeing up" the significant other from assumed duties associated with the injury and allowing this supportive other more independent time to pursue and accomplish activities of choice (free time)	• Not an adequate sample to "judge" method fully; however, pre-injury and current ratios of free and obligated activities in daily life do NOT realign fully; there is "significant" movement toward prior values, but not fully; likely "not" preferred after injury; aids in the "outward" appearance and the conducting of life, does not necessarily address more important "inward" personal effects of injury	(conclusion) • Again, important addition to restoring life's daily form and having current operations "feel" right and productive; less restorative of close personal ties between parties/ operationally, it may be helpful to embed these treatment processes into a theoretical framework that addresses more life system changes and how to achieve them for all persons closely affected by aphasia rather than individual/ separate treatment plans for everyone

(when)
• Late 1990s to present

(where)
• Real life settings

(references)
• LPAA, 2000
• Byng et al., 2000

(why)
• To enhance the living of life by identifying and reducing life barriers

(for whom)
• Months/years following end of traditional tx

(what)
• Based on LPAA treatment philosophy and framework, assessed life barriers of affected parties to see which interfere most in chosen daily operations; examine each scenario for ways to diminish/circumvent/remove obstructions so person can "partake" more easily and freely

(how much)
• All persons whose daily life is continually impacted by the absence of the uninjured self of the person with aphasia

• Provided a theoretical and practical framework in which to treat life participation; although the effects of disrupted communication "underlie" the life barriers addressed, it is not that, per se, that drives the remediation; instead, it is the enhancement of: feelings/attitudes, connections with others, and activities of choice
• When improved, so too is life's quality and daily pleasure

• Not treatment that's easily charted in conventional "cause-effect" accounting systems
• It often is NOT reducible to "how many" or "how much" of given constructs are present now that weren't prior to treatment
• Final results more generic, "my life today is far better than it was six months ago, I'm doing more, feeling better about what I do and my relationship with others; I'm confident more is possible"

(conclusion)
• Clearly a treatment framework that deserves more in-depth examination, i.e., in developing better ways of confronting life barriers and documentation of outcomes and their importance to the living of daily life

(what's next)
• More still needed in ways of keeping intimacy "alive" and "well" in the personal relationships of people confronting aphasia on a daily basis

Table 4.1 (Cont'd)

WHEN WHERE REFS	WHY FOR WHOM	WHAT HOW MUCH	WHAT WORKED	WHAT DIDN'T WORK	CONCLUSION WHAT'S NEXT?
(when) • Late 1990s to present (where) • Real life settings (references) • Coping model related to intimacy • Lyon & Shadden, 2001	(why) • To understand and determine what "coping" with the lasting effects of aphasia means and entails in everyday life; more specifically, it's effects upon relationship ties/ personal intimacy (for whom) • Months/years following end of traditional tx	(what) • "Coping" is NOT a personality trait or a preordained skill/ ability; little known, though, about the ways relationship ties "change" when aphasia is a constant in life and what self adopted methods of coping seemingly "work"; have begun examining "how" coping has or has not been of aid in preserving personal bonds/ties in key relationships in life (how much) • All persons whose daily life is continually impacted by the absence of the uninjured self of the person with aphasia	• Have only "begun" looking into personal intimacy in relationships in couples coping with the chronic aspects of injury associated with aphasia/stroke • Some "notable" results exist in normative literature to suggest that subcomponents (emotional, sexual, intellectual, recreational) must all be there and, to some degree, "well" to have entire package function • Wellness in these realms is likely linked to physical wellness	• Not looking for treatment interventions at moment • Looking instead for what has and has not worked to keep intimacy a part of life in couples long post-onset	???

adult—Communicative Drawing (Phase 2: Late 1970s to late 1980s). Next on my journey, I sought to enhance participation in life through novel partnerships—Communication Partners (Phase 3: Late 1980s to mid 1990s). Next, it evolved to include enhancing communication within two-person dyads in natural settings, along with making readjustments to the kinds and amounts of daily activities (Phase 4: Mid 1990s to late 1990s). More recently, my journey has addressed key life realms that slowly, and often insidiously, change for the worse due to the sustained absence and lack of continuity of daily communication (Phase 5: Late 1990s to present). Viewed as an evolution, the dominant progression over this 30-year period has been away from isolated repair of language and speech in the injured adult and towards methods that ensure long-term preservation of self and others, and participation in daily life, domains that erode due to chronically disordered communication.

Considering Ehrlich's claim that solutions to problems must evolve foremost from the selection of a proper organizational level, my own conclusion is that we, too, must address communication remediation within its rightful whole. Communication is not a free-standing entity or "thing". In this respect, it is not like an arm or leg that suddenly doesn't work due to paralyzing injury. The prime role in life of verbal communication is to help organize and mediate thought (past, present, or future), to share those thoughts with others, and to provide a medium for interpersonal interaction. As such, talking does not serve a central function outside its connections with the processes of living life. If the forms and actions of daily life were somehow suddenly removed, there would be no reason or need to "chit-chat" with others. Thus, communication is more a life-conduit, channel, or interpersonal medium than a separate, isolated entity. It is from such a view that Kagan (1998) has popularized the concept of aphasia as involving disruptions of communicative "access". When communication becomes disrupted in later life (e.g., through aphasia) and when permanently so (chronic condition), it does not solely, or even primarily, affect the act of communicating *per se*; it alters "access" to every major domain of daily life. Since the results of our restorative efforts (treatment of the communicative impairment) are only partially successful, our treatments must address life functions and systems in order to become more life-altering and sustainable (Byng et al., 2000; LPAA, 2000). In this way, the value and importance of daily life can be enhanced.

From my thirty-some years of intervening, the organizational level from which I now choose my entry point into rehabilitative efforts is that of the life processes that matter most to affected parties. This same organizational level also directs the search for both communicative and other strategies that permit the individual's safe and viable return to participation in life. Although it may seem like a subtle departure from traditional goals, this organizational whole actually emanates from augmentation of life processes, rather than communicative processes that best support daily function.

A REAL-LIFE EXAMPLE

Last spring I began seeing a 78-year-old woman named Patty. She had incurred a left cerebral occlusive infarction approximately a year before. She was left with a moderate/severe Broca's aphasia and a mild right hemiparesis. Patty was ambulatory and self-sufficient with her basic ADLs (Activities of Daily Living) at that time. Her functional speech was limited to "yes/no" and a few automatic phrases (I'd like that; how nice). Her auditory comprehension, although functional, was easily compromised, through either the quantity or complexity of language spoken to her. She recognized basic printed words and grammar, but had difficulty with reading comprehension beyond the sentence level.

Patty lived in the home of her daughter, Carol. Besides Carol, the household included Carol's husband, Martin, and their 10-year-old daughter, Megan. Patty, a long-time divorcee, had moved into Carol's home at the time Megan was born. And since the two of them, grandmother and granddaughter, had been with each other all Megan's life, they shared a very special and close bond. Patty had always been involved in the process of living life, and was an "on the move" type of person. Besides working full-time at a nearby bookstore, she had helped around the household and in the rearing and support of Megan. Patty had been an avid reader and enjoyed a variety of literary styles. She had actively sculpted with clay and took private lessons weekly. In addition, she had assisted in starting two community support groups for people with a history of chronic heart disease or failure, and remained an active member. She was adored by many persons with whom she had come to know and share life.

At the time I began my intervention, life's daily form and structure was quite sparse. Patty had just become a consumer of a Madison, Wisconsin, healthcare agency that provided total health care "in the home" of the elderly as an alternative to institutionalized care (a nursing home or an assisted living environment). That agency ran an adult daycare centre and Patty had begun attending their functions twice weekly. Otherwise, Patty was at home where there were no formal opportunities for activity. She might occasionally go with her daughter or granddaughter to lunch or to do some shopping, but basically she sat idle much of each day. She was not a television enthusiast.

Prime participants in Patty's life were approached as to the life barriers that stood between them and their desired involvement with Patty or their participation in their own daily life choices. From this process, lists were made of barriers that originated because of Patty's aphasia. Table 4.2 contains a summary of the items on these lists along with a list of others (life facilitators) who might be available and willing to assist with minimizing or circumventing these life barriers.

Note that Patty's list centred around feelings of disconnection from others and personal inadequacy in daily life. As well, she longed "to do"

Table 4.2 Directly affected persons: Life barriers and facilitators

PATTY		CAROL (DAUGHTER)		MEGAN (GRANDDAUGHTER)	
BARRIER	FACILTR	BARRIER	FACILTR	BARRIER	FACILTR
• Communication with Carol, Megan and others • Feeling "able" to act on her own behalf • Participation in life (in and outside home)	• Carol • Megan • Elder Care • SLP	• No assured way of knowing Patty's wishes or opinions in daily life • Wanting "more" quality and quantify engagement in daily life • Respite care	• Martin • Megan • Elder Care • SLP	• Missing her closest friend and confidante in life • *Unsure* whether she was responsible • If *still* possible, how to reconnect with grandmother	• Carol • Martin • Patty • SLP

Table 4.3 Treatment target/process/outcome

WHO/ BARRIER	TARGET	PROCESS	OUTCOME
• Carol and Patty	• Enhance their ability to interact comfortably and effectively	• Principles of Supported Conversation (Kagan, 1998) paper/pencil; key words written out choices/ratings of them/verification sketching	• Comfort in interacting; more reliable info exchange, not always complete
• Patty	• Increased engagement "of choice" in life	• OUTSIDE HOME – ceramics private lesson – volunteerism: former place of employment cardiac support group • INSIDE HOME – assisting: making bed daily sorting laundry/ folding clothes – talking books	• Greater pleasure in and anticipation of day's/week's offerings
• Megan and Patty	• Exploring new ways for them to connect	• Joint cartoon strip • Movie rentals	• Increased interaction in daily life

something of personal importance to her. Her daughter, Carol, was unclear as to whether anything more could be done interactively with Patty to discern her basic knowledge, desires, and wishes. She wanted more in life for her mother. And she needed more free time (respite) for herself. Finally, Megan deeply missed the companionship of her closest friend and confidante in life. She was desirous of anything that might allow her and her grandmother to have closer contact and interaction. Also, she was concerned that maybe she hadn't acted as fully and as quickly as she should have at the time of her grandmother's stroke. A year earlier, when returning from school, she had found her grandmother on the floor unable to walk or talk. It had taken Megan some time to realize that she should have called the emergency number. She wondered, "Did my delay cause my grandmother's condition?"

Table 4.3 contains an overview of treatment targets (life barriers selected), processes, and outcomes that followed. Since Patty and Carol both expressed a desire to connect more with each other, we began by addressing the adequacy and fullness of communication between them. What became immediately apparent to all parties was that there was much, much more that could be shared and ascertained (both in form and quantity of content) than either had previously thought. By slowing down their interaction, and by giving each of them a clearer role of how and what to do in order to negotiate their sharing, they began feeling more successful and even broaching novel topics. Strategies for this improved interaction centred around writing out key words (concepts and choices) which Patty could refer to as the conversation progressed. Besides giving her a way to rank or judge each idea (through accompanying numerical, lined ordinal scales, from "no interest" to "so-so" to "very interested"), it provided a quick and reasonable way to verify Patty's understanding and position on given topics. Such supportive or augmentative techniques to dyadic communication have been detailed elsewhere in greater depth (Kagan, 1998; Lyon, 1999b). In essence, though, Carol and Patty began interacting in realms never previously approached. Although shared informational content was not always complete or even certain, the quality of their "connectedness" in life had improved.

Next, we addressed a couple of "life barriers" on Patty's list. These selections focused on increasing her sense of personal value and participation in chosen activities in daily life. Outside the home, we re-established weekly private lessons with her former ceramics instructor. We set into motion the machinery necessary to allow Patty to return to her former place of employment, not as an employee but as a volunteer. We arranged for her to volunteer one morning a week, assisting in basic tasks of personal choice at her neighbourhood bookstore. As well, we found a productive role for her in her woman's cardiac support group, adding the names of new members to a computerized mailing list. Inside the home, she assumed more responsibility for her own self-care as well as for household chores. She made her bed daily and assisted with the family's laundry by sorting and folding clothes. Finally, we oriented her to "talking books" (audio cassette books), to help re-establish a preferred former activity. By everyone's assessment, the multitude and diversity of these endeavours increased Patty's participation and pleasure in daily life.

Next, we explored ways of bringing Patty and Megan together. One realm that immediately provided "a foot in the door" was interactive drawing. On a regular basis, Megan actively and adeptly drew at home, and designed cartoon strips of her own invention, with personal characters and plots. Since Patty could share in this modality, in that she possessed the ability to draw simple stick-like figures and, with Megan's help, could alter visual applications to differing scenarios, it was a natural arena where they could play and explore together. They quickly created a couple of cartoon strips and, within days of starting these activities, Carol reported that Megan was more attentive and responsive to her grandmother's needs in other life realms, like asking to assist her on trips outside the home. As another example of strategies to increase their interaction, we arranged for them to visit a video store together, selecting films for each other, viewing them together, and discussing the "appropriateness" of their selections.

This encapsulated segment of treatment does not attempt to capture the totality of intervention with Patty, Carol, or Megan. Instead, it serves solely to exemplify the organizational therapeutic level alluded to earlier. It involved approximately 12 one-hour sessions over a 3-month period (from the twelfth to fifteenth month post-onset). The costs of these services ($50/hr, approximately $250/month) met with the full approval of Patty's healthcare payer, who also sought her improved quality of life, as long as such services generated sustainable life differences at a reasonable rate. Note, too, that no treatment claims to this agency involved Patty's ability to communicate independently. All treatment targets centred, instead, around life systems for affected parties (the "disability" of aphasia, rather than just the "impairment"). Again, in terms of cost effectiveness, all goals achieved here were met at a total cost of around $600. Perhaps more importantly, the extent of sustainable, "life differences" (that truly mattered to those affected parties) exceeded what may have evolved from 12 hour-long sessions that focused solely on communication repair within the person with aphasia.

To clarify, this example is not intended to suggest that aphasiologists haven't advocated for inclusion of key natural life variables and settings as a crucial component of therapy. Notable in this respect are the works of Lubinski (1981, 1986), who eloquently detailed the importance of addressing chronic communication impairment at increasingly complex levels of social interaction in daily life. Termed a "systems approach", such schemas target communication repair within the affected person first and then move progressively outward to family, friends, work associates, and eventually to interactions in society at large (see Figure 4.1). The prime target of such treatment is "improved communicative use" within real-life contexts. As

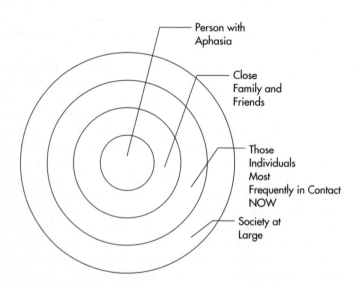

Figure 4.1 Systems theory: Treatment of more than communication repair. Treatment target: Communication efficiency and effectiveness at each life systems level.

such, this organizational "whole" aligns itself well with our prime professional role traditionally, as communication repair specialists.

The organizational level in Patty's case, though, is different. What was
targeted in this "whole" was the re-involvement of affected parties in chosen
pursuits in daily life. Once these systems became identified, the diminishing
of life barriers, communicative and otherwise, could begin, thus permitting
optimal function to return to preferred levels of daily use. Accordingly, the
therapeutic targets here align more closely with the goals of improved feel-
ings/attitudes, connections with others, and participation in daily activities
(Byng et al., 2000; LPAA, 2000).

As speech-language pathologists, we may wonder whether our professional expertise and training qualify us to be "life participation experts".
Originating from a medical model of managing acutely disordered communicative functions and their repair, such a role shift may seem incongruous. However, advocating for treatment of chronic dysfunction in life is
not, since these consequences arise largely from an absence of knowledge
about the nature and/or permanence of the communicative injury. Although
we may not possess sufficient knowledge of all aspects of life participation to
recommend precisely how life should proceed, we do possess:

- the knowledge of impaired communication and the skills necessary to
  help in the gathering of information from all parties;
- means of assessment of what is possible;
- ways to strategize and facilitate achieving these ends.

We are the professionals who can best serve in this role, as interpreter and
negotiator, to ensure that clarity of choice in life is understood, offered, and
pursued. From there, the implementation of these selections may begin.
Often, affected parties feel comfortable progressing in small steps of their
own making. Occasionally, though, such efforts may require the assistance
of other professionals (e.g., occupational therapists, physiotherapists, social
workers, and nurses) to ensure their optimal function and safety. Regardless,
broken life systems are not only justifiable therapeutic undertakings for SLPs,
they may represent the organizational level at which we are most apt and
able to yield sustainable, life-altering outcomes.

A LIFE PARTICIPATION DIAGRAM

Figure 4.2 contains a visual representation of the theoretic underpinnings
involved in Patty's case vignette. The theory for these constructs originates
from a Life Participation Approach to Aphasia (LPAA), and the seven clinical experts (R. Chapey, R. Elman, J. Duchan, L. Garcia, A. Kagan, J. Lyon,
and N. Simmons-Mackie) who authored that publication (LPAA, 2000). As
well, P. Fougeyrollas and his colleagues (Fougeyrollas, Cloutier, Bergeron,

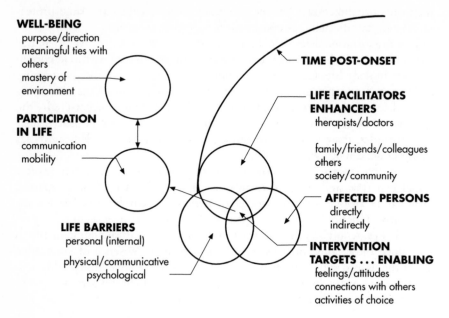

Figure 4.2 Diagram of life participation in aphasia (Lyon).

Cote, Cote, & St. Michel, 1997) directly influenced the form and content of this model. These latter model builders were obviously influenced by the World Health Organization's earliest efforts (1980).

Core components of my version of the LPAA model, displayed as overlapping circles in Figure 4.2, involve the interaction of three highly dynamic life domains over time post-onset: (1) affected persons, like Patty, Carol, Megan, and Martin, (2) life barriers, as just defined, and (3) life facilitators/enhancers, "others" in life who might enable affected persons towards reinvolvement in desired daily activities.

Affected persons not only include those directly impacted (the person with aphasia and close family, friends, and business associates), but may also include those indirectly involved (family and friends who are less present, and novel acquaintances who would like to share parts of life with the person having aphasia, yet, due to limited knowledge about the impairment, feel uncomfortable or uncertain as to how to proceed).

Life barriers involve curtailments "within" (personal) or "outside" (environmental) the affected person. Personal realms include physical differences in cognition, language, mobility, and sensation; or psychological differences to self-esteem, worth, confidence, growth, acceptance, intimacy and personal bonds, and wellness (happiness). Environmental realms involve physical differences like access to buildings, places, and activities of personal choice, and social differences like access to participation in societal, political, religious, judicial, or educational gatherings. Depending on the affected person and the time post-onset, any one of these, or a combination thereof, may obstruct or hinder access to preferred/chosen pathways in daily life.

Life facilitators/enhancers typically refer to trained professionals (medical and rehabilitative personnel) in the initial weeks and months post-onset. However, as the chronicity of impairment becomes known, facilitation of and within daily life increasingly relies on those parties "present" in daily life. Because of this, fostering "ownership" to act on one's own behalf (empowerment) is essential from the outset in this type of treatment. Such empowerment involves daily facilitators as well as affected parties. Whenever possible, this process begins by including such parties in all management decisions, since it is important that everyone knows and understands the form and course of treatment, and the potential outcomes and the roles each must assume.

Note, too, within my diagram, the overlapping areas between and among life domains. At times in the earlier case vignette, the treated life barrier focused more on the concerns of two-party relationships (e.g., between Patty and Carol or Megan and Patty). Each participant in these dyads also served as her own facilitator as well as assisting the other party. Carol needed to speak less while carefully attending to Patty's entire message. Such a focus "aided" Carol in staying better connected with her mother (facilitating her life barrier), but it also aided Patty in feeling equally valued in the communicative exchange and wanting to participate communicatively (facilitating Patty's life barrier). Finally, as shown in this figure, at any point in time, not all life barriers dominate preferred life choices and actions. Patty's inability to express her basic needs, for example, did not prohibit her desire/choice to eat out in public restaurants. Although she couldn't always be assured that the waiter would know how to discern her menu choice, she knew that her daughter would intercede if necessary. Overall that activity brought more pleasure, of choice, than displeasure from this life barrier. Thus, it is where these life domains (affected parties, life facilitators, and life barriers) merge, shown here centrally in the overlap of all circles, that treatment becomes an essential and viable remediation undertaking.

As a point of elaboration, here, treatment targets remain life-oriented . . . at all times. They address enhancement of attitudes/feelings, personal and social connections with others, and participation in chosen activities in daily life. Such ends were not randomly selected; they represent, according to noted social psychologists (Ryff & Singer, 2000a), those facets in life that we all must possess to act freely and fully in daily life.

It is from enhanced participation in life, that psychosocial wellness follows (shown here as well-being). The latter, according to Ryff and Singer (1998), entails having purpose and meaning in life, meaningful connections with important others, autonomy, mastery of the environment, and self-acceptance/love. These prime features of well-being, interestingly, may also be essential to physical wellness (Ryff & Singer, 2000a, 2000b).

Finally, the make-up or constellation of these life domains varies substantially as a function of time post-injury (shown here as an upwardly arching line labelled time post-onset). Such an approach to treatment relies on continuous assessment and prioritization of "current" life barriers, and which of those are most amenable to modification, either through restoration or circumvention. The continuing question to be asked is, "Which barriers if reduced or minimized would enable affected persons to act on their own behalf?". Management requires that we seek and develop effective and cost-sensitive ways that permit affected parties to move in and out of treatment over time, and to seek periodic "life adjustments" so-to-speak, that continue to support optimal interactions with, and in, life.

COMPONENTS TO ENHANCING LIFE PARTICIPATION

A dominant memory of mine from decades ago, when people with aphasia received hundreds of hours of restimulation/restorative language and communication therapy, was the termination of treatment. No matter the duration or success of treatment, when that moment arrived, it frequently came with a sense of total disbelief and denial on the part of the affected parties. It was not that they hadn't "heard" that treatment would end, or even the conditions under which this might occur. It was that they could not imagine that such a moment was now, and that much, much more function wasn't still possible just days or weeks hence. Clients often asked, either overtly or covertly, "How are we ever going to live life like this?"

Their plight and anguish dominated my thought too. Which of our prior clinical gains mattered now? Which of them could be counted on in daily life in the weeks and months ahead? What more might be done to make those skills work and feel harmonious and good, given their life scenarios at that moment? Thus, coming to grips with permanency of injury associated with aphasia and stroke was inescapable ... for everyone. Much for that reason, the latter segments of my therapeutic journey have focused on this process of remediation (making life work after communicative restorative processes ended). In our literature, that phenomenon is better known as "coping". Because it is a concept and process entirely of its own, and because our effectiveness in treating the disability of aphasia depends on our understanding and inclusion of coping, a brief overview follows.

COPING AND LIFE PARTICIPATION

In America, the permanent change resulting from acquired physical, mental, or psychological injury is not often formally treated, but is left instead to affected parties to sort through and decipher for themselves. "Chronic" is a bad word in our healthcare system because if you cannot fix it, it is seen as money wasted to attempt to teach people how to live with their unfixable impairment. If there is any intervention at all, it typically takes the form of either peer support groups or visiting a trained professional counsellor, knowledgeable about that impairment's course and life consequences. Both of these management aids may substantially benefit certain parties in re-establishing meaning and balance to daily life (Elman & Berstein-Ellis, 1999; Luterman, 1991). However, it is important to note that, alone, these aids neither represent nor capture what the process of coping is, or what it might be. In fact, "coping" is often interpreted as recognizing that you "are" your disability—for example, that one is "an aphasic person". This limited version of "coping" casts a bias that is both inaccurate and unjust. Limiting coping treatment to just peer groups or going to a counsellor reinforces the notion that its course is a long evolutionary process, almost a passive state of maturationally growing "to absorb" what life is and must be now, by "living with it".

To me, our literature on coping only condones this view. Much of it suggests that survivors must ascend a set of steps or stages like shock, denial, anger, bartering/bargaining . . . leading ultimately to acceptance (LaPointe, 1997; Tanner & Gerstenberger, 1988) of permanent dysfunction. Not only must affected parties "work through" these emotional barriers, their success is viewed as tied to particular personality traits and/or skills involved in overcoming prior life crises—temperament, hardiness, introspection, dispositional optimism, and locus of control (LaPointe, 1997).

This view of coping denies the therapeutic legitimacy of assisting people idiosyncratically with what is not working at the moment. It also implies that such endeavours are apt *not* to work, either because people aren't "ready" (they've not yet ascended the requisite adjustment steps to allow advancement) or they don't have the necessary requisites or "coping" skills to do so.

Nearly two decades ago, Lazarus and Folkman (1984), noted field psychologists and research experts in the study of coping, wrote the following definition of the coping process:

> . . . constantly changing cognitive and behavioral efforts to manage specific external and/or internal demands that are appraised as taxing or exceeding the resources of a person.
>
> (Lazarus & Folkman, 1984, p. 141)

What is most noteworthy about their definition, and later exposed through their careful analyses of the coping process, is the following:

- Coping is best represented as an ongoing, active, interactional process between person and environment, *not* a protracted, passive evolution that requires months or years to determine its form, value, or outcome.
- Coping "ability" is not a personality trait. Certain prior tendencies and perceptions about life may well influence its course and/or outcome, but those, too, typically are modifiable with time, desire, and effort.

- Coping is different from pre-established or automatized adaptive behaviours in life—things you have unconsciously learned to do or use under "trying" conditions or circumstances.
- Coping is not to be confused with outcome! Just because daily life doesn't return to a glowing, radiant sphere of joy, happiness, and fun, doesn't mean that treatment isn't yielding effective and sustainable gains. At any point in time, one must ask instead: "How would life be had we *not* made whatever adjustments (coping) we did?" If the living of life is better at the moment, even if it remains marginal, coping strategies and their enhancement have not only proven effective, but essential.
- The ability to cope at any moment in time does not necessarily predict what might be possible in the future, especially if affected parties are informed and aided in those very adjustment processes.

Given the earlier treatment example, my clinical sense is that almost all of Patty, Carol, and Megan's intervention centred around the support of coping. That is:

- There existed a specific set of external and internal life variables that were taxing or exceeding their current resources to function optimally or productively in daily life.
- Those breakdowns involved ongoing interaction among them and their specific life contexts.
- Piece-by-piece, everyone involved worked through a series of barriers that made their shared environments more comfortable, predictable and productive.
- Outcomes did not turn life into a glorious, ideal, or perfect state of being. However, they did yield a greater sense of value, purpose, and meaning for all affected parties.
- Outcomes did not rely solely on any party's prior maturation through a series of adjustment stages, or their tenacity to "work hard" through prior life crises. Maybe select parts of their past experience did help, but these alone did not determine the course of treatment here. Instead, this coping required a catalyst or catalysts—life enhancers—people willing to commit time and effort towards assisting stalled life processes to work again.

Short of interventions that either avert the initial physical injury to the brain or return damaged structure to its prior physical status (structurally and functionally), it would be my opinion that augmenting the process of coping represents the best therapeutic option for returning daily life functions to their optimal levels "of choice" and engagement. More importantly, as suggested earlier, it may well contain outcomes that move us closer, as providers, to supporting sustainable, life-altering differences. Because "coping treatment" offers promise, I'd like to speculate briefly on where we might need to look with future endeavours.

MANAGING "COPING TREATMENT" IN THE FUTURE

If we revisit the therapeutic outcomes of this case example, there is little doubt, especially when evaluated by those treated (Patty, Carol, and Megan), that such interventions enhanced daily life, making it more tolerable and "of choice". Yet, judged against a backdrop of normative life function (prior to injury with aphasia), there remains much that is still viewed as "less" or "undone". If asked whether today's picture of daily life compares favourably with its pre-injury form, Patty, Carol, and Megan would answer a resounding "No!". Even with the benefits of this treatment, measured on a 10-point scale of life satisfaction, post-treatment values fall at least 2 or 3 points lower than pre-injury levels. It is true that the permanent loss of access to many prime life domains, of personal autonomy and self-worth, and of ease of daily operations is too great to "fix" through these methods, and perhaps others, short of fully restoring prior function.

That said, however, there is another realm of "loss" that may be quite modifiable through treatment. This is fortunate, in that it permeates, often insidiously, daily life and its operations. I refer to the loss of intimacy in key personal relationships. There is an expanding body of "normative" literature on this topic—literature that is not about aphasia. The focus of this literature is on the importance of intimacy in life for all of us (Ryff & Singer, 2000a, 2000b; Ryff, Singer, Wing, & Love, 2001). Fundamentally, how well we establish, maintain, and keep key relationships in life may well affect our psychological, as well as physical, well-being. When communication ease and access become chronically disrupted, as with aphasia, the form and nature of intimacy is dramatically affected (Lyon, 1999a; Lyon & Shadden, 2001). Yet we know little of the evolving nature of such deterioration, or what may help or not in assisting those affected in remaining connected. This realm represents fertile ground for future examination and treatment.

RESTORATION OF LOST COMMUNICATIVE FUNCTION

When the prime therapeutic emphasis is on restoration of life functions, as opposed to communicative functions, where does communicative restoration fit in such a model?

The argument was made initially that communication subserves the mediation of sharing and living life, and thus is integrally bound to those processes. As well, presence of and access to communication often define who we see ourselves as being. Other than looking at one's face in a mirror and saying, "That's me," how one sounds when hearing oneself talk is likely the next associate feature in life that one identifies *as* oneself. When talking has been present for seven decades of life, as in Patty's case, and then is suddenly removed, it is not strange that affected parties seek first and foremost its optimal return. The life participation model does not disallow that.

It only maintains that we must target those life barriers (certainly disrupted communication being a prime one) that preclude daily involvement at any point in time.

For some parties, the duality of treating both life function and communicative function appears to be a dichotomy. How can one target adaptive life strategies (coping) until one is certain that restorative efforts (communicative) have run their full course? Why work on something that may not be needed, and something that feels terribly foreign and uncomfortable to their way of life and your accustomed way of offering service to clients? Only after permanency of injury is well known, internalized, and somewhat accepted, may the latter even seem justified. Although, in my experience, this has usually been true, the origin of this type of thought seems embedded in a rather restricted sense of what permanence of injury represents and how we, as therapists, elect to speak about it initially, i.e., immediate following onset. It is essential that such a conversation occur, not in any absolute terms but in relative ones. Since we're likely not to "know" the absolute limit of functional return for years (not months), and since such functional return (especially beyond the first 8 to 12 months post-onset) is apt to be gradual at best, working on current life forms and functions early post-onset is not wasted effort or time. It is, instead, essential to building an optimally strong foundation for self-sufficiency and autonomy in the years to come. Augmentative life systems do not interfere with augmenting disrupted communication systems, but they do provide a basis to live life should current function remain unchanged, and provide meaning to attempts to use augmented communication systems. They also set the stage for positive coping with what "is", even when what "is" changes.

LESSONS LEARNED EN ROUTE

Now, having spent some time recounting what I have learned about treatment en route to the journey's conclusion, let me attempt to share some of what I have learned from some special fellow travellers along the way. One of those most important "teachers" was a kindred soul, a golfer.

Over the past couple of years, I've begun playing golf more regularly. Nowadays I attempt to get out for several hours, four or five times per week, usually in the early morning. Some of my friends and colleagues may wonder, how can one attend to this, to that degree, and still be productive at work? The truth is, I learned this lesson from a client of mine (a man with aphasia). I consider this gentleman more a mentor than a patient. He ran a highly successful insurance agency with multiple offices in multiple cities and multiple states. However, his first order of business, each day, from the age of 19 until he suffered a stroke some 60 years later, was 18 holes of golf. That activity was not just about play or fun, although it was both of those. It was an essential part of daily life—it defined who and what he was and wanted to be. Furthermore, he was not an excellent golfer . . . ever, although he was very good. And this didn't matter to him! He sought this experience because he immediately became "lost" in the act of doing it, and he didn't really care about its outcome. He kept score and he wanted to shoot a good score, but even that was not his prime motivation. He loved the process and being in it, a phenomenon in life more formally known as "flow" (Csikzentimihalyi, 1990, 1997).

Now, part of getting "better" at golf, even at my age of 56, seemingly involves taking lessons. I've done that intermittently. Recently, I was out on the practice range with a golf pro because I wanted him to "make me" more adept at executing the golf swing, and he was there because he felt he possessed the skills to do just that. To begin, he asked me to hit several balls and then he began telling me what I needed to change in my swing to become a better golfer. I could tell from his assessment that he was well trained and well intentioned. He definitely knew what a proper golf swing entailed, and what of my swing needed correction. I could tell, too, he had thought about effective ways of sharing such information with his clients. So I began attempting to insert the suggested changes into my swing, and have succeeded to some lesser degree than instructed, although I will continue to try.

To my knowledge, though, this instructor never alluded to the fact that there are hundreds of thousands of ways of hitting a golf ball, or how "my swing", as it existed at that moment, might be maximally improved by minimally changing something within that structure. Nina Simmons-Mackie has long asserted that whatever we "do" in aphasia treatment has got to "fit" within existing ways of life function or operation for it to habituate (Simmons-Mackie & Damico, 1997). Real change has got to become potentially automatic in function. Accordingly unless we bring comfort and ease into the desired shift, whether involving a golf swing or living with permanent differences in our communication system, it is apt not to work in real life.

Over 30 years, I've been taught this very principle repeatedly: We need to be less concerned with complete repair of broken parts—unless of course, those functions are restorable—and more concerned with automaticity (ease, comfort, and pleasure) in life. To extend the lesson my clients have taught me, and that was well described by Simmons-Mackie, although my golf swing is apt never to look or feel like that ideal computer-generated model, I need to consider what I might change of what's already there, and what could, with time, become automatic.

Taken a step further, automaticity may mean "not needing" to change anything—unless of choice. Ram Dass, whose popular message in 1971 was "Be Here Now", recent completed another text, *Still Here* (Dass, 2000). Dass began writing a book on natural ageing, but prior to finishing, suffered a stroke that left him with aphasia. He stated in his book that this real-life event and experience gave him the ending that he was seeking. It made him realize that he wanted to be free to experience any age-related event in life fully and completely "as is". His notion was that having aphasia was not a penalty or bad misfortune; it was simply a natural part of his life course and process. As such, he didn't want therapists telling him, "You've got to get better" by learning to do such and such. He wanted time, and the freedom to learn, from whatever this turn of events had brought. He remarks that he spoke out frequently in life before this occurrence, but, because speech and language were not now readily at hand, he had been forced to listen more, and was learning from the experience.

To conclude, I feel that aphasia treatments need to be more life-oriented and life-altering to endure. They need to "fit" with the life schemas and agendas of those affected. They need ultimately to make those who receive them feel better about themselves, their lives, and their connections with others. Certainly, addressing disruptive communication is essential, both directly and indirectly. But we must place our first priority on what in life is most desired, what about that that is most obstructed or interfered with, and what of that might be changed. Finally, we need to ask ourselves, "How do we do all these things and have them fit comfortably into what exists rather than remake what doesn't?"

My journey has taken me to this juncture in the road. The path ahead has been "prepped" with an LPAA model, but the landmarks are yet to be established before paving begins. My hope is that, as speech-language pathologists, we will be instrumental in this future course, this next journey in living, and in enhancing lives of those with aphasia.

REFERENCES

Byng, S., Pound, C., & Parr, S. (2000). Living with aphasia: A framework for therapy interventions. In I. Papathanasiou (Ed.), *Acquired neurological communication disorders: A clinical perspective*. London: Whurr Publishers.

Csikzentimihalyi, M. (1990). *Flow: The psychology of optimal experience*. New York: HarperCollins Publishers.

Csikzentimihalyi, M. (1997). *Finding flow: The psychology of engagement with everyday life*. New York: HarperCollins Publishers.

Dass, R. (2000). *Still here: Embracing aging, changing and dying*. New York: Riverhead Books.

Ehrlich, P. R. (2000). *Human natures*. Washington, DC: Island Press.

Elman, R. J., & Berstein-Ellis, E. (1999). Psychosocial aspects of group communication treatment: Preliminary findings. *Seminars in Speech Pathology, 20*, 65–72.

Fougeyrollas, P., Cloutier, R., Bergeron, H., Cote, J., Cote, M., & St. Michel, G. (1997). *Revision of the Quebec Classification: Handicap creation process*. Lac St-Charles, Quebec: International Network on the Handicap Creation Process.

Kagan, A. (1998). Supported conversation for adults with aphasia: Methods and resources for training conversation partners. *Aphasiology, 12*, 816–831.

LaPointe L. L. (1997). Adaptation, accommodation, aristos. In L. L. LaPointe (Ed.), *Aphasia and related neurogenic language disorders, 2nd Edition* (pp. 265–287). New York: Thieme.

Lazarus, R. S., & Folkman, S. (1984). *Stress, appraisal, and coping.* New York: Springer.

LPAA. (2000). Life Participation Approach to Aphasia. *ASHA Leader, 5*(3), 4–6.

Lubinski, R. (1981). Environmental language intervention. In R. Chapey (Ed.), *Language intervention strategies in adult aphasia* (pp. 223–248). Baltimore: Williams & Wilkins.

Lubinski, R. (1986). Environmental systems approach to adult aphasia. In R. Chapey (Ed.), *Language intervention strategies in adult aphasia* (pp. 269–291). Baltimore: Williams & Wilkins.

Luterman, D. M. (1991). *Counseling the communicatively disordered and their families* (2nd Ed.). Boston, MA: Pro-Ed.

Lyon, J. G. (1995a). Drawing: Its value as a communication aid for adults with aphasia. *Aphasiology, 9,* 33–50.

Lyon J. G. (1995b). Communicative drawing: An augmentative mode of interaction. *Aphasiology, 9,* 84–94.

Lyon, J. G. (1996). Optimizing communication and participation in life for aphasic adults and their prime caregivers in natural settings: A use model for treatment. In G. Wallace (Ed.), *Adult aphasia rehabilitation* (pp. 137–160). Boston, MA: Butterworth-Heinemann.

Lyon J. G. (1997). Volunteers and partners: Moving intervention outside the treatment room. In B. Shadden & M. T. Toner (Eds.), *Communication and aging* (pp. 299–324). Austin, TX: Pro-Ed.

Lyon J. G. (1999a). *Coping with aphasia.* San Diego, CA: Singular Publishing Group.

Lyon J. G. (1999b). Treating real-life functionality in a couple coping with severe aphasia. In N. Helm-Estabrooks & A. L. Holland (Eds.), *Approaches to the treatment of aphasia* (pp. 203–239). San Diego, CA: Singular Publishing Group.

Lyon, J. G. (2000). Finding, defining, and refining functionality in real life for people confronting aphasia. In L. Worrall & C. Frattali (Eds.), *Neurogenic communication disorders: A functional approach* (pp. 137–161). New York: Thieme.

Lyon J. G., Cariski D., Keisler, L., Rosenbek, J., Levine, R., Kumpula, J. et al. (1997). Communication partners: Enhancing participation in life and communication for adults with aphasia in natural setting. *Aphasiology, 11,* 693–708.

Lyon, J. G., & Shadden, B. (2001). Treating life consequences of aphasia's chronicity. In R. Chapey (Ed.), *Language intervention strategies in adult aphasia* (5th Ed., pp. 297–315). Baltimore: Williams & Wilkins.

Lyon, J. G., & Sims, E. (1989). Drawing: Its use as a communicative aid with aphasia and normal adults. In T. Prescott (Ed.). *Clinical Aphasiology Conference Proceedings.* San Diego: College Hill Press.

Pound, C., Parr, S., Lindsay, J., & Woolf, C. (2000). *Beyond aphasia: Therapies for living with communication disability.* Oxford: Winslow Press.

Ryff, C., & Singer, B. (1998). The contours of positive human health. *Psychological Inquiry, 9*(1), 1–28.

Ryff, C., & Singer, B. (2000a). Interpersonal flourishing: A positive health agenda for the new millennium. *Personality and Social Psychology Review, 4,* 30–44.

Ryff, C., & Singer, B. (2000b). Biopsychosocial challenges of the new millennium, *Psychotherapy and Psychosomatics, 69,* 170–177.

Ryff, C., Singer, B., Wing, E., & Love, G. D. (2001). Elective affinities and uninvited agonies: Mapping emotion with significant others onto health. In C. D. Ryff & B. H. Singer (Eds.), *Emotion, social relationships, and health* (pp. 133–175). New York: Oxford University Press.

Simmons-Mackie, N. N., & Damico, J. (1997). Reformulating the definition of compensatory strategies in aphasia. *Aphasiology, 8*, 761–781.

Tanner, D. C., & Gerstenberger, D. I. (1988). The grief response in neuropathologies of speech and language. *Aphasiology, 2*, 97–84.

World Health Organization (WHO) (1980). *International classification of impairments and handicaps.* Geneva, Switzerland: World Health Organization.

5 Context, culture, and conversation

Claire Penn

> We inhabit the great stories of our culture. We live through stories. We are
> lived by the stories of our race and place. We are, each one of us, locations
> where the stories of our place and time become partly tenable.
>
> (Mair, 1991, cited by Evans, 2002)

This is my story. In this chapter I will describe the multiple influences that
have directed me forward as an aphasia therapist—the role of mentors, life
events, geographic context, and pure serendipity. I will consider the phases
of my own development in relation to some ideas about aphasia therapy and
highlight some lessons learned, using as illustration the personal narrative of
a person with aphasia. Finally I will offer some advice to the young clinician,
which I suppose is one of the indulgences permitted in this phase of my
career!

The context in which I have done most of my research and therapy has
been a very important influence on my development as a clinician-researcher.
As a South African I was often insecure and envious of my American and
European counterparts who (seemingly at least) had the benefit of team
interaction, resources, status, and opportunity to take part in large-scale
funded collaborative studies. My graduates often moved overseas and into
the supportive arms of a distant network and my life as an aphasiologist
became increasingly reliant on aeroplanes. By contrast I perceived my own
context as one that, like the Avis advertisement, forced me to "try harder"
and to evolve more ecological approaches to assessment and therapy by
having to:

- rely on and develop my own neurological and neuropsychological competence in issues of diagnosis;
- often operate independently of a team and understand the importance
  of working in a transdisciplinary manner;
- address issues of rapid turnover and quick effectiveness because of short
  hospital stay and no opportunities for follow up;
- work with a range of interpreters, assistants, and extended families;

- adapt and create assessment and therapy techniques in a range of ways to address the cultural and linguistic diversity of the caseload.

PHASES

The theme of this chapter is phases: the historical phases of aphasia therapy, the evolution of an approach to aphasia in myself, and the phases of recovery in the person with aphasia. These are certainly not separate constructs and I will argue that the therapeutic relationship is an exquisitely attuned interface between the phase of recovery, the personal phases of the person with aphasia and clinician, and the context of the interaction, defined historically and socio-politically.

One of the reasons that I chose speech-language pathology and more specifically aphasia therapy as my career was simply that I did not know what I wanted to do, and this career seemed to offer an opportunity to pursue my interest in language and art, in medicine and science, and to work with people. This turned out to be a happy motive and choice. In my career as a therapist I have had brief diversions into other areas, but it has been in aphasia that I have found the most growth and personal development; as a clinical coach it has been with aphasic clients that I have seen the most development in student clinicians; and with my colleagues working in this field, I have had the most meaningful professional interactions.

MY DEFINING MOMENTS AS AN APHASIA CLINICIAN AND THE LESSONS I HAVE LEARNED

While I was still a student, my crusty neurology professor declared one day during a ward round that speech therapy was as effective as chicken soup to the stroke patient—benign and doing no harm but of no proven good. I was profoundly indignant yet could not really at this stage extend a convincing or scientific argument to the contrary. I resolved that I would take up his challenge and I did so for the next 25 years! I met him again, long retired and living in Australia, and had a delightful lunch with him, thanking him for shaping my career in the way that he had.

This phase coincided with the harsh and startling reality of my uselessness in the context of Baragwanath Hospital in Johannesburg (the largest hospital in the southern hemisphere) where I did my hospital clinical experience as a student. I was allocated an aphasic client who spoke six languages—none of them my own. He had TB in addition to aphasia and was feeling very ill indeed. His family could not be contacted. He was in a ward of fifty patients many of whom did not have their own bed. Nothing I had read or learned prepared me for this experience and the harsh words of my neurology professor were ringing true. I remember clearly what I did with this man.

I bought him a pack of cards and a packet of cigarettes and played a game outside in the gardens of the hospital with him, while he smoked illegally. He was discharged shortly thereafter and I felt justifiable guilt and doubt about my role, and choice of career. (I also incidentally nearly failed my hospital practicum.)

But this was in many ways a defining moment, because it helped me understand the unique challenges of my context. When I became a clinical educator, this experience made me determined to provide adequate skills to my students for addressing such a challenge (Penn, 2000). Traditional assessment and therapy techniques had proved irrelevant to me, I was poorly educated in cultural aspects. I wished I could speak this man's language and understand what mattered to him. It provided me with a new respect for those disciplines (such as anthropology) whose methods include observation, and a growing awareness of how irrelevant I was in the grand scheme of things.

The choice of pragmatics as my field of endeavour combined my intrigue in context with my first love, linguistics. This was inspired by talented linguistics lecturers and also by my experience as a British Council scholar working in England with Maggie Hatfield, Steven Levinson, and David Crystal. I had a wonderful time in Maggie's department. On Thursday mornings her department was a busy and bustling activity centre which was attended by a large number of persons with aphasia from all over the county—they came for a range of therapies, group and individual, they came as volunteers to aid in the research of some of the famous names at Cambridge University, but mostly they came to "hang out": to drink tea and to meet together. It struck me that this was a healing and bustling creative warmth which reflected the personality of the person in charge. Even the tedious reading of a list of non-words on a set of little cards did nothing to detract from the moment.

It was during this time that I realized the link between clinician and researcher and that the most mundane of daily activities, if described and documented with careful precision, can form the basis of relevant evidence for clinical intervention.

When I had completed my doctoral research I spent an influential year in the US working with "big names" in aphasia, including my mentors Carol Prutting and Audrey Holland, who humanized my therapy. From Terry Wertz I learned that you can prove scientifically that therapy works better than chicken soup!

I came home fired up and helped start the Stroke Aid Society in Johannesburg, which is a volunteer-run group providing opportunities for persons with aphasia to meet socially and to receive therapy. One of the persons whom I saw in therapy was a very special man, LC who on the second anniversary of his stroke took his own life. I have written elsewhere about this case and its impact (Penn, 1993). In therapy we were working on goals of autonomy and reasoning. His return to work proved a debilitating event and his changed role in his family was more than he could bear. Despite what I thought (and the tests affirmed) was an excellent recovery, this un-expected act made me seriously reconsider my role as a clinician.

At his funeral one of his family members said something like: "Let us remember L for what he was before the stroke." I had only known him for the two years after the stroke and loved him for the intelligent unique person that he was. I was puzzled by the evident fact that society assumes there is no dignity and quality of life possible after aphasia, and I knew that this is just not so!

This was a very important milestone for me. I could not make sense of it at first. I went for counselling with professionals at the Hospice Society (a wonderful organization for assisting those coming to terms with terminal disease) and immersed myself in readings about autonomy and burnout. It led me to change very drastically the way I teach the aphasia course, and I now teach a substantial course on ethics to my students which includes, among other things, the topics of abortion and euthanasia. Such topics demand a process of coming to terms with one's own perspectives, under-standing the origin of others' perspectives, and examining routes of inten-tion, action, and consequence—all again very critical in clinical development.

For several years mid-career I was seconded by a research institute to explore and develop a sign language dictionary. While this was far removed from aphasia it also contributed directly to my aphasia track. I became aware of alternative views of the disorders that we had studied as students. Immersed in growing advocacy movements, issues of esteem and empow-erment as well as huge political changes, a cultural rather than a disability perspective emerged from this experience.

The socio-political transition that has happened in my country over the past ten years has been nothing short of a miracle and suddenly it became clear as never before that my role as an aphasia therapist was to fight tooth and nail amidst changing health policy and the redistribution of resources. No effective therapist can be neutral politically, and advocacy is a pivotal skill to learn given the profound impact that the social economic and polit-ical context has for those with illness. (For more on this point, the writings of Farmer, 1999, provide great clarity and insight.)

THE NARRATIVE JOURNEY OF VALERIE ROSENBERG

After my sortie into sign language, I gradually increased my amount of clinical work. In 1999 I shared with a British audience the recovery diary of Mrs R and how my own thoughts about therapy resonated with her insights (Penn, 1999). This was a personal reconstruction of a therapy experience with Mrs Valerie Rosenberg, whom I first saw for therapy in June 1998. From the outset, therapy was very much a joint enterprise and this paper described the evolution of the content and process of therapy from the perspectives of both therapist and client.

Detailed collaborative narratives of this nature are few and far between and become possible only when the powerful subjective experience of the client is accessible. Being able to self-reflect, to be meta-linguistic or meta-cognitive hopefully unravels some of the pieces that make up the therapy process and provides insights for other therapy dyads. I chose this particular client to describe because:

- Her symptoms were mild enough for us to access her personal insights. As an accomplished author, despite what she perceived as severe limitations imposed by her condition, she was able to describe her subjective experience with great clarity, honesty, and sensitivity using powerful metaphoric language. I have drawn liberally on her own quotations (in italics) and have, where necessary, provided commentary on her own experiences.
- She was very highly motivated to improve her abilities, and persistently addressed her difficulties. Her discipline in therapy as well as her detailed, honest, daily self-reflection provide a rigorous tracking of the evolution of recovery.
- Her initial cluster and combination of symptoms (including visual problems, organization, planning, and memory difficulties) make some of the therapy techniques and processes very relevant, not just for the person with aphasia but for other categories of cognitive and communication difficulty that we encounter as therapists (such as those caused by closed head injury) and highlighted for me that at the mild end of the severity continuum it might appear limiting to differentiate communication problems by aetiology.

Valerie insisted on keeping my notes as an adjunct to her diary and after a period of time I was able to recognize the patterns and process of what we were doing and was inspired to put them to paper. As we did this, I became aware of how many different perspectives of aphasia are required to understand the whole picture. At times, the focus had to be driven by strictly neurological considerations, at others an insight into principles of linguistics and psychology was required. A series of distinct phases of recovery emerged and each phase seemed to demand a very different balance of contributing disciplines.

Specifically, her insights help us to answer some of the questions that should be paramount in the aphasia therapist's mind:

- What does it feel like?
- What do we know about what works?
- What should we do?
- What should we not do?

Valerie Rosenberg developed aphasia after surgery for a non-malignant tumour. The midline tumour was accessed through the left temporal lobe, leaving Valerie with a cluster of symptoms which included a mild aphasia with receptive difficulties and expressive problems, manifesting in word-finding difficulty and poor topic control. She also had visual problems, memory and organization problems, emotional difficulties, and distractibility and fatigue.

Prior to her surgery she was a very active and intellectual author and playwright who had been nominated for two literary awards. She had a busy and enriched social life, was well travelled, and had many hobbies. She had a very well-established support system of family and friends.

Her own words describe her premorbid life:

> *I had reached my seventieth year privileged to be able to look back on What the heck—It was a golden life . . . one lucky lady*

Her narrative was marked by several milestones.

The Beginning

The neurological event was a terrible one for her. Once again, her own words are stronger than any other:

> *My first recollection after the operation was . . . well look I'm not really sure that's what it was. It was more a feeling.*
> *I was hovering above my bed . . . from the wall, watching myself in my blue prison pyjamas.*
> *Time was warped or it stood still as though there was no such thing as passage of time, I think.*
> *Like being in an egg.*
> *Or a bubble*
> *I didn't like it*
> *Was this delirium?*
> *An out of body experience?*
> *Or what?*
> *Slowly I began to work my way out*

The various symptoms she experienced were described in early and later diary entries. Of her visual problems she described the following:

> *I remember that first morning when I tried to confirm my new world in hospital, I asked for my spectacles and it showed a world that was definitely skewed with a large crack down the middle like that of a broken mirror.*

> *What is left of what I can see with my bad eye is like looking through a funnel and what is left of what I can see with my good eye is scarily reduced. (will need*

to speak to Claire about how not to injure myself). My first though was Yikes!
He did the wrong operation. Nobody tells you about this.

Still tunnel vision or funnel visions. Left eye very much narrowed. Warp like
a Picasso plate. Not constant. Shifting
I see only a segment at a time. Marry this to an inability to retain what I see
in my mind's eye and my garden planning is almost insoluble.

Of her expressive difficulties:

I feel there is a "sticky gap" in my mind.
Aphasia: the medical term for my post-surgery condition is like trying to wade
knee-deep through melted toffee. Sticky.

Cognitive symptoms:

As I start my journey out of my bubble I list the things that make me feel
muddled
Too much. Of anything. Like too much on my plate. Or too many choices of
dishes. Too much newsprint. Especially in the Sunday papers. It's like what's
left of my brain has a problem coping with too much in too little space.
ideas are spider web thin
My thoughts still seem tangled and I still feel as though there is a piece of my
head Dr S neglected to put back.

Affect:

This has been a horrid few days with increasing insomnia, lack of control
both physically and emotionally, crying jags and sudden bouts of temper. And
TERROR
It doesn't feel like me here inside this strange person's skin and I wish someone
would please come and help me to get out. It's so scary.
If the radiologist was delighted the tumour is satisfactorily excised, satisfactorily
for whom?

My philosophy for therapy with a client of this nature has evolved over
the years and has been based on a number of principles. If one were forced
to label my "approach" under an umbrella term, it would be "pragmatic",
based on the critical principles of assessing and treating language within the
context of the client, attending to holistic needs, working on the compensa-
tion, and adapting to dynamic and transactional processes, particularly through
conversation.

My belief is that communication transcends and mediates almost every
aspect of living and that one's role as a communication therapist cannot

therefore be restricted to commonly used techniques and processes. Attunement, flexibility, and empathy—the essential ingredients for positive therapy—became so easy in this particular therapeutic experience possibly because, as for Valerie, my business is words and I revel in their structure, and their role in conveying thought and emotion in healing. I believe that the subjective world of words defies any attempt to systematize and standardize a therapy approach, and that meaningful therapeutic interaction with and around words resonates with complexity and potential. Reflective thinking becomes the crux of the therapeutic process for both client and therapist and enables a negotiated partnership linked by communication.

The goals of treatment that we derived together and which seemed largely unspoken were to restore meaning to her life, to reconstruct her dignity and capabilities as an author, to "fake it" if necessary to the outside world while coming to terms with possibly permanent sequelae of the surgery. As a very proud person, she desperately wanted to demonstrate that she was in control of her recovery, and sought strategies that would allow her gradual and careful adaptations towards resuming her old life. For the purposes of this chapter, I will focus on Valerie's response both to therapy as a whole and to the specific therapy procedures we employed.

> *How long have I got I wonder before we know whether I'm permanently brain damaged? I mean is this permanent or what?*
> *And what happened to my bargain with God.*

Therapy was divided into some distinct phases which emerged as a function of the process of recovery and various environmental factors. Below using mostly Valerie's direct observations, we see how she gradually learned to live with aphasia.

Phase One: Finding the way out of the bubble

The first phase of therapy started as soon as Valerie returned home, and much of this therapy was observed by a caregiver who was closely involved in everyday routines and who from time to time, between sessions, phoned me and sought clarification and guidance. This phase of therapy lasted about two months.

> *So of course it was home. It just didn't behave like it*

A structured routine was established, Valerie preferring to work for several hours in the early mornings to accomplish her goals. Her two main props were a diary which she kept from the beginning and then eventually her old friend, the laptop computer on which she had produced so much creative work. This step was a difficult one to take initially and was fraught with technical challenges and uncertainty, but she later documented it as a lifeline.

It lines up your thoughts. It puts things in order.
My computer and by extension my writing remain a lifeline and hopefully my
way back to me.
My word processor is my best friend.
Yesterday the power went off and it was restored and I tried to recapture what
I had written for my diary only it was gone from my memory. Like a chunk of
life all leaked away. That's why I need to get it down fast. . . . encouraging me
to open a vein.

The medium of therapy was conversation, as "Conversational language reflects the natural workings of the mind more closely than language of any other kind" (Chafe, 1977, p. 52). Valerie's insights into the impact of her problems on conversation are seen clearly in her observation:

With my comprehension always behind everyone else's the keenest rapier grows
dull, when it takes too long to thrust home. By the time I am ready I no longer
grasp what seemed funny before I lost the point. That currency of life and food for
the source bites the dust and the magic of humour vanishes like mist in the sun

Much of therapy comprised the development of little "one-liners" which were intended to act as verbal mediators for everyday coping and for helping to re-script some of her problems (see Table 5.1). They drew on some of her premorbid strategies and work habits and often targeted a number of her difficulties at the same time. For example the phrase "keep grounded" was originally used as a reminder to stay on the line when practising writing, and was aimed to counteract the impact of the visual difficulties. However, it became a metaphor for much more than this—being used as a reminder to stay on track and in direction when facing some of the chaos and distractions of everyday life in tasks other than writing.

Management of the feelings and depression surrounding the experience formed an important part of therapy. Inevitably, as time went on, there were increased feelings of depression and the dilemma for both of us as to how to handle it is reflected here:

To block out the depression or not to. Last week after the scan I had two days
when I just cried and cried. First we tried Claire's way. To accept the feeling as
something positive and live through it. Go with the flow. I tried.

After commencing anti-depressant medication:

It certainly helped but I felt so stupid. As if I'd taken a step back into the fog
from which I'm trying to struggle free . . . I need my clarity of thought as much
as possible. But I also need not to be overwhelmed by misery. It seems a hell of
an equation. The way for me is to block these scared sad feelings with work.
Always has been.

Table 5.1 One-liners used in therapy with Mrs Rosenberg

Visual difficulties
- Use large print books
- Remember the left visual field
- Draw and attend to margins
- Use a ruler
- Work on an uncluttered surface
- *"Keep grounded"*

A number of these strategies were developed in consultation with an occupational therapist. Despite opportunity to have individual occupational therapy, Mrs Rosenberg indicated a preference to have only one therapist and I therefore attempted to incorporate some well-established techniques for visual field and perceptual difficulties into therapy with her.

Organization and planning
- Talk and then do
- Revise and check your work
- Diary (plan, write and check)
- Set up
- One thing at a time

Organization and planning difficulties pervaded most of Valerie's life and pointed to some difficulties with executive routines. Again, in consultation with an occupational therapist and a neuropsychologist, we targeted initially everyday activities (such as dressing or gardening) and analyzed the components of various tasks. Valerie found that planning (either by means of a diary or by verbally anticipating the stages of a task) considerably helped the pacing and sequence of acts. Her diary of events became at the same time a retrospective analysis and an important planning platform.

Memory and reading
- (Who? When? Where? What?)
- Research and discuss, then write

The primary materials used in these activities were novels, TV documentaries, films, magazines articles, and newspapers. Valerie was encouraged to interact with the texts read by asking specific questions (Who were the participants? When did this take place? etc.), if necessary talking about them and then trying to write a response to each question. Such activities encouraged both memory and organizational strategies and were formalizations of well-developed premorbid analytic strategies which she had used as author and playwright.

Conversational one-liners
- Let the words serve the idea
- Visualize
- Beat about the bush
- Strategies of delay and repair
  "I'll call you back"
  "I need more time to think about that"
  "Please say that again"
- Catch your ideas in a net (mind mapping)
- Don't repeat yourself

Table 5.1 (Cont'd)

Using conversational opportunities we together identified some of the strategies that helped organize and control both the transmission and reception of ideas. Many of these ideas stemmed from my work with other persons with mild aphasia and specifically from the ideas of Joseph Wepman who was a strong protagonist of "thought therapy". I encouraged Valerie to focus on the idea rather than the specific words (through techniques such as visualization) and we used some mind-mapping techniques (visual displays of main content nodes) to help her link content, and to compensate for memory lapses. She became aware of the impact of some of her word-finding struggles and her digressions and the importance of staying on topic. She also developed an appreciation for circumlocution (in the presence of specific word-finding problems) and of compensatory of delay and repair.

Coping
- Avoid distractions
- Chill out
- Go with the flow
- Fake it until you make it
- Keep energy and strength for what is needed
- Do one brave thing each day

As life situations arose, we analyzed Valerie's response to them and what worked and did not work. We soon discovered that there were certain contexts (places and interlocutors) that were to be avoided and that she was better at certain times of day than others. Strategies for coping with everyday challenges evolved over time. She soon learned to keep her space and her plans for each day simple and to avoid people and tasks that upset her. Using some teenage terminology from her grandchildren, "Chill out" and "go with the flow", proved very helpful. She discovered that much of her success relied on attitude encapsulated in such one-liners. Amusingly we both became hooked on some of the self-help books around at the time (some prescribed by her daughter) and we both benefited from some of these mantras.

Phase Two: "So this is the real world bit by bit"—Problems and solutions

A second stage of recovery started when Valerie left on holiday with her family. This lasted about four months and the process was carefully documented. I was available by telephone for consultation and the caregivers were briefed to continue with some of the activities on which we had worked before. This phase was the one in which Valerie began to encounter real-world challenges and devised many of her own strategies for coping.

Valerie continued to document in detail her main difficulties, some of which were resolving, as well as her solutions to them. Some examples:

I see only a narrow segment of a page at a time.
My third dimension is missing. If I close my good eye, I lose my third dimension depth. And if I close my bad eye the whole scene jumps to the right, recedes farther away and loses definition. Al this is quite dizzy-making. You better believe it.

I try to choose big print or print that breaks in the middle of a page. Also I need a ruler to keep the lines in position or they seem to float. I see that I have of brightly coloured ones so that they are unlikely to get lost.

Don't' trust my spelling and words often look wrong even when they're correct. Who there's a double letter, I have to count or ask someone if I' right. I know I should use a dictionary but every option is at the cost of something else time wise and concentration wise.

Reading is really difficult so I have to choose (what to read) carefully. Need to express time telegrammatically. A sketch of the clock face as opposed to the digital system. But if I want to meet a friend to walk at seven am I get anxious and start waking myself at five.

I am marooned without my diary. I have no memory in my head
"the act of physically making my thoughts visible and audible puts them in a shape I can deal with. The abstract thought has no reality I can grab. Now I know why elderly people talk to themselves.

With increasing social opportunities, difficulties with her personal relationships began to emerge and become important.

What is this terror? It haunts me and makes me really act like someone who's lost her marbles. I want to behave normally enough to "fake it until I make it" . . . and then along come the weepies.
I should grow up. But how do I trust? And how do I steer? It's such a "what's the use?" world right now.
I've learned to pace myself, simplify and dress real fast. And it is still better if I restrict myself to safe gentle people but I do miss people. It's lonely here.

Phase Three: Taking stock

Valerie returned from holiday and to regular therapy. This third stage seemed to represent a period of consolidation in which we worked specifically on problem areas while extending and discussing strategies for coping and setting goals for the future.

Valerie's presenting problems at about eight months since onset included difficulties with attention, persisting visual problems, and reading and conversational difficulties. Many of these problems could be subsumed as difficulties with executive functions and were worked on through a series of executive routines such as suggested by Ylvisaker and Feeney (1998), some of which are reflected in Table 5.1. Her writing played an increasingly important and satisfying part of her life and she also began to show increasing curiosity into the neurological and psychological mechanisms and explanations for the difficulties she was having.

> *The brain is a wonderful contraption.*

The important issues at this stage appeared to be those surrounding social and relationship issues. Although she indicated that she *"did not have many friends. I always wrote"* she was able in the months of her illness to see who was good for her and who did not help.

> *My solitary cut-off life is one of the worst aspect that has happened to me.*

She tried to reclaim some of the power and status she previously had in her family. This proved complex and required a re-negotiation of roles. She expressed a feeling of being "defenceless" and accurately and sensitively recognized what she called threats to her goal of renewed autonomy and dignity.

> *G shared with A few intimate sympathetic looks of fellow sufferers lumbered with aging relatives not right in the head. I hated him for his insensitivity and smugness. Make that present tense. And there's nothing I can do.*

> *Dear G It is hideous to see everything through this crooked fog, but it is also hideous to see how badly we each need to escape. And what a hideous prison I have become for you. It's a lousy trick for God to have played. You deserve better and I wish I could make it better.*

Coping with these aspects formed the next stage of therapy and led to a referral to psychotherapy for a period. My own time commitments, but more important an awareness of my own boundaries, led to this referral. My earlier experience with LC and my awareness that depression is a major, recurring, and potentially dangerous force, particularly in a person with great insight and at certain transitional phases of recovery, prompted this referral. Both of us became aware that the symptoms we had worked on together (including visual, language, and memory aspects) had responded well to the techniques that we had used. We both acknowledged, however, that though there was more work to be done, the impact of some of the emotional and relationship aspects was more pervasive and important.

Valerie continued to keep in touch and sent me her chronicle when she completed it. Her comment at the end of therapy with me said a lot:

It has been a great privilege to have you guide me through this journey. Your empathy and inventiveness have made all the difference between what was left us to work with and our reaching for the me I used to be.

Phase Four: Two years down the line

Valerie ended her chronicle with an anniversary:

I don't like life through the cracked looking glass . . . Thoughts out of synch and unrelated words to express them.

And it scares me that I may not write again. Because practical or not, that's still how I define myself. A writer with the need to write as urgent as the need to breathe.

Here an identity crisis rears its head. Because of my brain is impaired so is my mind. This assault on my soul has damaged that part of me that makes me.

But I have friends,
Grandchildren,
Puppies

And a garden, . . . and J is teaching me to photograph with the camera he helped me choose.

That magical weekend the trees just burst into blossom and the bulbs into bloom. Those two days were the happiest I've had since surgery.

So let's shake the kaleidoscope and see what new patterns form:

This surely reflects a level of transcendence and moving beyond *"crying at the moon"* (Valerie's words) and indeed, "beyond aphasia" (Pound, Parr, Lindsay, & Woolf, 2000). In going through her chronicle she has moved into partial acceptance, a recognition of what she has and what she can do and the challenge that her life presents. The way ahead is marked by significant events—working towards goals and establishing the human pattern of cycles and celebrations. Her narrative at this point appeared close to that described by Frank (1995) as the "restitution narrative", demonstrating a forward perspective and contrasting so markedly with that of Mr C at the two-year milestone.

How was this therapy different from what perhaps could be termed more traditional aphasia therapy? I never once did a standard test as I feel it is not necessary to highlight the deficit. Conversation, observation, and discussion with Valerie's family provided most of what I needed to know. I held hands and I tried to listen to the subjective world of this person, and we jointly solved the problems. Often I was on the wrong track and she told me so. Often my ideas were elaborated by her and lifted out of the mundane to more creative extensions.

I was her speech-language therapist, but also at times assumed the role of psychologist, confidante, occupational therapist, daughter, and friend. While being acutely aware of my own professional boundaries, in this particular case, the holistic nature of therapy required that at times I put on the hat of others. I know that I would have dealt with this in a different way at an earlier phase of my professional development, and no doubt I will handle things differently in the future. The special connection that we had, and her clear communication about what she needed, as well as the intellectual interests we shared, made the process a natural one. I sought supervision on this case (as I do on many others) and I became very aware that when one is dealing with life participation issues, no one discipline has the answer. The client herself called the tune, and the phases that emerged were probably unique to her. I felt that I learned a huge amount from Valerie Rosenberg about the timing and nature of therapy. There was a mutuality of purpose and I believe a mutuality of growth for us both. I would prefer to see my role as that of facilitator rather than therapist, and I believe that each profession and individual who focuses on such participation issues may have to act in a transdisciplinary way to remain truly centred on what is relevant.

The distinct phases became very important—and the intermediate one, in which she had no direct contact with me, fortuitously created an opportunity to practise what was discussed in therapy and to measure its impact. Her careful documentation served in this case as a profoundly useful "consumer-driven" quality check of therapy techniques.

The hallmark of this therapy was its interactive and dynamic nature. The topics, methods, materials, and props were established naturally and spontaneously as each session evolved. We stayed on track and yet the sidetracking became sometimes potent and alluring and enriched our interactions.

We can never hope fully to reach the reality in our clients' minds and to understand the subjective reality not only of aphasia but also of the many symptoms that follow brain damage. However Valerie Rosenberg's powerful account and the therapy process has provided a beautiful window on courage, the human spirit, and the power of words, which I feel privileged to have shared. Her account joins an increasing body of self-reports of persons who have recovered from aphasia and who point out what (and whom) they perceive as important in the recovery process (Parr, Byng, & Gilpin, 1997; Pound, 2000). A narrative such as this one serves as an important bridge between the worlds of the person with aphasia and the therapist and can provide the evidence for what should be done (Kleinman, 1988; Riessman, 1993). Focus on symptoms, either cognitive or linguistic, should never be at the cost of the goal of maximizing personal control and re-establishing autonomy and a sense of self. Therapy should work towards enabling choice, respecting dignity, preserving continuity, and enabling social interaction and enjoyment of activities. No person exists without others. This is reflected most aptly in the Zulu proverb: A person is only a person because of other people.

In an important article written two decades ago on the nature of suffering, Cassell (1982) reminds us that the subjective experience of illness is very different from the objective indices of disease. Suffering is increased if the physician ignores these subjective aspects. We should always take into account that the persons we treat have a personality and a character, a past, family ties, roles, culture, politics, regular behaviours, a secret life, and a perceived future. Although aphasia presents a tremendous challenge to communication, we should never make the mistake of not asking about these dimensions and trying to understand how they impact.

Perhaps ultimately the goal we search for is transcendence. Cassell (1982) described transcendence as being expressed directly in religion and traditions and comprising an intense feeling of bonding with groups, ideals, or anything larger and more enduring than the person. The spiritual dimension is important when meaning is assigned, and suffering is reduced when it can be located within a coherent set of meanings. Transcendence is the most powerful way in which one is restored to wholeness after an injury to personhood—it locates a person in a far larger landscape.

ADVICE FOR DEVELOPING CLINICIANS

The above musings about my own phases and the responsibilities of the aphasia clinician lead inevitably to how to teach students of the 21st century to access the landscapes of those whom they serve. While curriculum content probably needs to be changed in many ways, perhaps the above discussion brings us back to the question of whether therapists are born or made.

A few years back Audrey Holland and I sat down to write a paper called "Clinical Artistry in the Treatment of Aphasia". It remains (perhaps predictably because of its nature) under review, but we have made a start on what we think it takes to be a good aphasia clinician. It boils down to a list of suggestions which we hope might help (see Table 5.2). Aphasia therapy is not easy. It challenges your very core. For aphasia therapy to work well we have to leave the confines of the therapy room both psychologically and physically.

I have suggested in this chapter that to everything there is a season and that the notion of cycles and phases is one we should be very much aware of. While it may take courage to venture into "the larger landscape", the journey has certainly been worthwhile for me and has been facilitated by the wonderful persons I have worked with, who have taught me never to take life and words for granted, and have provided me with a lasting love for my profession.

Table 5.2 Penn and Holland's checklist for successful aphasia therapy: Some do's and don'ts

---

- The brain should fascinate you endlessly. (You should be challenged by explanations of what you see, and revere the complexity and unique fingerprinting of brain damage on communication.)
- Recognize the phases in yourself and merge clinical practice with your own fascinations.
- Be confident in saying that you don't know, but conscientious in rectifying that.
- You don't have to be the expert. There are far too many around already!!
- Do continue to read in and out of the field.
- Do keep hands on. Being with clients and knowing persons with aphasia will enrich you more than any textbook. Always remind yourself through contact with persons with aphasia about what it's like not just to have but to live with aphasia.
- Develop and use your sense of humour.
- Always ask what is wanted, rather than assume you know.
- Utilize creative methods of mentoring/shadowing/coaching as a method of teaching clinical skills.
- Address some real fears: Will I have another stroke? Will I die? Being able to cry with the client is more healing than being unrealistically joyous. Perkiness is not next to godliness.
- Develop insight into your own reactions, be in touch with your own feelings and be realistic about your capabilities.
- Anticipate, recognize and deal with burnout because it will happen and working with clients when you are in that phase is detrimental to everyone concerned.
- Accept ambiguity, uncertainty and change, for after all that is what life is.

The speech of the children of man is our interest
And the communion of man is our concern . . .
Therefore the duty we owe is sacred
And our calling is gravely important

Robert West (1961, p. 8)

ACKNOWLEDGEMENTS

I have gathered a posie of other men's flowers. Just the hand that binds them is my own.

Montaigne

I thank the following persons for their mentorship, past and present, and their influence and support in shaping my professional interests: Len Lanham, Tony Traill, Frances Hatfield, Steven Levinson, David Crystal, Martha Taylor Sarno, Carol Prutting, Audrey Holland, Timothy Reagan, Dilys Jones, and Rachel Chapman.

I pay tribute to Sally Byng, Carole Pound, and all those at Connect for their far-reaching vision.

Finally I offer profound thanks to Valerie Rosenberg for her courageous chronicle.

REFERENCES

Cassell, E. J. (1982). The nature of suffering and the goals of medicine. *New England Journal of Medicine, 306*(11), 639–645.

Chafe, W. (1977). Polyphonic topic development. In T. Givon (Ed.) *Conversation: Cognitive, communicative, and social perspectives.* Amsterdam: John Benjamins Publishing Company.

Evans, M. (2002). *Towards culturally appropriate speech and language services.* Unpublished Masters dissertation, University of Cape Town, South Africa.

Farmer, P. (1999). *Infections and inequalities: The modern plague.* Berkeley: University of California Press.

Frank, A. (1995). *The wounded storyteller.* Chicago: University of Chicago Press.

Kleinman, A. (1988). *The illness narrative: Suffering, healing and the human condition.* New York: Basic Books.

Parr, S., Byng, S., & Gilpin, S. (1997). *Talking about aphasia.* Buckingham, UK: Open University Press.

Penn, C. (1993). Aphasia therapy in South Africa: Some pragmatic and personal perspectives. In A. Holland & M. Forbes (Eds.), *Aphasia treatment: World perspectives.* San Diego, CA: Singular Press.

Penn, C. (1999). *It's a matter of meta-: A case study of Mrs Rosenberg.* Keynote address to the British Aphasiology Society meeting, London.

Penn, C. (2000). Cultural narratives: Bridging the gap. *South African Journal Communication Disorders, 47*, 71–78.

Pound, C. (2000). *Learning to listen and helping to tell: The role of identity narratives in aphasia therapy.* Paper presented at the 9th International Aphasia Rehabilitation Conference, Rotterdam.

Pound, C., Parr, S., Lindsay, J., & Woolf, C. (2000). *Beyond aphasia: Therapies for living with communication disability.* Bicester, UK: Winslow Press.

Riessman, C. K. (1993). *Narrative analysis. Qualitative research methods* (Vol 30). New York: Sage Publications.

West, R. (1961). To our new members—ave et vale. *ASHA, 3,* 6–8.

Ylvisaker, M., & Feeney, T. J. (1998). *Collaborative brain injury intervention.* San Diego, CA: Singular Press.

6 Just kidding! Humour and therapy for aphasia

Nina Simmons-Mackie

Humour has been defined as that which is amusing, comical, ridiculous, or ludicrous, and often connotes playfulness or fun (Berger, 1993). Humour is insidious—it pervades our day, yet we hardly notice it. Humour has been described as a process—the perceptual and cognitive ability to pick out something unexpected or funny about a situation (Wooten, 2001). Laughter is the behavioural response to humour. Laughter can be a mild pleasure or a hysterical whole-body response—the proverbial "laugh till you cry". Mirthful laughter is sometimes difficult to stifle once it starts and flows through the body like a current. In fact, the word "humour" derives from the word "fluid" (Merriam-Webster, 1995). In the Middle Ages it was believed that the body fluids or humours flowed through a person as aspects of feeling, mind, and spirit (Wooten, 2001). Thus, humour carries a sort of metaphysical feel to it—a union of the body and spirit.

People express humour in many ways. Humour is not restricted to telling jokes. It can be a quip, a playful look, or a shared laugh. My sense of humour tends to gravitate towards seeing the absurd in everyday life—like the hour my husband and I recently spent at an eccentric veterinarian's office discussing our sick dog, while a large yellow bird perched on my husband's head! I found the incongruity of this to be quite hilarious.

Humour is everywhere. We laugh during parties, movies, phone conversations, business meetings, and even during speech therapy for aphasia. Although humour pervades human communicative interactions, humour rarely holds the spotlight in the study of aphasia. In a review of the literature, LaPointe (1991) urged clinicians and researchers to explore humour and its effects. However, the literature continues to offer few references to humour and its roles (LaPointe, Katz, & Kraemer, 1985; Marshall, 1994; Norris & Drummond, 1998; Potter & Goodman, 1983; Williams, 1996). Perhaps humour is a topic that evades analysis, since as E. B. White (1954) suggests we can dissect humour like a frog, but the thing dies in the process and the innards are discouraging to look at. Or perhaps humour is deemed too frivolous to garner serious attention by speech-language pathologists. Although we tend to discount humour as "frivolous", it serves important functions in human communicative interactions, including speech therapy interactions.

The importance of humour in therapy became obvious to me as a result of an incident that occurred many years ago when I was a young aphasia therapist. At the time I was working in a rehabilitation centre with another young clinician. We loved our work. We couldn't imagine doing anything more emotionally and intellectually stimulating than learning from people with aphasia day after day. My colleague was a very funny person. We laughed a great deal, and our clients laughed a great deal. Even though we worked hard and were very committed, we had a good time. One day as we were walking out of our suite of therapy rooms with two clients, all of us laughing heartily, an administrator pulled me aside and said, "All this laughing is unprofessional and disrupts the business of this institute—you girls need to get *serious*." I was stunned! Being young and insecure, I believed her. My colleague and I embarked on a mission to get more serious. But the zest went out of our therapy, and we could see the effects on our clients and ourselves—we were getting bored and irritable. The impact of the change was tangible. It didn't take long for my inventive colleague to come up with a solution. One day, she came into my office with a dictionary and pointed to the word "serious" and said, "a synonym for serious is *grave*. That means DEAD!" So we decided to forget being serious! Since this experience I have consciously considered fun and humour to be very important elements of work.

Since this original encounter with the administrator who suffered from terminal professionalism (the stultifying belief that a professional must be grim and sombre), a large literature has arisen that attests to the positive impact of humour in health care. For instance, the nursing and psychology literature is replete with information on humour in health care (e.g., Brooks, 1994; Buxman, 1991; Herth, 1984; O'Malley, 1992; Wooten, 1996). Much of the focus of this literature is on using humour to cope with illness and stress. In fact, there is an American Association of Therapeutic Humour and journals that focus on humour as a part of health care (e.g., Murphy & Englehart, 1994). There is also information in the sociolinguistics literature. For example, conversation analysts have studied the structural characteristics of joint laughter and telling a joke (Glenn, 1991–92, 1995; Jefferson, 1979, 1985; Sacks, 1974), and identified humour and laughter as official conversational activities (Goodwin, 1996; Jefferson, Sacks, & Schegloff, 1987). Thus, humour is not simply random frivolity. It is an integral aspect of interpersonal communication. Humour is intensely social, and it is decidedly communicative. Therefore, it is an important topic to those concerned about promoting interpersonal communication and social interaction for those affected by aphasia.

APPLICATIONS OF HUMOUR TO APHASIA THERAPY

The topic of humour as it relates to therapy for aphasia seems to divide into two major content areas. First, one can investigate the role of humour in standard therapy sessions—that is, how humour serves as an interactive resource during routine speech therapy. Second, we can address the purposeful programming of humour into aphasia management and life with aphasia.

Humour as an interactive resource in therapy interactions

Humour bubbles up often during routine speech and language therapy. This is not the "falling down laughing" type of humour, telling jokes, or "wearing a funny nose" type of humour. Rather, humour appears as an "unplanned" part of therapy. Unexpected responses, subtle asides, or exaggerated facial expressions arise during interactions with clients, and create humorous interludes. What is the purpose of these humorous interludes during therapy? In order to more fully understand "what's going on" relative to humour in therapy, I initiated a research investigation employing qualitative research methods (e.g., Agar, 1986; Atkinson & Heritage, 1984; Goffman, 1974; Gumperz, 1982). I would like to share a few preliminary observations about humour during traditional, didactic, individual aphasia therapy interactions.

Routines of therapy

Therapy for communication disorders is an organized social event that carries with it certain expectations. When something unexpected or incongruous occurs during an organized social event, it is often perceived as funny. Therefore, observations of humour in therapy help expose the expectations and discourse routines of therapy. In therapy, when the client and therapist laugh at a deviation from the expected, it is clear that they "know" what the expected routine is and recognize when it is altered. Thus, humour foregrounds expected therapy practices. The following is an example of a deviation from therapy routine that is perceived as humourous.

> The clinician is trying to guess what a client is describing.
> *Clinician:*   So someone's at the barbershop?
> *Client:*   Yes, yes, yes, yes
> *Clinician:*   And they're getting their hair cut?
> *Client:*   Yea, GOOD! (points at the clinician)
> Clinician & client laugh

Here the humour lies in the reversal of the typical therapy sequence. Usually the therapist evaluates the client with a "GOOD". Here the client does the evaluation of the therapist—an atypical discourse sequence. Both client and therapist recognize implicitly that the therapist is expected to do the evaluating, not the other way around. So this unexpected discourse sequence is funny! In fact, the more rigid the routines of a particular event, the more likely a deviation will seem funny. The humour in such sequences highlights the relatively rigid discourse structure of therapy interactions.

Participant roles in therapy

Humour can also highlight the expected roles of participants in therapy. For example, seeing your therapist doing something absurd is funny because of the therapist's expected role as a "professional" and an expert.

> *A therapist and client are taking turns drawing cards from a stack in a Promoting Aphasics' Communicative Effectiveness (PACE) activity (Davis, 1993a). The therapist is supposed to communicate the contents of the card to the client. The therapist pulls a card from the stack, looks at the card, then furtively replaces the card in the deck. The client gives her a stern look, and the therapist loudly whines, "I'm not cheating!"*

Both the therapist and client laughed after this incident. Why? Perhaps because we don't expect a therapist to cheat and then lie about the cheating! This is not consistent with the role of the professional or expert.

Another interesting clue to roles in therapy is gleaned from who initiates humour—who jokes? Preliminary analyses find that of the therapy sessions studied, the overwhelming majority of the humour occurrences were clinician-initiated. This is interesting since the literature suggests that humour relates directly to power and superiority in society (Berger, 1993; Brown & Levinson, 1987; Davis, 1993b; du Pre, 1998; Emerson, 1973). Who jokes and who is the target of joking discloses the social hierarchy. When the power structure favours one individual over another, the more powerful individual has more "joking rights". In the samples studied, the therapists did more joking. Perhaps the distribution of joking in these sessions is an example of the asymmetrical social structure of therapy in favour of clinicians.

This brings us to another interesting question. Who laughs in response to attempts at humour in therapy? In the therapy sessions studied to date, the most common response was shared laughter. That is, both therapist and client laughed. Clients routinely laughed at therapist-initiated humour. However, there were examples of therapists not laughing at client attempts at humour. Although not common, therapists on occasion did purposefully decline client attempts at humour. Here is an example of a therapist ignoring a client's attempt at humour (Simmons-Mackie, Damico, & Damico, 1999, p. 225):

Clinician:	Show with your hand how you brush you teeth.
Client:	(Bares gums in an exaggerated fashion, laughing—he has no teeth)
Clinician:	Show with your hand.
	(Lifts client's hand and moves it towards his mouth)
Client:	(Moves hand across mouth in brushing motion, frowning)

The therapist ignores the client's humour and reorients to the task. The subtle implication is that the client is not allowed to joke during the task. This is a very powerful example of subtle cues to who has the right to joke. It is possible that in some cases clients learn that they do not have "joking rights" in therapy or that they are not permitted to initiate humour during the work of therapy.

Values in therapy

The content of humour in therapy is also interesting. In the sessions studied so far, the humour was benign. There were no sarcastic jokes or off-colour quips. The overarching theme seemed to be "therapists used humour for good". In other words, it appeared that therapists used humour to help manage therapy sessions and make clients feel better about therapy. In addition, humour typically did not "stand alone" and did not derail or replace the activity at hand. Rather humour was tucked within larger discourse units. Humour served as a temporary respite that shifted the tone of the session. The humour appeared to be a covert way of managing interaction and adding a more positive valence.

The positive use of humour in standard therapy sessions seemed to fulfil several functions including (1) mitigating embarrassment, (2) motivating clients to cooperate, (3) reinforcing affiliation, and (4) relieving tension. The funnier sessions definitely had a more positive and enjoyable feel. However, there was an asymmetry to humour. Clinicians did most of the joking, suggesting that in order to "do good work" these therapists controlled the sessions, established the discourse structures and "called the shots".

Why is asymmetry in "who jokes" or who controls therapy important? The ability to exert power over others and take control of events is an important aspect of maintaining autonomy and reinforcing self-esteem. If expressing humour is an expression of power and contributes to self-esteem and autonomy, then a more equal distribution of "joking rights" in therapy might be important. Equality of joking could help equalize the relationship and help build self-confidence in the person with aphasia. Perhaps as therapists we might examine our own subtle interpersonal use of humour in therapy and make sure that sessions are fun, that we use humour to advantage, and also that clients are empowered to use humour in therapy.

Let me share an anecdote to demonstrate the power of well-managed humour in standard therapy. Kit, a lady with very severe aphasia, had worked with two prior clinicians before she began working with Margie. She had made very little progress and, in fact, often did not even show up for therapy. Her husband said she did not like therapy. When Kit began to work with Margie there was a change in her attitude about therapy. Therapy videotapes of Kit with a prior clinician and Kit working with Margie revealed that both therapists employed similar therapy tasks; however, the tone of the sessions was notably different. With Margie, the session was replete with humour.

Kit was empowered to have fun—and she was very funny on the videotape with Margie. Even though Kit was virtually nonverbal she used gesturally conveyed jokes, prosody, and facial expressions to be funny. Kit's husband reported that her attitude towards therapy and her self-confidence soared after starting to work with Margie. She was able to express her personality and individuality. She became a person instead of a patient. Although this is anecdotal it gives a sense of what humour might add in standard therapy— and does add with many empowering therapists.

PREMEDITATED HUMOUR

Incidental humour within regular therapy tasks is not the only way to use humour in aphasia therapy. The second major topic focuses on "premeditated humour". This is humour that is purposefully planned as a therapy task or as the therapy itself.

Humour as a therapy task

Humour can be programmed as a therapy task—that is, the stimulus in therapy. Thus, humour serves the same purpose as picture cards or written questions. Humour becomes the context for working on individual communication goals. For example, therapy with an individual who is working on reading comprehension might include funny stories or written jokes as the reading stimuli. A client might practise specific spoken discourse strategies while describing a funny picture or a series of cartoons. Clients and family members can practise use of conversational supports such as drawing, gestures, or writing while discussing a humorous event.

   Why would we do this? Other than just being fun, the literature suggests positive benefits to programming humour into goal-oriented therapy.

Humour and brain activation

Humour creates interesting activation effects on the brain, perhaps stimulating right hemisphere activation and drawing more brain processing into a given task (Davis, 1993a). For example, one study demonstrated that a large portion of both hemispheres is engaged in the processing of jokes (Derks, Gillikin, Bartolome-Rull, & Bogart, 1997). In fact, broad patterns of activation probably occur for most types of humour. It would seem that therapy that focuses on cerebral reorganization might be able to capitalize on the activation patterns inherent in humorous stimuli.

Humour and memory

It has also been suggested that humour can improve learning and memory (du Pre, 1998; Wooten, 2001). When something is funny it heightens and focuses attention and provides added salience. Humour is both intellectual and emotional, so it possibly draws on multiple processing systems. Humour is a potential tool for teaching compensatory strategies or teaching communication partners. For example, I have worked with clients to come up with memorable names for their compensatory strategies, such as the "come hither stare" to request help in word finding from partners, or the "killer grab" to describe a rather aggressive turn-taking strategy.

Humour and stress relief

Humour as the context of therapy also helps "lighten up" the hard work of therapy. It relieves stress and heightens positive emotions. In fact, physiological studies have highlighted the positive effects of humour on health and stress relief (e.g., Berk, 1989a, 1989b; Fry, 1992). Tasks that achieve communication goals and simultaneously relieve stress are practical and efficient.

Humour as a communication facilitator

Humour has been touted as a way to facilitate communication by lubricating the interactional process (Volcek, 1994). This seems to support my own observations that when people with aphasia "lighten up", when they don't try so hard, they often do better at communicating. Success in therapy tasks and enhanced motivation support the use of humorous therapy materials.

Humour as a social bond

When people laugh together the social bond is reinforced (Buckman, 1994; du Pre, 1998; Jefferson et al., 1987). In groups, shared humour serves to build group identity and promote interaction. Humour is fun; thus, motivation is enhanced both for clients and for clinicians. Clearly, there are many potential benefits for using humorous therapy tasks.

HUMOUR AS THERAPY

Humour can also be therapeutic itself. If we believe in holistic, person-centred programming for aphasia, then we must not ignore spiritual and emotional health. Many have discussed the depersonalizing experience of being a patient, the feelings of helplessness and loss of dignity, and the high incidence of depression among stroke survivors (e.g., Cousins, 1979; LaPointe, 1997). Clearly these psychosocial consequences of illness could markedly affect outcomes from aphasia therapy. Therefore, taking humour a step farther we might actually consider it *as therapy* to decrease depression, raise morale, and build a positive sense of self (Clark, 1988; Richman, 1995; Wooten, 2001).

In fact, laughter is one of the four basic antidotes to tension and depression within the strain of modern living. These stress antidotes are (1) drugs, (2) exercise, (3) spirituality, and (4) laughter (Berk, 1998). Of course, I feel compelled to add a fifth antidote to this list: (5) eating junk food and chocolate! In fact, I recently found the perfect "no stress diet" (Berk, 1998, p. 97):

Breakfast
$\frac{1}{2}$ grapefruit
1 slice toast
1 cup skim milk

Lunch
4 oz broiled chicken breast without skin
1 cup steamed broccoli
1 cookie (biscuit)
1 cup herb tea

Afternoon Snack
Rest of package of cookies
1 quart chocolate ice cream
1 jar hot fudge sauce

Dinner
Double quarter pound burger with cheese
Super large fries
Jumbo soda
Bag of chocolates
Entire frozen cheesecake eaten directly from box

Since it is not recommended that speech therapists ply their clients with drugs or chocolate, laughter is one stress antidote that we can easily program into aphasia intervention. The following are potential benefits of humour as a therapeutic regime and life enhancer.

Healing the body and preventing illness

Chronic syndromes such as aphasia can create a cycle of stress and anxiety that negatively affect the body, exacerbate illness, and reduce the effectiveness of therapies. Laughter has positive effects on our physiological response to stress. Mirthful laughter enhances the immune system and positively affects chronic illness (e.g., Berk, 1989a, 1989b; Fry, 1992; Kamei, Kumano, & Masumura, 1997; Lefcourt, Davidson-Katz, & Kueneman, 1990; Martin & Lefcourt, 1983; Soloman, 1987). Laughter can stimulate endorphins, acting as a mood elevator and tranquilliser (Volcek, 1994). Humour actually helps heal the body and promote recovery.

Promoting well-being

When we expose people to humour it raises spirits and invokes positive emotions (Erdman, 1993; Freud, 1960; Herth, 1984; Wooten, 1993). For example, a research study of elderly people showed that a three-week humour programme significantly improved morale, and decreased agitation and loneliness among the participants (Tennant, 1990). Thus, humour has the potential to promote well-being.

Humour as defence mechanism and stress reliever: Coping through humour

Humour has been described as the highest and most mature of all the defence mechanisms—the indispensable little shock absorber (Buckman, 1994). Humour helps deal with pain, grief, embarrassment, anger, and prolonged stress. By seeing something as funny we minimize it and gain power over it. Self-deprecating humour helps us and others deal with anxiety and is a good way to model taking risks and being imperfect. For example, when I make a mistake while teaching I often use humour to minimize the mistake and my own embarrassment. I always seem to end up with chalk somewhere on my anatomy while teaching classes; the "chalk check" at the end of my classes is a form of "joke's on me" that students enjoy. Clients can learn to use humour to minimize their own imperfections and soften embarrassment. This brings us to another benefit of humour: humour can help build a positive sense of self.

Humour and the sense of self

A sense of humour and a sense of future are partners.
(Volcek, 1994, p. 120)

Humour can encourage a more positive perspective on ourselves and our world. It has been said that using humour is like having inverse paranoia— you think the world is out to do you good (Volcek, 1994, p. 116). Humour can improve perspectives by fostering objectivity about ourselves and our situations. That is, if I view an event or some characteristic of myself as funny, then it is not as dreadful as I thought. Humour builds a sense of personal control over life. One might not be able to control the aphasia, but one can control emotional responses to aphasia by substituting humour and positive emotions for negative emotions. By controlling one's emotions, the locus of control shifts from the external world to the individual. Feeling a sense of control is very important to well-being. When we learn to use humour as a coping mechanism, we gain a sense of control over ourselves, feelings of helplessness and anxiety are reduced, and a positive sense of self is reinforced.

Humour also helps build insight. When someone pokes good-natured fun at a behaviour, it can help the recipient identify a self-defeating or irritating behaviour. In fact, sometimes I worry that aphasia therapy is too supportive, that we don't foster the growth of strong identities because we feel the need to nurture and coddle clients. When therapists become caretakers and nurturers, helplessness and poor self-esteem might be promoted. Well-timed humour can raise difficult issues and provide a context for gaining insight and for self-actualization. Humour can communicate to a person that "I know you have the strength to deal with this situation". Thus, humour might provide an acceptable medium for challenging clients to undertake something difficult or deal with a difficult issue. In fact, psychotherapists sometimes use humour to raise topics that might otherwise be too difficult to introduce into a discussion, making humour an excellent tool in counselling (Buckman, 1994).

Humour as a learned cultural behaviour

Humour reflects one's perspective on life and cultural beliefs. What is deemed funny varies, from person to person and from culture to culture. There are many factors that influence one's appreciation of humour, such as ethnic background, occupation, socioeconomic status, gender, age, political affiliation, race, even hair colour. Dumb blonde jokes are usually not quite as funny to blondes! And anyone with children is well aware that little boys find anything related to bodily functions to be hilarious. Therapists might help ensure that humour is personally and culturally appropriate for those affected by aphasia (Volcek, 1994).

While the propensity for humour is probably innate, like language, humour can be learned and expanded (Berger, 1993). Humour can be cultivated, and one's sense of humour flowers with exposure. Groups or families breed humour among themselves and instil particular humour styles such as puns or word play versus practical jokes. Families or groups also often have ritualized themes that bubble up all the time. For example, my husband and I have a "speaking dog" theme as part of our family humour. We communicate things from the perspective of one of our dogs. "Guess what Lou Lou told me? She thinks it's time that you take me out to a nice restaurant" or "Whitie wants to know where you put the peanut butter!" This ritual humour helps us avoid directly saying what might be fuel for conflict. Therapists can help identify and promote ritualized themes in groups and within families as an expression of humour. Also, therapists can assist families in incorporating humour styles that are aphasia friendly.

DOING THERAPY

So how do we do humour *as* therapy? Humour as therapy involves a concerted effort to teach the benefit of humour, provide exposure to humour and an effort to teach others to seek out humour, appreciate humour, and even produce humour. Humour involves learning to search the world for comic possibilities. My mother who is retired now calls me often to "report in". She always asks, "So, how are the dogs" and I always relate a funny dog story (dog humour is indeed a big theme in our home). She looks forward to our shared laugh over these dog stories. Then she relays the stories to her friend, Agatha, who in turn tells her friends. In fact, my dog stories probably entertain much of elderly New Orleans. This funny dog report has become a very important ritual. Not only does it bring enjoyment to others, but also I enjoy it—seeking out funny things to report brightens my days. Thus, a key to building humour into life is learning to see the humour that is all around us. Working with clients and family members in using methods to inject humour into their lives is a possible goal in itself.

Humour therapy might start by introducing the concept of humour as therapeutic. For example, information on the physical and psychological benefits of humour can be provided. There is a huge literature on the benefits of humour and the internet abounds with humour information and resources. Passive exposure to humour in the form of videotapes, audiotapes, books, and cartoons can be provided. The idea can be introduced that humour is an important form of communication. So, for example, the therapist might help others focus on how people react to humour—what do you do when you are really happy or tickled? What does your face look like? What do you sound like? How does your body move? How do you feel? Clients and/or family members can listen to or try to produce various laughs and talk about how they communicate different things—the scary laugh, the Santa Claus laugh, the silly giggle, the howl. Typically, people start to laugh just by hearing laughter! Dr Paul Berghoff (2001), a psychologist, works with clients and families to develop a special "celebration strut"—a sequence of behaviours that shows appreciation or joy. The celebration strut (it need not involve walking) is like a personal version of a high five or football strut. Such activities help those affected by aphasia recognize various forms of communicating humour and joy.

Strategies for adding humour into daily life can be introduced. Like most therapy recommendations, merely giving a client or family a list of humour activities does not fulfil the goal. Rather, the process should be participatory and fun; folks do best if guided through the process. They can learn to enjoy and seek out humour as a part of life. Most of all, we all need to learn how to adapt humour to aphasia. Obviously humour does not need to be spoken. Visual jokes, vocalizations, facial expressions, and gestures are great. The following are a few examples of ways to introduce humour into daily life for those affected by aphasia, caregivers, and healthcare professionals.

- Create a humour-charged atmosphere. By providing an environment that reinforces and cultivates humour and fun, we can model this atmosphere for those affected by aphasia, for students, and for other health professionals.

- Keep a journal (e.g., via writing, drawing, pictographs) that depicts at least one funny thing from each day to help focus on the humour around us.
- Provide access to video or audiotapes of comedians (public libraries sometimes loan these free of charge).
- Provide access to humorous movies or television shows (old silent movies or old "I love Lucy" shows are often hilarious and very visual).
- Join "on line" joke lists. For example, sites offer jokes, cartoons, or even audios of people laughing.
- Read and collect cartoons.
- Read humorous books (e.g., "healthcare" humour, cartoons, jokes).
- Facilitate access to performances such as clowns or mimes.
- Provide weekly humour "prescriptions" such as the following (Herth, 1984).

> If you do not laugh regularly, you may suffer from humourrhoids. This is a condition that starts with the hardening of attitudes and may actually lower your laugh expectancy. Suggested cures include taking a mild laughsitive every day or laughing at one's own every-day unintended humour. These should restore you to regular hilarity.
> (Erdman, 1993, p. 66)

- Create a "humour centre" at your facility. This can be as simple as a bulletin board of funny cartoons, pictures or sayings, or as extravagant as a "laugh room" where people enjoy comedy videos, books, cartoons, funny hats and noses, or gags.

In addition to providing access to humour enjoyment, therapy might involve working on producing humour. The following are a few examples of humour-production activities.

- Work on "humour" discourse such as telling jokes or story telling. This might involve learning to use supports to tell a joke or story (e.g., pictures, props). For example, therapists might employ conversational coaching (Holland, 1988) to practise telling a funny story or to practise getting the punch line of a joke.
- Practice using nonlinguistic humour such as pantomime, gestures, or facial expressions.
- Keep a daily cartoon, joke, or funny newspaper story in one's pocket to show others. One man with aphasia collected funny newspaper headlines to share with friends. Another collected jokes from his email network and printed these to share with aphasia group members.
- Draw caricatures of situations or people. An excellent group project is to work on drawing caricatures of events or famous people to grasp humorous characteristics (but drawing caricatures of each other has the potential to be embarrassing or hurtful).

- Wear a hat or T-shirt with a funny saying or picture.
- Keep a humour journal to share with other people. Once per day, think about your day and find something funny about it. Write it down or draw it, or work with a partner to represent it. The journal is then shared with friends or a humour "buddy".

While most of these examples focus on the person with aphasia, humour as therapy is quite universal. It is a tool that is appropriate for people with communication disabilities, caregivers, students, and healthcare providers. For example, support groups for carers or rehabilitation team meetings might incorporate humour as a "therapeutic" tool to reduce stress, enhance co-operation, and improve the living of life.

THE HUMOUR ASSESSMENT

If we wish to incorporate humour into speech-language therapy, then it might be appropriate to determine what we find funny and what our clients deem funny. It is interesting that therapists spend time assessing the ability to retrieve words, form sentences, or understand simple instructions, but we rarely make a direct effort to assess how clients deal with difficult situations or how they view the world and themselves. Richard Dana (1994), a psychologist, suggests that humour can be a tool for assessing adaptive potential and attitude towards change—attributes that are potentially important to life participation and communicative reintegration.

A humour assessment might be in order to help gauge the humour of those affected by aphasia. This might include observational assessment to determine aspects of humour enjoyment, production, and style.

- Observe "receptive humour". Are there clues that indicate if the individual is receptive to humour? What does this individual laugh at? Is this individual offended or hurt by certain humour?
- Observe "expressive humour". How does this individual express or share humour? Can this be expanded?
- What type of humour does the client seem to favour (e.g., irony, word play, puns, sarcasm, slapstick, absurdities)?
- What modalities and humour characteristics might encourage humour sharing (e.g., gesture/pantomime, graphics/cartoons, written jokes, pranks)? Are there adaptations or accommodations that will enhance humour appreciation and production?
- Are there any humour "themes"? Are there topics that are "taboo" for this individual/family/group?
- Are there favourite comedy artists (e.g., comedians, clowns)?
- Observe changes in humour appreciation and/or production. Does the client or carer show increases in appreciation or use of humour? When

clients make jokes it can signal diminished anxiety, increased assertive-ness, and increased self-esteem and self-confidence (Buckman, 1994, p. 19). Such changes are important outcomes to be documented.

HUMOUR CAVEATS

For every advantage of humour, there is probably a flip side. Humour is not always funny to everyone. Humour is not always kind. In fact, humour can be used for all sorts of wicked purposes such as exerting power or control over others, minimizing and embarrassing a person or a whole group of people, or expressing hostility. Therefore, any application of humour must follow rules to ensure that it is appropriate and positive.

* Humour rules should be understood and reinforced. Humour should never belittle or mock. Rapport and respect are the highest priority.
* Humour should be well timed and appropriate. When I worked as a speech-language pathologist at a rehabilitation centre, I encountered a good example of this maxim. One day while I was visiting in the occupational therapy clinic of the centre, one of the vocational place-ment counsellors (a lovely, feminine woman) walked into the room with a theatrical moustache glued onto her face. The staff and clients in the busy gym laughed uproariously. The incongruity was very funny. Apparently, bolstered by the huge success of her prank, the counsellor then went to her office and attempted to conduct an interview (mous-tache still in place) with her next client. The client happened to be a young man with aphasia who had been anxiously practising for this interview for weeks. To him this interview was extremely important and serious. When he walked in and saw the counsellor with her moustache, he was totally undone and at a loss for words. The result was terribly disappointing to the man with aphasia. A humorous prank in one setting did not generalize well to the second situation.
* Maintain sensitivity to the interaction of social power and humour. If a "joker" has more power than the recipient of the humour, then insens-itive humour will increase the recipient's sense of helplessness and inferiority—this could easily happen in therapist–client relationships. The humour in such cases becomes a method of controlling and keeping the client in a low position. Similarly denying the client the "right" to use humour can be a means for the therapist to keep control. Thus, potential social consequences of humour must be considered.
* While humour can effectively draw attention away from a mistake or error, humour loses its comedy when it is repeatedly used as a cover for poor preparation or bad therapy.
* Humour should not be used to ignore or minimize a client's feelings or requests.

- Since humour is individual and cultural, then sensitivity to diversity is important in order to avoid offending others.
- Remember to be sensitive to overhearers. I must admit to feelings of inadequacy and paranoia after recently leaving a meeting room only to hear the participants break into laughter as the door closed behind me. Overhearers might think you are laughing at them!
- Forced humour tends to create awkwardness. Incorporating humour in the management of aphasia should be fun. This happens when the atmosphere fosters lightheartedness and openness. If professionals and students promote the enjoyment of humour among themselves, then this atmosphere more easily generalizes to therapy situations.

This discussion of humour in aphasia therapy extends beyond the typical realm we think of as speech-language therapy. However, improved communication must occur in the context of enhanced life satisfaction, participation in a social world, and a robust sense of self. Humour can play an important role in this broadened context of intervention. Humour is intensely social and intensely communicative. If used appropriately, it has great potential for improving one's quality of life, coping with stress, and adding fun to life for people with aphasia, carers, and those of us who offer services to people affected by aphasia.

REFERENCES

Agar, M. (1986). *Speaking of ethnography*. Newbury Park, CA: Sage.

Atkinson, M., & Heritage, H. (Eds). (1984). *Structures of social action*. Cambridge: Cambridge University Press.

Berger, A. A. (1993). *An anatomy of humour*. New Brunswick, NJ: Transaction Publishers.

Berghoff, P. (2001). *Open the door and let humour in: Rediscovering laughter*. http://www.uncp.edu/home/berghoff/humour.html

Berk, L. (1989a). Eustress of mirthful laughter modifies natural killer cell activity. *Clinical Research*, *37*, 115.

Berk, L. (1989b). Neuroendocrine and stress hormone changes during mirthful laughter. *American Journal of Medical Sciences*, *298*, 390–396.

Berk, R. (1998). *Professors are from Mars, students are from Snickers*. Madison, WI: Mendota Press.

Brooks, R. B. (1994). Humour in psychotherapy: An invaluable technique with adolescents. In. E. S. Buckman (Ed.), *The handbook of humour: Clinical applications in psychotherapy* (pp. 53–73). Malabar, FL: Krieger Publishing.

Brown, P., & Levinson, S. (1987). *Politeness: Some universals in language usage*. Cambridge: Cambridge University Press.

Buckman, E. S. (1994). *The handbook of humour: Clinical applications in psychotherapy*. Malabar, FL: Krieger Publishing.

Buxman, K. (1991). Make room for laughter. *The American Journal of Nursing*, Dec., 46–51.

Clark, P. (1988). Autonomy, personal empowerment and quality of life in long term care. *Journal of Applied Gerontology, 7*(3), 279–297.

Cousins, N. (1979). *Anatomy of an illness.* New York: W.W. Norton & Co.

Dana, R. S. (1994). Humour as a diagnostic tool in child and adolescent groups. In E. S. Buckman (Ed.), *The handbook of humour: Clinical applications in psychotherapy* (pp. 41–51). Malabar, FL: Krieger Publishing.

Davis, G. A. (1993a). *A survey of adult aphasia and related disorders.* Englewood Cliffs, NJ: Prentice Hall, Inc.

Davis, M. S. (1993b). *What's so funny: The comic conception of culture and society.* Chicago: University of Chicago Press.

Derks, P., Gillikin, L., Bartolome-Rull, D., & Bogart, E. (1997). Laughter and electro-encephalographic activity. *International Journal of Humour Research, 10,* 285–300.

du Pre, A. (1998). *Humour and the healing arts.* Mahwah, NJ: Lawrence Erlbaum Associates Inc.

Emerson, J. (1973). Negotiating the serious import of humour. In A. Birenbaum & E. Sagarin (Eds.), *People in places: The sociology of the familiar* (pp. 269–280). New York: Praeger.

Erdman, L. (1993). Laughter therapy for patients with cancer. *Journal of Psychosocial Oncology, 11,* 55–67.

Freud, S. (1960). *Jokes and their relation to the unconscious.* New York: W.W. Norton.

Fry, W. F. (1992). The physiological effects of humour, mirth, and laughter. *Journal of the American Medical Association, 267*(13), 1857–1858.

Glenn, P. J. (1991–1992). Current speaker initiation of two-party shared laughter. *Research on Language and Social Interaction, 25,* 139–162.

Glenn, P. J. (1995). Laughing at and laughing with: Negotiating participant alignments through conversational laughter. In P. ten Have & G. Psathas (Eds.), *Situated order: Studies in the social organization of talk and embodied activities* (pp. 43–56). Lanham, MD: University Press of America.

Goffman, E. (1974). *Frame analysis: An essay of the organization of experience.* New York: Harper Colophon.

Goodwin, C. (1996). Transparent vision. In E. Ochs, E. Schegloff, & S. Thompson (Eds.), *Interaction and grammar.* Cambridge: Cambridge University Press.

Gumperz, J. (1982). *Discourse strategies.* Cambridge: Cambridge University Press.

Herth, K. A. (1984). Laughter: A nursing Rx. *American Journal of Nursing,* Aug., 991–992.

Holland, A. (1988). *Conversational coaching in aphasia.* Presentation at the Deep South Conference on Communication Disorders, Baton Rouge, Louisiana.

Jefferson, G. (1979). A technique for inviting laughter and its subsequent acceptance declination. In G. Psathes (Ed.), *Everyday language: Studies in ethnomethodology* (pp. 79–96). New York: Irvington Publishing.

Jefferson, G. (1985). An exercise in the transcription and analysis of laughter. In T. A. Van Djik (Ed.), *Handbook of discourse analysis* (pp. 25–34). London: Academic Press.

Jefferson, G., Sacks, H., & Schegloff, E. (1987). Notes on laughter in the pursuit of intimacy. In G. Button & J. Lee (Eds.), *Talk and social organization* (pp. 152–205). Clevedon, UK: Multilingual Matters.

Kamei, T., Kumano, H., & Masumura, S. (1997). Changes of immunoregulatory cells associated with psychological stress and humour. *Perceptual Motor Skills, 84*(3/2), 1296–1298.

LaPointe, L. (1991). Brain damage and humor: Not a laughing matter. In T. Prescott (Ed.), *Clinical aphasiology* (Vol. 20, pp. 53–60). Austin, TX: Pro-Ed.

LaPointe, L. (1997). Adaptation, accommodation and aristos. In L. Lapointe (Ed.), *Aphasia and related neurogenic language disorders* (2nd ed., pp. 265–287). New York: Thieme.

LaPointe, L., Katz, R., & Kraemer, I. (1985). The effects of stroke on appreciation of humor. *Cognitive Rehabilitation, 6,* 22–24.

Lefcourt, H., Davidson-Katz, K., & Kueneman, K. (1990). Humour and immune system functioning. *International Journal of Humour Research, 3,* 305–321.

Marshall, R. C. (1994). Management of fluent aphasic clients. In R. Chapey (Ed.), *Language intervention strategies in adult aphasia* (3rd ed., pp. 389–406). Baltimore: Williams & Wilkins.

Martin, R., & Lefcourt, H. (1983). Sense of humour as a moderator of the relationship between stressors and moods. *Journal of Personality and Social Psychology, 45,* 1313–1324.

Merriam-Webster (1995). *Webster's dictionary of word origins.* New York: Smithmark.

Murphy, J., & Englehart, P. (1994). Healing through the power of humour: A hands on approach to developing a humour project for patients in health care facilities. *Therapeutic Humour: The Newsletter of the American Association for Therapeutic Humour, 8*(2), 1, 3.

Norris, M. R., & Drummond, S. S. (1998). Communicative functions of laughter in aphasia. *Journal of Neurolinguistics, 11*(4), 391–402.

O'Malley, B. (1992). *Levity for longevity: Guidelines and sourcebook for humour, laughter and creativity in geriatric settings.* Saratoga, NY: The Humour Project.

Potter, R., & Goodman, N. (1983). The implementation of laughter as a therapy facilitator with adult aphasics. *Journal of Communication Disorders, 16,* 41–48.

Richman, J. (1995). The lifesaving function of humour with the depressed and suicidal elderly. *Gerontologist, 35*(2), 271–273.

Sacks, H. (1974). An analysis of the course of jokes telling in conversation. In R. Bauman & J. Sherzer (Eds.), *Explorations in the ethnography of speaking* (pp. 337–353). Cambridge: Cambridge University Press.

Simmons-Mackie, N., Damico, J., & Damico, H. (1999). A qualitative study of feedback in aphasia therapy. *American Journal of Speech-language Pathology, 8,* 218–230.

Soloman, G. (1987). Psychoneuroimmunology: Interactions between the central nervous system and the immune system. *Journal of Neuroscience Research, 18,* 1–9.

Tennant, K. (1990). Laugh it off: The effect of humour on the well-being of the older adult. *Journal of Gerontological Nursing, 16,* 11–17.

Volcek, M. K. (1994). Humour and the mental health of the elderly. In E. S. Buckman (Ed.), *The handbook of humour: Clinical applications in psychotherapy* (pp. 111–132). Malabar, FL: Krieger Publishing.

White, E. B. (1954). *The second tree from the corner.* New York: Harper & Bros.

Williams, S. E. (1996). Psychosocial adjustment following stroke. In G. L. Wallace (Ed.), *Adult aphasia rehabilitation* (pp. 303–324). Boston: Butterworth-Heinemann.

Wooten, P. (1993). Laughter as therapy for patient and caregiver. In J. Hodgkin, G. Connors, & C. Bell (Eds.), *Pulmonary rehabilitation.* Philadelphia, PA: Lippincott.

Wooten, P. (1996). *Compassionate laughter.* Salt Lake City, UT: Commun-A-Key Publishing.

Wooten, P. (2001). *Jest for the health of it!* http://www.mother.com/JestHome/

7 Learning from Roger Ross: A clinical journey

Audrey L. Holland and Amy E. Ramage

Roger Ross was a big man, in almost all ways larger than life. We learned an incredible amount from him over the course of the six years we worked with him, collectively and individually. Roger Ross had incurred a stroke at the age of 62, 3 years before I[1] met him in 1994. Although he had exhausted his benefits for reimbursed services, he continued to seek help. Ruona Bertaccini, of Martha Taylor Sarno's staff, referred him to me when he moved from New Jersey to Scottsdale Arizona, 120 miles from Tucson. A few months later, he began coming to our clinic weekly, to participate in our aphasia groups, and to continue individual treatment. He was a linchpin in our programme until September 1999, when he suffered a second stroke that left him unable to drive the 250-mile weekly round trip. This second stroke seemed to "move about the wiring in my head" (to quote him) so that his speech, if not slightly better, was certainly no worse. I remained in frequent contact with him until his untimely death resulting from complications of a fall, in October 2000. I last saw Roger Ross in late August of that year. We will always miss him as our friend and teacher. He was our partner on a 5-year journey we took to unravel his aphasia and what could be done about it.

We want to talk about that journey, emphasizing what we did, and what we both learned from it. We begin by describing Roger's aphasia and the clinical interventions that were attempted; what worked and what failed to work, and why. Then we will describe attitudes and beliefs, and conclude by discussing what have become very dominant themes in our work. Some of these beliefs he simply reinforced; others he helped us to develop.

ROGER ROSS' APHASIA

A volumetric reconstruction of Roger's brain revealed extensive left hemisphere damage lesion with virtual destruction of Broadmann's areas 22, 39, and 40. He had no residual motor impairment, although he reported that his voice felt tight and lacked its pre-stroke vocal range. The reconstruction also

---

1 The use of singular personal pronouns in this chapter refers to ALH, its first author, or when appropriate, to Roger Ross himself. AER will be used to refer to the chapter's second author.

shows a very healthy right hemisphere, as well as the areas surrounding the infarct. This healthy tissue appears to be partly responsible for his capacity for change and learning following the stroke.

Rather than test scores, which have been described in a previous publication (Holland, 1998), we summarize these findings with an impression of Roger Ross' language. The most striking initial observation was how easily Roger wrote the words he could not say. He carried small pads of paper on which he wrote troublesome words for his hearers to read as he continued on. All of us, even his fellow aphasic group members improved our ability to read upside down as a result of frequent talking to Roger. This writing strategy, supplementing his laboured speech, made him a skilled communicator. His word retrieval was limited, and he overused his few words with impunity. For example, a spectrum of good things was typically described as "interesting" or "terrific" depending on his degree of enthusiasm. Bad things were "terrible". If he could not say the word he searched for, he correctly and effortlessly wrote it on one of the many small pads of paper he always carried, trusted his listeners to read the word (from any angle) and just continued to talk—about a wide range of topics. He made very few spelling or perseverative errors in his writing, and the errors he did make were often correctly chosen and spelled words in Portuguese, a language he spoke fluently before his stroke. Proper names were particularly pesky. Paraphasic errors almost never occurred, and long silences often occurred, seemingly in their stead. He could almost never read aloud the single words he wrote correctly. He spoke slowly, with false starts, revisions, and pauses. He did not write phrases or sentences spontaneously (and still did not at the time of his death). As hinted earlier by his inability to read aloud the single words he wrote, he could not read text aloud. However, his silent reading comprehension was excellent, and he reported it to be "almost back to normal". He read daily for at least an hour with a discipline and motivation that were his hallmarks. Finally, his comprehension of single words, when they were spoken in isolation with little or no context, was poor. But his ability to understand spoken discourse, jokes and puns, conversation, theatre and so forth was as good as ours.

Thus, this puzzling man could: (1) retrieve the written form of single words when he could not say them BUT then could not read them aloud; (2) comprehend difficult text when read silently BUT failed totally to read text aloud; (3) speak in laboured, complex sentences BUT could not repeat or say the alphabet; and (4) follow normal conversation BUT had difficulty understanding single spoken words and proper names.

Extensive testing, with a variety of instruments—The Western Aphasia Battery (WAB), reading, writing, and semantic subtests of the Psycholinguistic Assessments of Language Processing in Aphasia (PALPA), written and spoken tasks designed and described by Berndt and colleagues (Berndt, Mitchum, Haendiges, & Sandson, 1997; Raymer & Berndt, 1996)—extensive observation, and interaction, all coalesced into a pattern suggesting that, although Roger could be classified as having conduction aphasia, he suffered

Table 7.1 Roger Ross' strengths and weaknesses from tests and observations

	Evidence	Interpretation
Strengths		
Excellent comprehension for discourse and text reading	WAB, conversational skills, ability to read advanced fiction, nonfiction, newspapers and magazines	Context enhances linguistic performance
Spontaneous single word writing	WAB, Berndt tests, conversation	Semantic system largely intact
Lexical decision	PALPA	Phonologic/graphemic input largely intact
Weaknesses		
Cannot reliably access semantic from minimal acoustic cues	Observation, WAB	Questionable single-word auditory comprehension skills
Poor phonological memory	WAB, PALPA, repetition tasks	Acoustic to phonological conversion fails when three syllable span is exceeded
Poor grapheme/ phoneme conversion	WAB, PALPA, conversation	Cannot write nonwords to dictation, minimal ability with real words while talking
Cannot rhyme	PALPA	Minimal internal sound patterns

from a severe phonological access impairment. We believe in looking at both strengths and weaknesses and how they balance in linguistic and personal terms. The language strengths and weaknesses listed in Table 7.1 come from both formal testing and observation. Also listed here are sources from which the strengths and weaknesses were derived along with their effects on Roger's communication.

Roger described his own problems as: "I have no sound patterns in my head." His description reminds us that professionals can sometimes save a lot of time by listening to what our aphasic friends tell us is wrong. Indeed, it is a clearer, less jargonistic description than the professional version, which might be something like: "Difficulty in accessing the phonological lexicon."

ROGER ROSS, THE PERSON

In addition to language strengths and weaknesses, personal character-istics and coping styles must be considered if one wishes to describe an individual's particular aphasia comprehensively. Personality and character play a role, not only in treatment planning, but also in living with aphasia. Here are some of Roger's characteristics that were influential.

Roger Ross could be described by vibrant adjectives—intelligent, courtly, difficult, self-disciplined, loyal, motivated, funny, for starters. His careers, as an international book publisher and consultant, as the mayor of the town in which he lived, and as a foreign affairs expert, spanned three continents over 30 years. In addition to English and Portuguese, he also spoke Spanish and French fluently. He was avid about food, theatre, dance, history, sports, and politics. He read the *New York Times* daily, and consistently shared its op-ed articles concerning the brain with his aphasia group. He also read Camus and Garcia Marquez and other difficult authors. One of my responsibilities to him ultimately turned out to be keeping up with him in worldly matters and serving as his discussant and sounding board.

Long before Worrall coined the term "Participating in Choice" (2000) Roger Ross was insisting on it. He was an object lesson in clinical decision making: clinicians who decided to "work on something" without consulting him about his desires and goals were simply rejected. So were clinicians who were unaware of their own limitations. (Remember that he was paying for his therapy.) For example, he undertook some private therapy closer to his home, and quit following a session in which he used the word "pert" and his clinician informed him "there was no such word". He apparently attempted to disagree with her, and she did not honour his challenge. He reported that he went home upset, looked up "pert" in his dictionary, and called to terminate treatment. "She made me doubt myself," he told me. "I don't need it."

No description of Roger Ross could be complete without noting his passionate belief in the power of aphasia groups. He disdained what he called "cake and coffee" groups, but worked throughout his post-stroke life to develop and participate in groups focused on coping with aphasia. When I met him, he had formed and had run at least two aphasia groups, and continued to do so for the rest of his life. His style was to get a group up and running, then move on to develop another. In all, he probably initiated six or eight aphasia groups. He wrote and published, with the help of his fellow aphasic group members or his clinicians, two articles on the group experience (Holland and Ross, 1999; Ross, 1996). In one of these articles he states, "I did not begin to get over aphasia until I became part of a group" (Holland & Ross, 1999, p. 116).

THE INTERVENTION

What did we work on? In retrospect, I feel lucky in that, for some time, I have been committed to the notion that ideally the clinician should facilitate working on what the person with aphasia wants to work on. When this is not possible, then it is mandatory to explain as clearly as possible, and to provide some counselling concerning why such treatment is not likely to be helpful, for instance, when clinical experience dictates that the aphasic person's chosen goal is probably unachievable. A relevant example might be that of an individual with severe apraxia of speech who insists on working on speech rather than on compensatory strategies that have some likelihood of success.

We also believe aphasia treatment should be designed to maximize strengths. This is in contradistinction to approaches that pinpoint and attack where in the processing schema things break down, as in many standard cognitive neuropsychological approaches to treatment. Thus my preferences would have been to keep the writing strategy foremost, make it even stronger, and complement this single-word writing ability with more extensive emphasis on writing longer units, or possibly to teach Roger to use computers more effectively, given the silent reading skills he so obviously possessed.

But Roger wanted to be able to access words in spoken speech more easily. He did not want to work on writing connected discourse, nor pursue computers. My choices bored him, and he decided that neither avenue was interesting or likely to be worthwhile to him. He wanted to substitute speech for his single-word writing strategy.

Of all eight cases who resembled Roger Ross, and who have been described in the literature (Shelton & Weinrich, 1997) not one clinician had even considered trying to improve spoken word retrieval. Nonetheless we undertook treatment aimed at efficient spoken word retrieval. (This is called *Fools Rush In*.) And I had to choose another strength to focus on if we were to make any noticeable inroads on spoken word retrieval. I tried to bolster Roger's phonological weakness by using a technique that potentially could work with an individual whose strengths were essentially personal, not linguistic. In this case, the strengths were his motivation, his fascination with being challenged, and his obvious intelligence.

The first approach was Autocue, first described in relation to writing by Marie-Pierre de Partz (de Partz, 1986), and then more fully explicated for word retrieval by Nickels (1992). Essentially as a phonological self-cueing procedure, Autocue seemed a very sound tactical approach. The goal was to use phonemic self-cueing first in an obvious, out-loud, up-front way until it became firmly established. Then the next step would be to instruct Roger to internalize the steps, to visualize the word "in his head" so to speak, and apply the cue silently, and then say the word without the necessity of writing it on paper.

Because the Autocue procedure has been well described in the above references, as have its modifications for Roger (Holland, 1998), it is only briefly summarized here. The clinician (in our case, in consultation with Roger) finds a key word for each letter of the alphabet that the aphasic subject can access consistently. For example, because Roger could consistently access "terrific", he was taught that if the word he was attempting to access through his writing strategy, say "tarantula" began with /t/, he was to whisper "terrific", /t/, /t/ . . . "tarantula". Thus, the /t/ in "terrific" became the bridge whereby he could cue himself to access and orally produce the word "tarantula". Eventually, Roger was able to access /t/ without use of the bridge word.

We taught each alphabet letter this way, beginning with consonants and working with four or five letters and sounds at a time. We adapted the cue cards from Hooked on Phonics for this purpose. Some of his bridge words included Pat, enter, and bell. At one point during training, Roger noted that he could not produce oral form of the word "p-r-a-y-i-n-g" by commenting "I haven't learned the (gestured praying, wrote /p/) thing yet." It took approximately 50 one-hour training sessions in which Autocue and dependent activities were featured, to master his bridge words and phonemic cues. That is, once learned, his therapy focused on each cue to reading word lists and naming pictures in confrontation tasks, with relatively good success. As he progressed with phonemic self-cueing, the contingencies were tightened, and Roger was expected to visualize ("inside his forehead") the way the word was written, apply the phonemic cue, and say the word without writing it. This was not easy, but with effort and time he could do it fairly well. Each session ended with a conversation, geared to promote this internalized use of Autocues spontaneously.

However, there was minimal generalization to conversation, probably because the Autocue procedure competed poorly with his already effective writing strategy. Even at its most successful the cueing was quite slow. Further, practice with confrontation naming and with oral reading of word lists was very different from on-line retrieval of words Roger wanted to use in conversation. (Lesser, 1989, noted that retrieval of the words in confrontation naming tasks was very different from the self-selection involved in conversational word retrieval. This was the problem we were encountering.) Thus, at the end of each session, when we moved to spontaneous conversation, bridges and autocues were abandoned in favour of the more efficient and worldly writing strategy.

The Autocue procedure is laborious and challenging to any but the most dedicated of aphasic persons. Roger was one of these. He truly enjoyed the intellectual nature of the activity, and we decided to confront the generalization chasm directly. An important and relevant observation was that not only Roger, but also listeners like me, inadvertently played into his writing strategy by failing to *require* him to say the words he wrote. In effect, the writing strategy seduced us all.

To approximate conversational word retrieval more closely, we moved from confrontation naming and word lists to categorical naming. An even more critical feature was that both Roger and I made a mutual commitment to apply the Autocue strategy in our conversations. He would not write until he had tried to say the word via his Autocue training, and if he initially wrote the word, I would refuse to read it. This was at least as difficult for me as it was for Roger—perhaps even more so, since I quite liked and was intrigued by his writing strategy to begin with. The writing was comparatively fast and effective—and along with most of his listeners, I was content to say the words he wrote for him. It was *Roger* (and the trees that he killed with his endless consumption of writing pads) who was dissatisfied.

Each of the 11 treatment sessions that followed had five phases, detailed in Table 7.2. They were designed to illustrate to Roger (and to me), the effectiveness of the phonemic cueing and to provide extensive practice in using it for self-selected words.

I took responsibility for the categories for the naming tasks. They were deliberately selected to be difficult, and thus to have potential to evoke proper names, as well as to challenge Roger intellectually: they are also included in Table 7.2.

Table 7.2 Phases of treatment

Phase 1	Pre-test "Say words you can think of that have something to do specifically with the Renaissance" (5 minutes). Start and end times, words generated, and total words documented and reported to RR.
Phase 2	Demonstration "This time I want you to write and then say words relating to the Renaissance" (5 minutes). Time recorded, words generated, and total words documented and reported to RR.
Phase 3	Practice "Now we are going to practise writing and saying. You are going to use a new category. This time come up with words that relate to drama and dance. I will help, but we will not go to a new word until you have said the one you wrote" (25 minutes). Data gathered and reported to RR.
Phase 4	Post-test "Its time to go back to Renaissance words. Remember that a pen is available. Use it if you need to. But try to SAY these words" (5 minutes). Data gathered and reported to RR.
Phase 5	Conversation "Let's talk about _____. Your pen is there to help if you need it." Substantive words generated were tallied and reported to RR.

TOPICS FOR CATEGORY NAMING

Three topics for each session Phases 1, 2, 3, 4, Homework

(1) Medical terms, Religion, Wild West; (2) Latin America, Russia, Movie Titles; (3) Buildings and Monuments, Natural Sites, World Holidays; (4) Music, Printing/Publishing, Politicians; (5) Renaissance, Drama and Dance, Break—no homework; (6) WWI, Weather, Famous Animals; (7) Cleaning terms, Cooking, Herbs and Spices; (8) Sports, Travel, Time and Space; (9) Media, Television, Insects; (10) Tools and Utensils, Emotions, Water; (11) Vehicles, Body Parts, Games.

Table 7.3 Crib sheet

- Do not hold your breath
- Speak on exhalation
- Breathe out
- Get the first sound under control before talking
- Give yourself permission to
  - Be flexible. If you can't say the word you want, let go and think of an alternative
  - Relax
  - Take a chance. Paraphasias are at least in the ballpark

Table 7.4 Comparison of pre- and post-test phases and conversation

Session #	Pre	Post	Conversation
1	5	7	6
2	6	13	11
3	6	8	6
4	4	5	10
5	4	6	7
6	8	8	9
7	2	9	13
8	9	10	not tested
9	5	10	14
10	5	10	14
11	6	14	not tested

Roger also had homework to do daily, alone. This is a consistent feature of much of the work done in our clinic, where a general goal is to have aphasic individuals develop a sense of responsibility and ownership, not only of their problems, but also of solutions to them. (Roger always did his homework avidly, provided it appeared to him to be sensible.)

Finally, Roger also had a crib sheet, illustrated in Table 7.3 for use with his homework, as well during sessions, and presumably whenever he chose to use it. (He almost always had it with him, in his briefcase, or in the form of a wallet card.) It included reminders for maximizing speech production.

We formally evaluated our treatment approach by comparing Phase I (Pre-test) and Phase 4 (Post-test) for each session. The data appear in Table 7.4. It can be seen that consistently higher performance was generated in the post treatment phase of each session. Pre treatment phases were variable—the dip in Session 7 was probably due to Roger's insistence on naming cleaning products, rather than words related to cleaning (that is, for example, to say "Boraxo" instead of "soap powder" or "broom"). He relaxed this self-imposed criterion during that session's post-test. I should note that typically, only about half of the words generated in Phases 1 and 2 showed up in the post-test, indicating that he was generating words from a much larger semantic pool that he could access at any one time.

Because this was a fairly rigorous experiment—done that way because this was part of a federally funded research project—I have more extensive reliability data, as well as data from conversation that showed Roger using increasing numbers of words. These data have also been described elsewhere (Holland, 1998). Here, because we are describing a clinical process, we emphasize some observations that began with this treatment and became part of Roger's consistent strategies.

First, he was increasingly skilled at saying the words he wrote, and less reliant on his listeners to say them. Second, he began to permit himself to make paraphasic errors. This suggests that he was beginning to become more tolerant of his errors, or that he was actually getting closer, somehow, to his phonological lexicon. In either case, paraphasias gave listeners more clues than did silence, so they facilitated conversation. Throughout the course of his previous treatment, I urged him to take chances with paraphasias. It was to no avail until after these generalization sessions, when he could see their advantage directly. This represents a lesson in the power and importance of person-relevant explication and demonstration. A third change was that, with increasing frequency, Roger could use a *single written letter* to cue oral word retrieval. In some instances, simply moving his pencil towards paper was sufficient.

Although Roger continued until he died to use writing both as a phonemic self-cue and as a substitute for oral word retrieval, we all believed he had increased his ability to communicate orally. Why did it work? One reason had to be our mutually increased discipline in trying to use phonemic cueing to facilitate oral word retrieval in our therapy. Another reason was related to incorporating conversation into every session as a trial balloon right after the treatment. (Roger and I were never able to deny ourselves conversation, usually going on and on before and after our more formal exchanges. But here, building it in directly after cueing was required proved to be advantageous.)

Following Autocue, we changed focus to developing and carrying out specific training on scenarios and bits of real-life interactions that gave Roger particular and consistent difficulty. In our research we have recently been exploring the effects of what is referred to as "context" building on the work of Hinckley, Carr, and Patterson (2001). Context-based training can be contrasted to more traditional training in which components of bigger behavioural units are systematically taught, and expected to generalize to a wide number of behaviours in context. This is referred to in the skill acquisition literature as "part task training". For example, when we practise word retrieval skills, we often target words (for example, family names) that we expect the person will use in many settings. In contrast, the procedures of context-based approaches specifically target the content words and grammatical structures that might be appropriate for a single scenario, such as making a toast at a wedding, and drill the explicit scenario.

This concept can be used to characterize contemporary approaches to second language acquisition, where the focus has shifted away from learning vocabulary and sentence types and grammatical rules, to approaching dialogues appropriate to specific contexts, such as finding out where the post office is, or ordering your favourite meal in a restaurant.

We approach context-based training by first conducting an interview, designed loosely in consonance with Linda Worrall's procedures for her functional communication therapy planner (1999). The goal of this interview is to choose some specific scenarios and scripts as stimulus material for the training. Examples include such things as buying a specific gift at a store, ordering in a restaurant, telling a joke, using a photo album to cue self-disclosure, talking to a travel agent, and many other short transactions, interactions, or monologues. The clinician writes the scenario, and modifies it as a result of consultation with the aphasic person who intends to use it.

Next, the scenario is practised intensively, with the goal of making it automatic. In Roger's case, he chose some explicit scenarios that gave him particular trouble. They were giving directions to his house over the phone, and instructing a bartender or friend to make Roger's idea of a perfect Martini. We wrote the scripts with Roger's input. He approved or modified them as he saw fit and we changed the explicit language to accommodate his aphasia. Then we practised and practised and practised them, with Amy and me, with other people we could collar into listening, in aphasia groups, and, in the real test case, the real world. And of course, Roger practised daily at home with a tape recorder to check his own work.

He was extremely successful with his scenarios, and we were preparing to continue with more of them when the second stroke occurred and he was forced to terminate formal therapy.

Roger Ross has substantiated our beliefs in some basic principles of intervention with people who have aphasia. These include the following:

1 To the fullest extent possible, make the focus of treatment a joint decision, of the aphasic person, his or her family and only lastly, you.
2 Therapy is a collaborative undertaking, and a collaborative commitment.
3 Ensure that your rationales are clear, not only to you, but to the aphasic person. That is, if you can't explain what you are doing to the aphasic person's satisfaction, you probably shouldn't be doing it.
4 Provide demonstrations of effectiveness of what you are doing, in addition to rationales.
5 Challenge, encourage personal responsibility and ownership, and lighten up.
6 Attend to strengths before weaknesses.
7 Be flexible. When something doesn't work, try something else.
8 Remember that it is never too late to change.

Roger Ross also taught us other things, but they were about us, not therapy, and not Roger. Here are two of them:

1   We are not experts in anyone's aphasia. We may bring collective information, gleaned from many aphasic individuals with whom we have worked, but the true expert in one's own aphasia is oneself.
2   Often, in clinical interactions with aphasic persons, the behaviour that needs to be changed is our own.

Finally, Roger Ross was largely responsible for helping us to recognize and understand that acceptance of a problem, fitting aphasia into one's life, and recognizing aphasia as a player and as a reality, are crucial aspects to learning to live both with, and around, aphasia. This is an evolving process, which probably takes some amount of time to grow into.

In a stunning interview near the end of his life, Roger Ross basically said that he doesn't think about aphasia anymore. He is just who he is, doing what he has to do. More than just aphasia, acceptance is an essential feature in surviving any of the many tragedies that life can, and often does, deal to any or all of us.

ACKNOWLEDGEMENT

This work was supported by the National Multipurpose Research and Training Center Grant DC-01409 from the National Institute on Deafness and other Communication Disorders (USA).

REFERENCES

Berndt, R., Mitchum, D., Haendiges, A., & Sandson, J. (1997). Verb retrieval in aphasia, 1: Characterizing single word impairments. *Brain and Language*, *56*, 68–106.

de Partz, M. (1986). Re-education of a deep dyslexic patient: Rationale of the method and results. *Cognitive Neuropsychology*, *3*, 149–177.

Hinckley, J., Carr, T., & Patterson, J. (2001). Differential effects of context-based and skill-based treatment approaches: Preliminary findings. *Aphasiology*, *15*, 463–476.

Holland, A. (1998). A strategy for improving oral naming in an individual with a phonological access impairment. In N. Helm-Estabrooks & A. Holland (Eds.), *Approaches to the treatment of aphasia*. San Diego CA; Singular Publishing Group.

Holland, A., & Ross, R. (1999). The power of aphasia groups. In R. J. Elman (Ed.), *Group treatment of neurogenic communication disorders*. Boston: Butterworth Heinemann.

Lesser, R. (1989). Some issues in the neuropsychological rehabilitation of anomia. In X. Seron & G. Deloche (Eds.), *Cognitive approaches to neuropsychological rehabilitation*. Hillsdale, NJ. Lawrence Erlbaum Associates Inc.

Nickels, L. (1992). The autocue self generated phonemic cues in the treatment of a disorder of reading and naming. *Cognitive Neuropsychology, 9*, 155–182.

Raymer, A., & Berndt, R. (1996). Reading lexically without semantics: Evidence from patients with probably Alzheimer's disease. *Journal of the International Neuropsychology Society, 2*, 340–349.

Ross, R. (1996). Aphasia groups: A view from the inside. *Advance Magazine*, May 3, 1996: 18.

Shelton, J., & Weinrich, M. (1999). Further evidence of a dissociation between output phonological and orthographic lexicons: A case study. *Cognitive Neuropsychology, 14*, 105–129.

Worrall, L. (1999). *FCP: Functional Communication Therapy Planner*. Bicester, UK: Winslow.

Worrall, L. (2000). *The Participating in Choice (PIC) approach to aphasia rehabilitation*. Talk given at the 12th World Aphasia Therapy Conference, Rotterdam, The Netherlands, August.

8 Group treatment and jazz: Some lessons learned

Roberta J. Elman

Life evolves. And so too does speech-language treatment. Or at least it should. Twenty years ago my approach to working with aphasia focused on structured drills that could be represented on Base-10 forms. It was the same approach that was accepted and taught to young clinicians in universities throughout the United States. And looking back at the treatment I provided two decades ago, I truly regret that the people with whom I worked were so rarely given the opportunity to learn how to communicate and move forward with their aphasia.

Twenty years is a long time. And thankfully life has brought me to the Aphasia Center of California. It is in this setting where I continue to learn that structure continues to be desired by therapists. Structure is safe and predictable and allows the therapist to be in control. But most human communication is not structured in this way. And by imposing artificial structure on communication we create an environment that has little to do with communication in the real world.

As a youngster I played the piano. My piano lessons over a 6-year period revolved around classical pieces by composers such as Bach, Beethoven, and Mozart. With practice, I became quite expert at playing these pieces from memory. However, if my piano teacher had asked me to write my own classical piece or to create a variation of a piece that I had memorized, I wouldn't have had a clue how to do it. My biggest frustration was with the need to practise the same pieces over and over. My piano teacher's goal was perfect performance of the music at recitals. Looking back I realize that I wasn't able to articulate my goal at the time—but I think it was the desire to create something new. By the age of 13, my piano lessons ended when I told both my parents and my piano teacher that I had no further desire to memorize classical pieces.

My experience with piano lessons mirrors my early experience of providing aphasia treatment in the 1980s. My treatment with Mr C is illustrative: An outgoing man, Mr C was in his 60s when he had a stroke resulting in Broca's aphasia. I was his first outpatient speech-language pathologist, and he was motivated and eager to regain his language skills. Just out of graduate school, I created a variety of treatment tasks that included inserting prepositions in phrases, stringing together SVO sentences, comprehension of written sentences and paragraphs of increasing length, and writing basic biographic information such as name and address. This treatment was provided in the days before significant healthcare cutbacks in the United States, so Mr C and I worked together for almost a year. We both became frustrated when no matter how hard Mr C tried, the overall result of our therapy was improved "rote" performance on treatment items with little generalization to novel items. I must admit that Mr C did not improve significantly in his ability to become a better communicator outside the specific treatment tasks or treatment environment. The end result was similar to my piano-playing experience—good rote performance with little ability to create novel material.

After additional years and clients, I started to think more about language use. My epiphany came while watching a documentary by Ken Burns on jazz. This television series follows the evolution of jazz over time in the United States. As I watched each episode, I realized that language shares much more with jazz music than with classical music. Language and jazz are improvisational in nature with the language topic or jazz piece rarely the same. And both require creativity and context. In fact, musicians often liken jazz improvisation to "telling a story" (Sabatella, 1996). My piano lessons would have been dramatically different (and ultimately more satisfying for me) if the goal had been to create and improvise rather than memorize.

As a speech-language pathologist, I believe that our ultimate goal is to improve language use so that individuals can participate more fully in life (LPAA, 2001). In most societies, spoken language use equates with conversation. Conversation in the 21st century is ubiquitous. It seems that people are constantly talking, with mobile phone use accelerating the amount of time people are engaged in conversation. Conversation is the main way that human beings create and maintain relationships, and serves as the primary interface between an individual and society (Kagan & Gailey, 1993; Pound, Parr, Lindsay, & Woolf, 2000). Therefore, if a key goal is for clients to be able to participate more fully in life, they will need to increase their skills in conversational speech and other creative uses of language.

It shouldn't come as a surprise that clinician-imposed structure in language tasks does not typically result in improved language use in natural contexts such as conversation. There is an enormous mismatch between what is being taught and what is in fact needed. The question I continue to ask myself is how can I as a speech-language pathologist facilitate language improvisation?

Group treatment has provided me with one vehicle. Groups can provide a safe context for members to improvise language and to create new ways of communicating. In addition, groups provide an opportunity for people with aphasia to observe and learn language patterns and strategies from one another. Other benefits of group treatment include the support and confidence to improvise language that group members provide. In a conversation group, each member has the opportunity to "solo" and feed off another member. It is important for conversation groups to be both natural and cohesive (Elman, 1999). The ideal group is one in which its members express genuine interest in the conversational topics and one another.

In a foreword to a book I edited on group treatment I wrote:

> Group dynamics are complex. If individual treatment can be compared to teaching a musical instrument, group treatment is much like conducting an orchestra. The clinician must keep in mind the communicative strengths and weaknesses of all group members. In addition, personality issues are overlaid, because group dynamics and group process are more than a sum of their individual parts.
>
> (Elman, 1999, pp. xiii–xiv)

My music analogy has evolved further in the last few years: rather than conducting an orchestra, I believe that a speech-language pathologist who facilitates a group is more akin to a musician who facilitates a jazz ensemble. This is because the language score is unknown in conversation, group members play off and bootstrap onto one another's language, and on the best days, the result is dynamic and truly improvisational in nature. Group treatment provides people with aphasia with an opportunity to practise their improvisational language skills.

Group treatment has become the environment of choice for my current treatment (Elman, 1999; Elman & Bernstein Ellis, 1999a, 1999b). I believe that group treatment provides individuals with aphasia an excellent vehicle to learn to improvise their communication skills. At its best, group communication treatment resembles a wonderful jazz combo—with each member riffing, elaborating, or interrupting. I watch a creative process unfold that is as much art as science. And thankfully group treatment has provided members with the opportunity to communicate and improvise again.

However, group treatment is not foolproof. As I listen to therapists talk about the type of group treatment they conduct, many gravitate towards increasing the structure in the group, making the group treatment become the same process as traditional individual treatment, but executed in a group. Why do therapists gravitate towards such structure? One reason may be that structure returns control and dominance to the therapist, and may serve to reduce the discomfort that some therapists experience when unknowns are introduced into treatment.

Another reason may be that therapists believe that facilitating conversational skills is not truly therapy. I remember working with Mrs W (during the same time period as Mr C) who was a brilliant woman with Wernicke's aphasia. Although her jargon and semantic paraphasias certainly made communication difficult, Mrs W was often able to use her own creative strategies and props to get her message across. Mrs W had travelled the world and owned several Berlitz guides that translated everyday words and phrases into foreign languages. She had discovered that if she used the English side of the pages, she could let workers at her retirement residence know what she wanted to order for her meals or what everyday chores were needed. Upon entering my treatment room, Mrs W enjoyed starting each of our treatment sessions with discussion of world events and recountings of some of her amazing life stories. As a young clinician, I was fascinated by these conversations, and amazed at how well Mrs W was able to convey so much information given her severe aphasia. However, I felt extremely guilty talking with her in this way, because I felt that I wasn't "doing" therapy. I realize now that the conversation that we engaged in was vital for Mrs W to improve and improvise her language abilities. She somehow knew that intuitively; unfortunately, at that time I did not.

Language and music are not the only areas in life that require improvisational skills. An inspired cook invents new dishes and combinations rather than following an exact recipe. A mathematician finds a new way of solving a mathematical problem rather than using the tried and true method. An artist creates a novel work of art rather than copying a previous painting or drawing. In fact, the ability to improvise is essential to all creative thinking.

Clark Terry, a jazz musician, is quoted as saying that the best way to become a great jazz player is to "imitate, assimilate, innovate" (Sabatella, 1996). If we extend this thinking to language, an individual begins by acquiring basic language structures. The process does not stop there, but continues with using these language structures in creative and innovative ways. Today I believe that our focus as speech-language pathologists should be to help individuals with aphasia become improvisational language users.

REFERENCES

Elman, R. (Ed.). (1999). *Group treatment of neurogenic communication disorders: The expert clinician's approach*. Woburn, MA: Butterworth-Heinemann.

Elman, R., & Bernstein-Ellis, E. (1999a). The efficacy of group communication treatment in adults with chronic aphasia. *Journal of Speech, Language, and Hearing Research, 42*, 411–419.

Elman, R., & Bernstein-Ellis, E. (1999b). Psychosocial aspects of group communication treatment: Preliminary findings. *Seminars in Speech & Language, 20*(1), 65–72.

Kagan, A., & Gailey, G. (1993). Functional is not enough: Training conversation partners for aphasic adults, In A. L. Holland & M. M. Forbes (Eds.), *Aphasia treatment: World perspectives* (pp. 199–225). San Diego: Singular Publishing Group, Inc.

LPAA Project Group (2001). Life participation approach to aphasia: A statement of values for the future. In R. Chapey (Ed.), *Language intervention strategies in aphasia and related neurogenic communication disorders* (4th ed., pp. 235–245). Baltimore, MD: Lippincott, Williams & Wilkins. [Originally published in the *ASHA Leader*, 5(3), 4–6.]

Pound, C., Parr, S., Lindsay, J., & Woolf, C. (2000). *Beyond aphasia: Therapies for living with communication disability*. Bicester, UK: Winslow Press.

Sabatella, M. (1996). *A whole approach to jazz improvisation*. Lawndale, CA: A.D.G. Productions.

9 The value of therapy: What counts?

Julie Morris, David Howard, and Sinead Kennedy

Change is central to the idea of aphasia therapy. Whenever we (as therapists) engage with a person with aphasia, we hope to be able to offer some kind of intervention that will improve their quality of life, will improve their language skills, and will give them the means to change the way they interact with the world. We have a multitude of assessments, both quantitative and qualitative, that can be used to assess these changes. Because therapy is not simply "the delivery of treatment", but an interactive process engaging and challenging both the person with aphasia and the therapists, we, as therapists, need to be equally open to change. One aspect of this is the willingness to drop or adapt therapy methods in the light of accumulating evidence of both their (in)effectiveness and (perhaps not unrelated) how they are seen by the client. More interesting is the challenge to what we value in therapy and what we count as "success" when there are mismatches between the different kinds of change (in assessments, targeted skills, quality of life, social engagement). Then we need to question which we value and why.

In this chapter we describe the process and progress of a course of therapy with one man with aphasia (Lawrence), not because the therapy was conspicuously successful (as we will show, it was not), but because it raises a number of issues that do, we believe, relate to the real-life, ever-changing process of therapy. These issues include:

- What counts as improvement? And from whose perspective?
- Whether complex strategies for circumventing problems are effective.
- What is the role of therapy many years after the person became aphasic?
- What are the roles of group and individual sessions?

First, however, we briefly describe the context—how we organize and "deliver" therapy. This is because it is rather unusual, providing its own, quite specific challenges and opportunities, and its constraints are necessary to understand the process of therapy with Lawrence.

The clinic was established in 1999, with the aid of a grant from the Tavistock Trust for Aphasia. Clients come for a 12-week block of treatment, attending 3 days a week from 10.15 to 3.30 pm. In each day they have one 45-minute individual (one-to-one) therapy session in both the morning and the afternoon. The remainder of their time is spent in therapy within a group with, usually, seven other clients. In total there are 12 clients in a clinic, of whom 4 will be having individual therapy sessions at any one time. There are specific aims for both group and individual therapy sessions for each client. The long-term aims for the clinic are negotiated individually with each client.

LAWRENCE: THE CASE HISTORY

Lawrence had a CVA 7 years before he came to the clinic, at the age of 50. A CT scan showed a large left temporo-parietal infarct. He has a resulting right hemiparesis and walks with a stick.

Before his stroke, Lawrence worked as a sales director at a national bakery. He is married and lives at home with his wife, Patricia. They have two grown-up children. Lawrence enjoys outings with close friends and family, but tries to avoid social contact with strangers without someone to support him. Lawrence and Patricia enjoy frequent holidays abroad.

After his stroke, Lawrence had excellent speech and language therapy that is described by Grayson, Franklin, and Hilton (1997), focusing first on word comprehension and retrieval and then on sentence comprehension. He was seen immediately post-stroke by a therapist, and when he transferred to a rehabilitation unit for 3 months he had continuing in-patient therapy. After leaving hospital, Lawrence had further therapy at home for the remainder of the first year. This was followed by a break and then attendance at a support group. After a further break, he referred himself again for therapy via a computer course organizer. This was for advice about accessing basic computing courses. The speech and language therapist then referred him to us. He and his wife had continued to do work at home, sometimes using their home computer, since discharge from therapy.

LAWRENCE'S COMMUNICATION

When we first saw him, Lawrence's spoken output was non-fluent (in the sense of being slow and broken rather than being agrammatic), with mostly high-frequency content words and frequent pauses. He relied a lot on stereotypic phrases; for instance, "wait a minute now"; "oh god it's . . .". There were also some semantic errors.

Lawrence's spoken output is illustrated by his description of the picture from the Comprehensive Aphasia Test (Swinburn et al., in press [2004]). In this picture, a man is sleeping in an armchair. Just above him are three bookshelves. A cat on the top shelf is reaching down with its paw to try to catch a fish in a bowl on the shelf below. In doing this, the cat has dislodged two books from the top shelf that are falling towards the man's head. A small boy, playing with a car on the floor, is pointing towards the cat:

Lawrence:	It's a sleep . . . like (points to man) (pretends to sleep and snore) like that . . . and it's the the . . . the er . . . wait a second, wait a second . . . it's the the cat . . . and it's (made sound about books and gestured falling) like that and its there and its oh look at it (LAWRENCE pretends to point like boy) look at it, and its /flə/, and that's it I think
Tester:	Um?
Lawrence:	Look at it just like that as well . . . and it's er, like it's (pretends to snore) . . . that's all I think . . . there, there, there (pointing) . . . that's it
Tester:	. . . What's the cat doing in the picture there? (Tester points)
Lawrence:	its erm . . . wait a second, it's er . . . like that, what's it called now, wait a second now . . . the fish, the fish like /ku/!
Tester:	. . . What's it going to do to the fish?
Lawrence:	just eat eat like that (gestures eating)
Tester:	. . . Yeah . . . anything else? Is that everything? I think, isn't it?
Lawrence:	and this like (points to man and pretends to sleep and snore) like that and there . . . and I think that's it

In conversation, he gave the impression of having generally good comprehension of language, although with some misunderstanding. He was unable to read and, indeed, unwilling to attempt to do so. He had very limited written output; he would, however, sometimes write the first letter of a word.

In his communication, Lawrence relied heavily on others. He and Patricia communicated relatively successfully, but this relied heavily on their shared knowledge and his wife's ability to fill the gaps or guess his meaning. Lawrence appeared to expect Patricia to understand and was frustrated if she did not, appearing to perceive this as *her* failure. This pattern was also seen with others, with the listener usually required to do a great deal of the communicative "work", unacknowledged by Lawrence. This was not always as successful as with Patricia. He sometimes used gesture, and sometimes spelled first letters with his finger, although not always accurately.

PRE-THERAPY ASSESSMENT RESULTS

Lawrence's language abilities and disabilities were formally assessed 3 months before starting the clinic and again at its start. The assessments used were the Comprehensive Aphasia Test (CAT; Swinburn et al., in press [2004]), spoken and written word–picture verification (using semantically related distractors; Morris unpublished), the Nickels naming test (in both spoken and written form; Nickels, 1992a), and retelling of the Cinderella story (Saffran, Berndt, & Schwartz, 1989), as well as other tests (including measures of conversation and social participation) not reported here.

These formal assessments showed that in auditory comprehension, Lawrence made a small number of semantic errors with single words, and had difficulties in understanding complex sentences. He performed at chance level in the comprehension of reversible sentences, choosing reverse role distractors in the Birkbeck Reversible Sentences Comprehension Test (Byng, Black, & Nickels, unpublished). In written language comprehension, Lawrence had problems at a sentence level. He was able to copy but not generate written words.

In tests requiring spoken output, Lawrence was good at single word repetition (14/16 correct), but very poor at reading single words aloud (2/24). Picture naming was also poor (11/24).

Analysis of his Cinderella narratives showed relatively normal phrasal structure, but much reduced thematic complexity, with 30% of arguments omitted. He relied to a great extent on light verbs (*do, make* etc.) and pronouns whose reference was not clearly established. In real life, his wife Patricia, who shares the context, can find this much more comprehensible than others.

Further investigation of Lawrence's reading and letter knowledge showed that letter cross-case matching was relatively good (22/26; PALPA test 19; Kay, Lesser, & Coltheart, 1992) and that he had partly preserved knowledge of letter–sound correspondences (19/26; PALPA test 22). He was very poor at blending phonemes (with three-phoneme items scoring only 4/40 correct). On a test of word reading he was able to read only 2/24 items correctly. Errors tended either to be no responses or to give some semantic information about the target. For example:

HOSPITAL   *the /dak/, the doctor there, not the doctor, it's the ... the ... the house, not the house*
RIDICULE   *its er ... good god ... no!*

In naming pictures, he was able to retrieve the names of 11 of the 24 items correctly, with errors again comprising mostly semantic information and no responses. When he tried to write object names, in his incorrect responses (almost all—51/52—were incorrect) the first letter was right on 11/51 occasions.

Figure 9.1 summarizes Lawrence's performance on the CAT Language Battery. The results are expressed as T scores (mean 50 and standard deviation of 10 in a large unselected sample of people with aphasia, using a non-linear transformation). It shows relative strengths in cognition (using screens of Raven's coloured progressive matrices, and non-verbal tests of

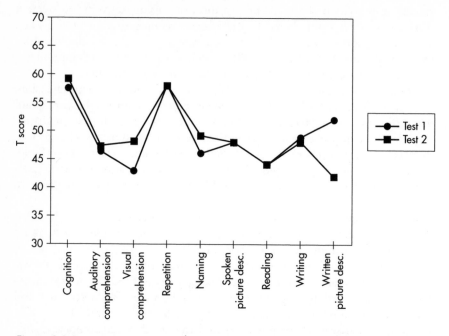

Figure 9.1 Lawrence's scores on the CAT Language Battery, tested 3 months before therapy started (Test 1) and at the start of therapy (Test 2).

semantic and episodic memory), and repetition, with an approximately equal degree of disability across the other modalities.

The CAT Disability Questionnaire investigates the *perceived* degree of difficulty in a number of areas. First, it probes the perceived degree of *handicap* in different situations in comprehension, expression, reading, and writing. Then it probes the perceived degree to which difficulties *intrude*, "get in the way of", understanding, talking, reading, and writing. It then asks about the degree to which the language difficulties affect the client's *self-image*, examining worry, confidence, self-esteem, and feelings of isolation. The final sections asks questions to assess the degree to which the language difficulties cause *distress* ("emotional impact") with feelings of frustration, sadness, anger, helplessness, feelings of unfairness, pessimism, dissatisfaction (and so on).

The results of the CAT Disability Questionnaire are shown in Figure 9.2, again expressed as T scores relative to the aphasic population (this test was only done at the first assessment, 3 months before starting the clinic). It is clear that Lawrence perceives himself as particularly impaired in reading. His feelings about his aphasia, on the other hand, are commensurate with his degree of language disability, with very similar T scores to those shown in the CAT Language Battery.

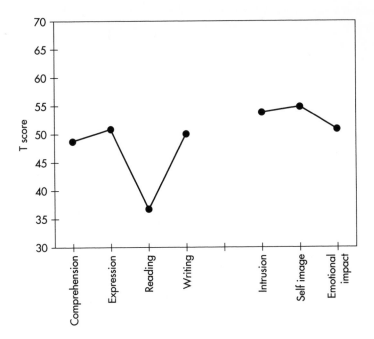

Figure 9.2 Lawrence's scores on the CAT Disability Questionnaire 3 months before therapy started.

GOAL SETTING

Lawrence and his wife Patricia had two main concerns. First they both wanted Lawrence to be able to say more; understandably they both felt that his difficulties in word retrieval were a major impediment to effective communication. Second, Lawrence wanted to be able to try reading.

Initially, Lawrence had been very resistant to any reading task. For example, the following exchange occurred after a single word reading test:

Tester:	. . . A bit more reading next time?
Lawrence:	Cause I can't read that's all
Tester:	No, no . . . its good to try though isn't it?
Lawrence:	But I can't read, so
Tester:	Its just part of the assessment . . . you did all right there
Lawrence:	But it's this now *(pointing to sheet of written words he has just had to read)*, it's not very good, you see

He often refused to do tasks involving written words in the initial stages of being seen.

After discussion, we adopted the following as aims of the therapy with Lawrence:

- To achieve the best communication possible.
- To widen his communication strategies, so that he is less dependent on Patricia.
- In individual sessions, "part-task train" reading and word retrieval, by learning the individual elements for a strategy.
- In the group, reinforce the above in communication (conversation) with different people ("whole task training"?).
- To gain support from others, and see other ways of managing living with aphasia.

We decided that, in the individual therapy sessions, we should focus on:

- helping Lawrence develop letter–sound relationships that would facilitate his reading (including of function words);
- helping Lawrence develop strategies to facilitate his word-finding difficulties (via practice of naming and the development of a self-cueing strategy).

We agreed we should not focus on either his difficulties with word comprehension or his difficulties in reversible sentence comprehension, because Lawrence did not see or experience these as problems. The real obstacle to communication, in everyone's view, was his difficulty in word retrieval.

LAWRENCE'S THERAPY

First we describe what we did in individual therapy. For his reading, we concentrated on developing his knowledge of letter–sound relationships, and then on blending phonemes. The therapy was based on that described by de Partz (1986; see also Nickels, 1992b).[1] This depends on using a self-selected relay word for each letter of the alphabet, chosen so that the first phoneme of the word corresponds to the most common realization of the first letter. The client learns to associate each letter with its relay word, and then to segment off the initial sound from that word. This is done first overtly and subsequently covertly (i.e., without the need for the relay word strategy). The aim is that by overlearning the task, letters will be automatically associated with their sounds. These relay words were chosen by Lawrence himself, with guidance from the therapist. For example, Lawrence chose "apple" as his relay word for A and "ink" as his relay word for I. Initial clusters were avoided, short vowels were used for initial vowels, and the right phoneme

1 With roots, though, that go back at least to Goldstein (1948).

was used (C for cat not city). A number of digraphs were also included (CH, SH, TH, and NG).

Having established letter-to-sound correspondences so that Lawrence could produce most letter sounds promptly and accurately, we introduced blending. Like de Partz (1986) we started with non-words. To facilitate the process of blending we started with vowel and consonant combinations (VC); the vowel can merge into the final consonant with minimal need for blending. Lawrence, however, objected to being asked to practise reading using non-words. He was not persuaded by our explanations that this was to ensure that he had good non-lexical skills that could be learned well before applying them to real words. We therefore complied with his wishes and moved on to practising these skills using short real words.

In designing therapy for Lawrence's word retrieval difficulties, we initially adopted a "multi-modal" therapy approach. This was built around evidence from Weigl (1961), Howard, Patterson, Franklin, Orchard-Lisle, and Morton (1985), and others that processing of a target picture name in relatively well-preserved modalities (in this case word-to-picture matching, word repetition, and copying) can make the word available for speech production (in this case) naming. The procedure, aimed at an initial target set of 25 nouns and 10 verbs, was as follows. First, we would ask Lawrence to name the target picture without help. This was to allow us to monitor progress and to offer treatment only for the items he found difficult. Then, if he had failed to name the picture correctly, we would ask him to do written word–picture matching (with one written word and a choice of four pictures), then to copy the word, cover it and write it, then cover the written attempt and produce the spoken name, providing progressive phonemic cues if necessary.

We abandoned this after 3 weeks, because Lawrence was making little progress with the target items, and because he didn't like the task. Despite our attempts to explain, he didn't see the point of word-to-picture matching which he found—or thought he found—trivially easy. We also abandoned this because he had started to fingerspell targets, very often getting the first letter right; he had acquired fairly competent letter-to-sound correspondences, and it was clear that he benefited from phonemic cues.

This meant that he had developed into the position where he had all the component skills to benefit from Nickels' (1992b) "autocue". This is an approach where, when retrieving a word, the client thinks of the first letter, sounds it, and then uses this self-generated phonemic cue to prompt word retrieval. Lawrence had all the skills necessary to develop this approach. Moreover, it has the advantage that it offers a *general strategy* to deal with word retrieval difficulties that can be used with any word that is problematic. Lawrence responded much more enthusiastically to this approach, partly perhaps because it built upon and acknowledged his developing skills and it had surface plausibility as a way of dealing with his word retrieval problems.

The third area targeted in Lawrence's individual therapy sessions was function word reading, introduced after 4 weeks of therapy. This was because he found reading function words especially problematic (probably because of their lower imageability and higher syntactic load), and this was a real impediment in his moving towards reading and understanding sentences and text. Here we used a "relay phrase" strategy based on work by Morton and Patterson (1980) and Hatfield (1983). Together with Lawrence, we generated relay phrases for common function words (e.g., fish *and* chips; I want *that* car). The aim was that Lawrence should learn to associate the relay phrase with a function word, and use this to cue production. In practice, he used this in conjunction with, as well as an alternative to, his letter–sound-based strategy to support function word reading.

Within the group setting, Lawrence was frequently perceived by the clinicians and other group members as "self-centred". Initially he was intolerant of others' communication difficulties, and sometimes laughed at their problems. This was an issue that had to be addressed for both Lawrence and a second client. Lawrence took the comments made in discussion on board and did seem to modify his behaviour. Alongside this, Lawrence expected the others to understand his communication. As many were unable to do as much communicative "work" on Lawrence's behalf as, for example, Patricia did, communication often broke down. This may have led to Lawrence's resistance to tolerating the difficulties of others. Their feedback to him was direct and unqualified!

Lawrence was usually motivated within the group, although this was dependent on topic and task. He continued to rely on his listener, focusing this predominantly on the group facilitator and a friend within the group. By the end of the therapy period, in the group Lawrence demonstrated an increased awareness of others' needs and difficulties. There was evidence that he used a self-cueing strategy. He would use fingerspelling (often of the first two or three letters) and then try and sound the word out. As his assessment results would suggest, this was not always successful (both in word finding and reading). He showed increased confidence, and was now willing to attempt most tasks.

OUTCOME OF THERAPY

The first way we assessed changes as a result of therapy was using the Comprehensive Aphasia Test, first at the end of the 12-week period of therapy, and a second time 3 months later. The results are shown, for the different functions of the CAT Language Battery in Figure 9.3. It is immediately apparent that Lawrence's results at the post-therapy assessments are not substantially different from those pre-therapy. This applies both to tasks that were focused on in therapy (naming and reading, for example), and those that were not (e.g., repetition and comprehension). This failure to observe improvement in the scores on a general aphasia test might be because Lawrence has, indeed, not improved. It might, on the other hand, be because

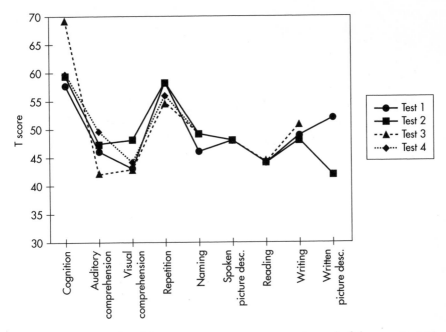

Figure 9.3 The results of the CAT Language Battery at the end of therapy (Test 3) and at follow-up 3 months later (Test 4). Scores 3 months before therapy (Test 1) and at the start of therapy (Test 2) are also shown.

this test, like others, probes performance in each domain with a very limited number of items, and has, as a result rather limited sensitivity to change.

Lawrence was tested with the Disability Questionnaire of the CAT on three occasions: once when we first saw him, once at the end of therapy, and again at the 3-month follow-up. The results of this are summarized in Figure 9.4. In terms of rated disability, there is a small amount of improvement after therapy. On the intrusion sub-tests there is virtually no change between tests 1 and 3 (before and after therapy), but substantially greater rated impact at the 3-month follow-up; we are not sure quite what to make of that.

Lawrence's treatment in one-to-one sessions had two main focuses: word retrieval and reading. Changes in word retrieval were tested in two ways. The Nickels naming test probes retrieval of 130 items with different numbers of syllables in the targets. The strategy that Lawrence had been taught— writing down the first letter(s) of the word, either in his head or on paper, and using his newly developed letter-to-sound correspondences to generate a cue for himself—would be expected to work better with shorter words where it would yield proportionately more information about the target. Changes in his naming scores are illustrated in Figure 9.5. Overall he improves from 20% in the pre-therapy assessments to 29% in the post-therapy

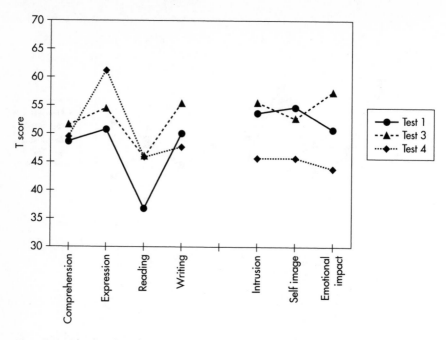

Figure 9.4 The results of the CAT Disability Questionnaire at the end of therapy (Test 3) and at follow-up 3 months later (Test 4). Scores 3 months before therapy (Test 1) are also shown.

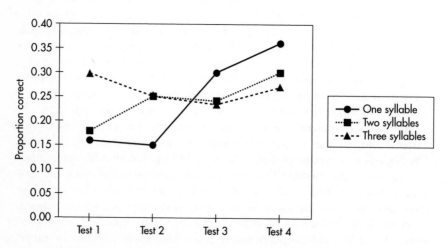

Figure 9.5 Naming accuracy for one-, two-, and three-syllable words over the four testing sessions in the Nickels naming test (n = 130).

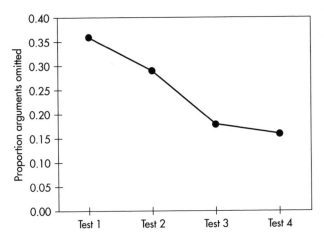

Figure 9.6 The proportion of obligatory arguments omitted in re-telling the Cinderella story over the four testing sessions.

assessments. This change, while small, is statistically significant (Wilcoxon matched pairs, $z = 2.14$, $p = .016$, one tailed). As Figure 9.5 shows, however, this change differed as a function of the syllable length of the target: one-syllable words improve by 18%, two-syllable words by 6%, and three-syllable words decline by 3%. This relationship between the amount of change and target syllable length is significant (Jonckheere trend test, $z = 3.05$, $p = .001$); there is greater improvement with shorter target words.

To assess whether there were any changes in word retrieval in a less structured task, we examined his telling of the Cinderella story, focusing on the proportion of obligatory arguments that were omitted. The results are shown in Figure 9.6. It is clear that the improvements in naming in the Nickels naming test are accompanied by a reduction in the numbers of arguments omitted in narrative speech.

The main thrust of reading therapy was based on the use of grapheme correspondences followed by blending of the phonemes to facilitate reading. This was supplemented, as described above, by a specific programme to aid reading of function words. Overall scores on the CAT reading sub-tests show no significant change in the reading of content words, but a small but reliable improvement with function words (see Figure 9.7). Further assessments concentrated on the components of reading that had been treated. Letter-to-sound correspondences showed only marginal, and non-significant improvement, from 19/26 pre-therapy to 22/26 at the end. These numbers conceal some more qualitative changes. Whereas before therapy he had only been able to produce a sound if he could think of a word that began with that letter—a process that was laborious, time consuming, and prone to error—after therapy he could do this with much more facility, without, in

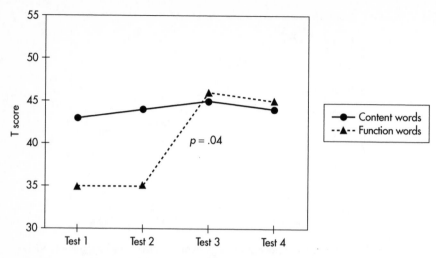

Figure 9.7 Lawrence's scores on the content and function word reading sub-tests of the CAT over the four testing sessions.

almost all cases, producing a relay word overtly. His blending ability was tested before and after therapy, using a 40-item test, all with CVC targets. This included both items where the onset had to be blended with the rime, resulting in a real word or a non-word, and where three individual phonemes had to be blended to produce either a word or non-word. Each of the four sets of trials was presented in separate blocks. Lawrence had scored very poorly on this blending test before therapy, but showed a dramatic improvement as a result of the therapy, as can be seen in Figure 9.8.

Much of the therapy involving blending had focused on short words. However, assessments used contained a mixture of short and long words. It appeared to be the case that Lawrence was able to sound out the letters of longer words but then failed to blend them, presumably because he had forgotten what the initial sounds were by the time he reached the end. Although there was little change in Lawrence's scores on reading, examination of his error patterns showed a different set of results.

As can be seen from Figure 9.9, only a small number of items led to either orthographically or semantically related responses. Similarly, few responses were unrelated to the target. In contrast, in the two pre-therapy tests, "no response" errors predominated, and these were usually Lawrence simply responding "no". Following therapy, Lawrence no longer failed to make an attempt but rather there was a dramatic shift in strategy, with him attempting to sound out many items. Note that this has been scored as a sounded-out attempt if Lawrence tried to sound out the first letter. On some items he sounded out more than this, but the first letter has been taken as a sounded-out response.

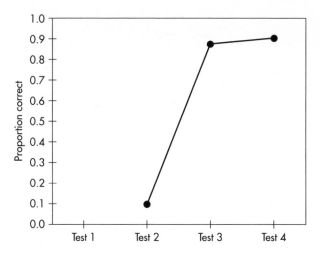

Figure 9.8 Lawrence's scores on the blending test.

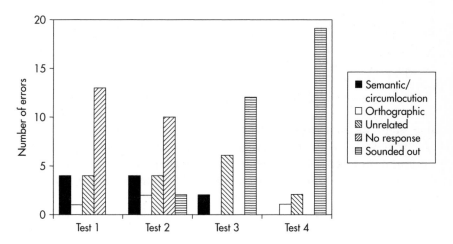

Figure 9.9 The distribution of reading errors on the CAT content word reading sub-test, over the four testing sessions.

These lengthy attempts characterized his responses in reading aloud following therapy. However, they were not always successful. Whilst Lawrence's ability to both sound out and blend the sounds from written words improved on testing, his reading failed to improve in terms of number correct. It is not clear how automatic these skills need to be in order to be incorporated into the reading task. Lawrence was able to carry out these "skills" in the test situation, but was unable to bring them together within a reading aloud task. In particular, while he achieved reasonable accuracy in sounding out the letters, he had much more difficulty in blending them (despite the dramatic improvement he had shown in blending when the to-be-blended phonemes were given to him by the examiner).

The overall pattern in changes shown in these assessments is clear. Lawrence showed small, but statistically significant, improvements in all the target areas worked at. The improvements were particularly prominent in the very specific skills worked at. These changes were not reflected in scores on the CAT Language Battery, mostly because a general language battery cannot be sensitive to small changes in specific areas, but also because Lawrence's language impairments were largely unchanged.

LAWRENCE'S PERCEPTION OF THERAPY

Despite little quantitative change in his spoken output, both Lawrence and Patricia perceived significant change in his abilities, especially in relation to his reading. There were qualitative changes in the kinds of responses he made, but these did not result in him being able to read more items correctly. Despite this, Lawrence became much more positive about reading—he would willingly attempt the reassessments and reported trying reading at home. This was in stark contrast to his frequent refusal to cooperate in reading tasks initially. This mismatch between actual test scores and perceived change is what became of interest.

One aspect that appeared to be important to Lawrence was that he felt he had at least some "control" of the situation; i.e., that he was influencing therapy via his comments. He had strongly disliked initial assessment ("imposed" and potentially highlighting failures), but as therapy progressed and his input was listened to, he became increasingly positive.

In an interview approximately 3 months after the end of his therapy at the clinic, Lawrence and Patricia were asked about his communication. This interview was unrelated to the clinic and carried out by an unbiased interviewer who sought to find out information about the kinds of strategies Lawrence had developed in relation to his communication generally. In this interview several comments were made about Lawrence's reading. When asked what Lawrence did when he could not think of a word, Patricia responded:

> *You usually write the first letter if you can't think of the word, because it's in your, you know what the word is.*

This demonstrated that Lawrence did use a fingerspelling strategy spontaneously in his communication.

A more extended—but unsolicited—reflection on the clinic by Lawrence and Patricia came later in the interview:

Interviewer:	What are your impressions of the therapy you received during your individual one-to-one sessions?
Lawrence:	Oh fantastic, really nice
Interviewer:	Did you enjoy them?
Lawrence:	Enjoyed them because, because A, B, C and that and its good
Interviewer:	Ah-ha, cause you were working on your letters
Lawrence:	Yes, oh-yes
Interviewer:	Do you feel anything changed in your time at the clinic?
Lawrence:	. . . Oh I don't know, it's it's everything
Interviewer:	Ah-ha
Lawrence:	It's everything
Interviewer:	What, what do you think did change Lawrence?
Patricia:	. . . There was one main thing wasn't there, that changed
Lawrence:	One main thing, yes
Patricia:	What was the main thing that you can remember that you couldn't do before you came to the clinic?
Lawrence:	A B C D E F G
Patricia:	You could actually relate to the letters
Interviewer:	Um-hum
Patricia:	Which he couldn't do before, whatever word you were trying to think about you'd say, what letter does it begin with or does it begin with /d/ "D" he says, doesn't matter, that didn't help him
Lawrence:	That's right
Interviewer:	Right
Patricia:	But that was the one thing
Lawrence:	And now now it's good
Patricia:	Yes, that was the one thing that you did learn
Lawrence:	Yes
Interviewer:	Ah-ha
Lawrence:	Smashing, really is
Patricia:	Even now, you still do that if he's thinking of a word he'll say the letters. You did that yesterday in the shop
Lawrence:	Yes
Patricia:	He'll write, either write the letters down but more now you actually say them whereas before you couldn't say the letters
Interviewer:	Right, yes
Lawrence:	And it really is good
Patricia:	Yes, it helps obviously, if you can't think of the word
Interviewer:	When you went to university to do speech therapy?
Lawrence:	Yes I think that's good that
Patricia:	That's when it got a lot better
Lawrence:	That's good
Patricia:	From er when he started there in February

Interviewer:	Really?
Lawrence:	Mm-mm . . . Cos it's
Patricia:	He couldn't think of the letters of the word 'till then
Lawrence:	It's like nothing, nothing at all
Patricia:	Couldn't think of the alphabet at all when we were reading
Lawrence:	Mm-mm
Interviewer:	Right
Patricia:	And you used to say it was like the word began with a B. He'd say, "It doesn't matter" it didn't help him at all
Lawrence:	No
Patricia:	He knew the word in his mind, he just couldn't say it, but me saying what letter it began with, it didn't help, until he went to the university. And it wasn't 'til after that, it's the first time you've ever been able to say the letters haven't you?

A little later the interviewer asked:

Interviewer:	Is there anything you feel able to do now that you could not do before?
Lawrence:	Oh its great
Interviewer:	Specific things Lawrence, try and pin it down. Do you think there is anything that you do either on or your own or with Patricia that you didn't do before?
Lawrence:	Yes
Interviewer:	Or do you think you do similar things?
Lawrence:	Well, er, Woolworths
Interviewer:	Ah-ha
Patricia:	Walk to Woolworths on your own. Yes, you wouldn't have done that normally, I've tried all ways
Interviewer:	Ah-ha
Patricia:	Give you more confidence in other words?
Lawrence:	Yes
Patricia:	Do you think its give you more confidence to go out on your own
Lawrence:	That's right yes
Patricia:	Like to buy something in a shop
Lawrence:	. . . Woolworths and er . . . camera as well
Patricia:	Sorry, you picked up, yes you did you picked up the films for the camera as well
Lawrence:	Yes

These comments show that Lawrence views his involvement in the clinic very positively. During the interview he described his experience at the clinic as "fantastic" and "really good". It appears that he sees himself as less handicapped in some areas, for example reading, and is willing to do things independently that he could or would not before.

FOLLOWING DISCHARGE FROM CLINIC

Lawrence now regularly attends a Speakability meeting once a month. Speakability is a national aphasia charity that co-ordinates self-help meetings which run approximately once a month. These are led by the people with aphasia themselves and have mixed content depending on what the group members wish. Lawrence has also been seen by his speech and language therapist to continue the reading work. There was a considerable gap following the end of clinic, but then he began an 8-week block of therapy, being seen once weekly. The focus of this block was discussed with Lawrence and Patricia and it was agreed it would focus solely on reading. Lawrence and his wife generated a list of personal words—family names, local place names, and shopping items—that he wanted to practise. They work on these during the week and progress is reviewed once weekly. Words that break letter-to-sound correspondence rules are marked with an exclamation mark.

The aim was to move him on from sounding out each letter to trying to get whole word recognition for a small set, or for Lawrence, at least, to be able to communicate what he did know of the word. Strategies such as use of rhyme have been developed, for example, if he is able to read the "at" of "cat" then he could use rhyme to generate which item he was reading.

In the future therapy may drop to once monthly with Lawrence and Patricia working on items together in the interim period. He is extremely motivated to work in his own time. It has also been recommended that therapy include work on developing the strategy of sounding out sufficient of the word to provide himself with a phonemic cue.

ISSUES RAISED IN THERAPY

What changes matter?

The central issue raised, for us, by our therapy with Lawrence is what we value in change. Ideally we, as therapists, would "provide treatment" that resulted in improvements in all of: global aphasia impairment measures (e.g., the CAT Language Battery); assessments of impairment in the target functions worked on; and assessments of disability (e.g., the CAT Disability Questionnaire). And we would hope to find that the client viewed the experience of the "treatment" positively, and saw it as resulting in real life changes in what they were able and willing to do.

It is not common, of course, to attempt to evaluate the effects of therapy at all these levels at once. We have tried to do so, and Table 9.1 summarizes the results that we have presented. We could view the results with satisfaction.

Table 9.1 A summary of the effects of therapy

Domain	Target	Source of evidence	Change
Overall language impairment		CAT Language Battery	No change
Impairment in target functions	Word retrieval	Nickels naming test and Cinderella narrative	Small, but statistically significant improvement
	Letter-to-sound correspondences	PALPA letter sounding	Improved ability; changes qualitative
	Blending	Blending test	Large improvement
	Content word reading	CAT word reading sub-test	No change
	Function word reading	CAT function word reading sub-test	Small, but statistically significant improvement
Language disability		CAT Disability Questionnaire	No significant change
Experience of therapy		Client interview	Very positive
Real life changes		Client interview	Some noted

Lawrence has improved in the target skills in a way that shows that what we did "worked". And Lawrence is very positive about the experience and, at least in some areas, feels that he can engage in a wider range of activities. Defending this position, one could argue that overall language batteries are not sensitive to the kinds of very specific changes that the therapy was designed to achieve; nevertheless, these specific changes may have effects in real life (cf. Howard, 1986).

A more sceptical view would point out that despite, in British terms, a huge amount of therapy (12 weeks × 3 days × 4.5 hrs = 162 hours), we have not managed to make any real change in his overall language abilities. That Lawrence said positive things about being part of the clinic can easily be discounted. He put a huge amount of time and effort into it; it is very hard to see something in which so much has been invested as anything other than worthwhile. Moreover, Lawrence is well aware of the time and effort clinicians put into the therapy; simple politeness requires that he say positive and appreciative things about the clinic. The sceptic could go on to argue that the only measurable result was that Lawrence could pick up the films from Woolworth's by himself—for some perhaps, not a change worth the effort.

The discordant pattern of results simply raises the question of what we mean by "benefit" from therapy. Subjective comments on change may not match objective measures of change. This may occur in either direction. What do we count as improvement? Improvement could be in targeted skills, formal testing, conversation, psycho-social aspects, the client's view of change, or any combination of these. One might protest that all of these are valid, and change in any is a worthwhile objective. Or one might put primary weight on one particular kind of evidence: perhaps on "formal" testing of language impairments because these measures are stable and reliable; perhaps on changes in social participation because the ultimate aim of the therapy is at just this level—although, as Elman and Bernstein-Ellis (1999) noted, it is very difficult to document such changes at more than an anecdotal level. These questions may have no simple answers, but they raise a number of uncomfortable issues about what we value and why.

When considering how we evaluate change, we must recognize that different kinds of evidence will be more likely to be persuasive to different audiences. For people with aphasia the perceived changes and benefits are, presumably, the most important outcomes. People commissioning services, on the other hand, are much more likely to be persuaded by more solid evidence from grounded assessments. Many therapists are, like us, anxious to explore the complex relationships between changes at different levels, recognizing that each has value, but of different kinds.

The "autocue" strategy

The therapy approach for word retrieval we ended up using with Lawrence was based on Nickels' (1992b) "autocue" method. Where a person with aphasia can access the initial letter(s) of a word they can't produce, they can fall back on the strategy of using their knowledge of letter-to-sound correspondences to generate a phonemic cue to aid word retrieval. Like Nickels (1992b) and Bastiaanse, Bosje, and Franssen (1996), we were able to show that this method was effective, to the extent that picture naming improved during therapy. And we know from the interview with Lawrence and Patricia that he does attempt to use this strategy at home. In the group we encouraged Lawrence to use this method when he had word retrieval problems. While this was sometimes effective, often it was not. The process of course requires that the correct initial letter is found; that the correct phoneme is generated from the letter; and that the person with aphasia can use this cue to produce their target. If any of these goes awry, failure is likely to follow. Moreover, engaging in this sequence is attention- and time-demanding. Speaking is itself attention-demanding (holding what you are trying to communicate, how far you have got in this, and so on). It is not straightforward to combine this with the complex word retrieval strategy. Because it is time-demanding, even in the tolerant context of the group, there is a danger that during the (possibly lengthy) pause the speaker will be interrupted and lose the floor. As Holland (1998) notes, this process can be "extremely laborious" and difficult to integrate into conversation.

The more the use of this strategy can become automatic, the less time- and attention-demanding it will become. As Luria (1947) emphasized, there is a real need to overlearn the component skills so that they can be combined relatively effortlessly in the reconstitution of function. It may be that Lawrence was less successful with this strategy because he had not acquired all the component skills with enough skill and automaticity. But it may be the case that this strategy can never be truly automatic. Its role may be more as a fall-back to use when confronted by moments of conversational breakdown and when it is successful as a form of self-therapy—producing a word in response to a phonemic cue does make it more likely to be retrieved later (Hickin, Best, Herbert, Howard, & Osborne, 2002).

While strategies such as this are attractive methods to use in therapy, because they provide a general (non-item-specific) means of dealing with word retrieval failures, we need to recognize that implementing them in real-life conversation may be more problematic than in formal tests of naming.

Group and individual therapy

Coming to the aphasia clinic involves a combination of group and individual sessions. In describing Lawrence's therapy we have provided much more detail about the content of the individual sessions. This is because the individual sessions are highly structured. The benefits, as we see them, of the group sessions are less tangible and less easily described and measured; and, indeed, as others have noted it is very hard or impossible to identify the important elements. In our view, the individual and group therapy play complementary roles and both are important.

During group sessions, people with aphasia have the opportunity to practise and implement techniques learned in individual sessions, in a social context that approximates more closely to the "real" outside world; it has the advantage that it is a relatively safe, sympathetic, and supportive environment. Other members of the group, both people with aphasia and therapists, can give real feedback on the successes and failures of communication. It offers opportunities for learning from, and sharing with, other people with aphasia about communication strategies that can be used, about ways of dealing with being a person with aphasia. In particular, it is possible to learn from other people with aphasia about activities that one can do, such as fishing, tennis, computing, and so on. This is a much more effective way of extending the range of activities that people can engage in than any kind of support and encouragement from a therapist. And, perhaps most important, it offers support, sharing of experiences, and solidarity.

Our clients are more sceptical than we are about the value of group therapy. While we see the group sessions as complementing and building upon the individual sessions and particularly offering opportunities for learning from each other, many of our clients are much less convinced of their value. For most of our participants, the group sessions they feel to be most beneficial are therapist-centred. Lawrence was fairly typical in seeing the real therapy as taking place in one-to-one sessions. He had little positive (or negative) to say about his time in the group, describing it simply as "too easy".

Therapy 7 years post-onset

As has been widely documented, the period immediately after a stroke that results in a person becoming aphasic is a turbulent time. The person with aphasia needs to come to terms with changes to their social role and activities they can participate in, and to cope with possible physical problems, in addition to the language difficulties. They also, typically, have a complex series of involvements with different therapies and different stroke services. This is also the period when the majority of input from speech and language therapists happens.

The early period after a stroke is also the period of most rapid "spontaneous" recovery, which typically happens most rapidly in the first few months post-onset and then at a decelerating rate, although this pattern is undoubtedly variable between individual people. The rationale for early intervention is, as Schuell, Jenkins, and Jimenez-Pabon (1964) argued, that one might be able to capitalize upon and shape the progress of spontaneous recovery, using perhaps the brain plasticity that may be greatest in these early stages.

While Lawrence had had organized, intensive, and effective therapy in the early period post-onset (see Grayson, Franklin, & Hilton, 1997), he had, at the point when we saw him, only the vaguest of memories of this early therapy that lasted for more than a year.

In the 7 years since the onset of his aphasia, Lawrence had inevitably come to some kind of accommodation with the limitations and difficulties this imposed on him. He relied heavily on his wife Patricia, as a communication partner and communication facilitator. But he was also anxious to engage in the world outside, as exemplified by his wish to undertake a computer course.

When he started his therapy with us, Lawrence had a strongly felt need to have more help, and both he and Patricia felt this would not have been possible earlier. Even when he spoke negatively about therapy, he continued to attend for 3 days per week and returned for his final assessments. While he was very positive about the idea of more intensive therapy before it happened (in prospect) and after it had happened (in retrospect), there was a mismatch with how he responded during his therapy, when he was often not especially positive. While this might have been because his experiences during therapy did not meet his needs and wishes, it may have been because the process of therapy challenged a set of established views about him as a person with aphasia, and a well-developed set of strategies for dealing with his communication needs. Willingness to engage with a process of change does not make that change any less difficult.

This raises issues of when therapy is appropriate for clients, given that Lawrence did have considerable amounts of therapy in the early stages following his stroke. So, one aspect of this is considering the "window(s)" of time when therapy might be appropriate. It is possible that, at least on average, large-scale language change is unlikely when therapy is undertaken at a point very long post-onset. Change may be limited by, at brain level, limited plasticity, and by effective and well-developed strategies for living with aphasia. However, there is substantial evidence that even a long time post-onset, motivated people with aphasia can make substantial improvement with well-organized and intensive therapy (e.g., Basso, Capitani, & Vignolo, 1979), and we have seen the same, but they do not always do so.

Nevertheless, one has to question why, in this country and elsewhere, such a small proportion of speech and language therapists' time and effort is used to engage in therapy with people with aphasia once they are over the early turbulent period. People who have come to terms with being language-disabled, who know about the limitations and possibilities it places on their lives, may be able to engage with more dedication and motivation in structured and intensive therapy to address particular areas that are of concern to them. It may be that intensive therapy may be more efficient at this stage; as far as we know there is no convincing evidence on this issue yet.

Education in Britain is seen as a life-long process, where people should be able to undertake courses to meet their educational needs at any point in their lives. This aim is largely, although perhaps not wholly, met. Rehabilitation, on the other hand, is seen as something that is undertaken in the early stages after the onset of the "disabling condition", and then ceases. We do not see why (aside from difficulties about the limitation in resources that really only reflects political will), therapy for people with aphasia should not be a service/process that people can access when they want to address particular needs at any point in their lives.

ACKNOWLEDGEMENTS

We are grateful for the help and cooperation of Lawrence and his wife Patricia (both names are pseudonyms); The Tavistock Trust for Aphasia for financial support; Janet Webster for help in data analysis; Alison Furness for permission to quote from her interviews with Lawrence and his wife; and all the students and staff working within the clinic.

REFERENCES

Basso, A., Capitani, E., & Vignolo, L. A. (1979). Influence of rehabilitation on language skills in aphasic patients: A controlled study. *Archives of Neurology, 36*, 190–196.

Bastiaanse, R., Bosje, M., & Franssen, M. (1996). Deficit-oriented treatment of word-finding problems: Another replication. *Aphasiology, 10,* 363–383.

Byng, S., Black, M., & Nickels, L. A. (unpublished) *The Birkbeck Reversible Sentences Comprehension Test.* London; Birkbeck College.

de Partz, M. P. (1986). Reeducation of a deep dyslexic patient—rationale of the method and results. *Cognitive Neuropsychology, 3,* 149–177.

Elman, R. J., & Bernstein-Ellis, E. (1999). The efficacy of group communication treatment in adults with chronic aphasia. *Journal of Speech Language and Hearing Research, 42,* 411–419.

Goldstein, K. (1948). *Language and language disturbances.* New York: Grune & Stratton.

Grayson, E., Franklin, S., & Hilton, R. (1997). Early intervention in a case of jargon aphasia. Efficacy of language comprehension therapy during early intervention. *European Journal of Disorders of Communication, 32,* 257–276.

Hatfield, F. M. (1983). Aspects of acquired dysgraphia and implications for re-education. In C. Code & D. J. Muller (Eds.), *Aphasia therapy.* London: Arnold.

Hickin, J., Best, W., Herbert, R., Howard, D., & Osborne, F. (2002). Phonological therapy for word-finding difficulties: A re-evaluation. *Aphasiology, 16,* 981–999.

Holland, A. L. (1998). A strategy for improving oral naming in an individual with phonological access impairments. In N. Helm-Estabrooks & A. Holland (Eds.), *Approaches to the treatment of aphasia* (pp. 39–67). San Diego: Singular Publishing Group.

Howard, D. (1986). Beyond randomised controlled trials: The case for case studies of the effects of treatment in aphasia. *British Journal of Disorders of Communication, 21,* 89–102.

Howard, D., Patterson, K. E., Franklin, S., Orchard-Lisle, V. M., & Morton, J. (1985). The facilitation of picture naming in aphasia. *Cognitive Neuropsychology, 2,* 41–80.

Kay, J., Lesser, R., & Coltheart, M. (1992). *Psycholinguistic Assessments of Language Processing in Aphasia.* London: Lawrence Erlbaum Associates Ltd.

Luria, A. R. (1947). *Traumatic aphasia.* [Translated from the Russian by D. Bowden, 1970.] The Hague: Mouton.

Morton, J., & Patterson, K. E. (1980). Little words—no! In M. Coltheart, K. E. Patterson, & J. C. Marshall (Eds.), *Deep dyslexia* (pp. 270–285). London: Routledge & Kegan Paul.

Nickels, L. A. (1992a). *Spoken word production and its breakdown in aphasia.* Unpublished PhD thesis, University of London.

Nickels, L. A. (1992b). The autocue—self-generated phonemic cues in the treatment of a disorder of reading and naming. *Cognitive Neuropsychology, 9,* 155–182.

Saffran, E. M., Berndt, R. S., & Schwartz, M. F. (1989). The quantitative analysis of agrammatic production—procedure and data. *Brain and Language, 37,* 440–479.

Schuell, H. M., Jenkins, J. J., & Jimenez-Pabon, E. (1964). *Aphasia in adults: Diagnosis, prognosis and treatment.* New York: Harper & Row.

Swinburn, K., Porter, G., & Howard, D. (in press). *The Comprehensive Aphasia Test.* Hove, UK: Psychology Press. [To be published 2004].

Weigl, E. (1961). The phenomenon of temporary de-blocking in aphasia. *Zeitschrift für Phonetik, Sprachwissenschaft und Kommunikationsforschung, 14,* 337–364.

10 Consumers' views of what makes therapy worthwhile

Aura Kagan and Judith Felson Duchan

Speech-language pathologists have long advocated for consumer involvement in setting goals and evaluating the success of therapies. One would be hard put to find a practising clinician or researcher in our field who would fail to see the advantages of involving clients in their own goal setting or in evaluating their own therapy progress.

Many speech-language pathologists use tools that are specifically designed to elicit input from consumers. For example, clinicians have conducted individual interviews with clients to find out their goals and their judgements about therapy progress (Pound, Parr, & Duchan, 2001; Simmons-Mackie & Damico, 2001). They have also interviewed individuals in groups and have used consumer satisfaction surveys and questionnaires to learn what consumers think about the services they have received (Rao, Blosser, & Huffman, 1998). They have designed therapies, such as Person Centered Planning, that require consumer input for evaluating success (Duchan & Black, 2001; Mount, 2001; Sanderson, 2000).

Information from individual interviews and groups has been used to conduct research as well. Clinicians have involved clients in self-evaluation research (Pound et al., 2001), action research (Horton, 1999), and research leading to the design of evaluation instruments (Lomas, Pickard, & Mohide, 1987).

These approaches to evaluation represent a move towards more consumer-led approaches and stand in contrast to objective and clinician-controlled approaches to evaluation that are typically used to judge the worthiness of therapy approaches. Generally speaking, objective controlled approaches do not take into account evidence having to do with the personal experience of consumers. (Note: The term "consumer" is one that is in common use in North America to refer to those to whom services are provided.)

This chapter reflects our interest in the views of consumers who still have aphasia post therapy; consumers who can reflect on what constitutes successful outcomes, based on their years of experience in living with aphasia. We will divide the chapter into several sections. First, we will examine clinical and research frameworks that facilitate or inhibit authentic consumer input to therapy evaluation. We will then describe examples of consumer consulting approaches that have been used to evaluate aphasia therapies. Following that, we will offer some methods that we specifically designed to overcome barriers to contribution by those with aphasia and will present the views of selected consumers who are experienced in living with aphasia on what makes therapy worthwhile. Finally, we will contrast the ideas of success put forward by these consumers with those found in existing consumer consulting approaches. We will conclude by suggesting ways to obtain authentic input from consumers about complex topics related to therapies.

EXAMPLES OF EVALUATION FRAMEWORKS USED IN RESEARCH AND CLINICAL PRACTICE

Speech-language pathologists, like all practitioners, base their evaluation practices in conceptual frameworks (e.g., Byock, 1999; Duchan, 2004). These frameworks govern the dimensions evaluated, and methods of evaluation, as well as the degree to which consumers are consulted in the creation of evaluation instruments and in the determination of their own success. They also influence the larger issue of who is regarded as the "expert" in the evaluation of outcomes. The influence of different frameworks provides possible reasons for the gap between what clinicians think should be done and what they are actually doing to involve consumers in therapy evaluation.

Perhaps the most commonly used framework is the *medical model*. Based on the diagnosis and elimination of physical disease, the medical model tends to portray the goal of intervention as a return to health. The aim of therapy and definition of success is to cure a disease or eliminate its symptoms. The approach to evaluation is influenced by the fact that this model is grounded in a restitution narrative in which a person's progress is seen as being along a pathway of return to an original, normal self (Becker, 1997; Frank, 1997; Pound, Chapter 3, this volume). There is little attention given to evaluating how patients cope with incurable diseases.

The medical model rests on the assumption that professionals are the experts who should be in charge of therapy decisions. It is argued that professionals have knowledge of research literature as well as the clinical experience needed to make informed clinical decisions. It follows from this line of thinking that professionals are in the best position to select and evaluate therapies. Consumers are seldom given an opportunity under this model to provide information about what else might have been done that would have made a difference in their lives. Nor are consumers consulted about their personal judgements about their improvement even in those areas being targeted in the study.

The medical model, when used to evaluate the success of treatment, is often associated with evidence-based practice, an approach that relies primarily on the use of objective standardized measures (Robey, 1998). Most researchers and agencies engaged in evidence-based practice call for well-controlled experiments with repeated trials. Performance of clients is

measured before and after the administration of a given therapy to determine whether the therapy produces statistically significant effects. The research is often based on the performance of large groups of individuals on
objective tests. The measures of improvement have been ones decided upon
by clinicians or researchers, with little attention paid to whether the changes
have had an impact on the ability of consumers to participate more fully in
society. The focus of these studies is often on what has been accomplished
by a very specific therapy.

A second framework commonly used by speech-language pathologists to
determine treatment and therefore indicators of clinical success, is the
psycholinguistic model. In this framework, communication is seen in terms of a
linguistic code made up of various levels of linguistic information (phono-
logy, morphology, semantics, syntax) that is used to comprehend or express
messages. Therapy success in this framework involves improvement in
processing linguistic information. Clients are evaluated for changes in their
abilities to comprehend or produce sounds, words, or sentences or to process discourse.

Although the psycholinguistic model differs from the medical model in
that it does not focus on illness, it does implicitly adhere to the restitution
narrative and also regards the clinician as the expert. Consumers may be
asked to rate their own improvements in various areas of linguistic competence, but in very general ways, since a full evaluation would require detailed
knowledge of linguistic systems and of language processing. In other words,
there is an information barrier to consumers in either providing expertise in
the construction of evaluation tools or participating meaningfully in the
evaluation of their own progress.

Subscribers to the psycholinguistic model also tend to favour the use of
standardized instruments and well-controlled experiments as a means for
obtaining evidence of the success of therapies. In this case, the dimensions of
success are psycholinguistic ones, and the instruments and experiments are
designed to reveal improvements in one or more psycholinguistic domains.

A third framework evaluates changes in *functional communication*. The main
emphasis in this framework is to evaluate a client's communicative independence in situations of daily living (Holland, Frattali, & Fromm, 1999).
An item on an evaluation instrument cast in this frame might involve rating
a person's ability to order food from a menu in a restaurant. Those with
aphasia have been found to perform better on functionally based tools than
they have on ones that focus primarily on their language abilities (Aten,
Caliguiri, & Holland, 1982). Tools in this framework often aim to capture
the degree of independence and/or burden of care.

A fourth clinical evaluation framework has been called a *person-centred
approach*. The name originates with therapists working with individuals
who have severe communication disabilities (for recent reviews see Holburn
& Vietze 2002; Mount, 2001) and involves evaluation of services from the
point of view of the clients receiving them. This framework has also been

Table 10.1 Core values in the life participation approach to aphasia (adapted from LPAA, 2000, 2001)

- The explicit goal is enhancement of life participation
- Everyone affected by aphasia is entitled to service
- Both personal and environmental factors are intervention targets
- Evaluation of outcome includes documented life enhancement changes
- Emphasis on availability of services as needed at all stages of aphasia

---

part of the thinking in a recent model proposed by The World Health Organization (WHO, 2001). WHO's *International Classification of Functioning* (ICF) represents a significant advance in its recognition of the importance of evaluating "participation" as well as body function and activities. Participation, however, is very narrowly defined and grouped together with activities. Furthermore, participation is evaluated by the healthcare professional, as in the medical and psycholinguistic models, rather than by the consumer. This is reinforced by the fact that the evaluator using the ICF must become familiar with the technical codes. Nonetheless, the ICF framework does leave considerable room for consumer input and, in our view, in order to be true to the model, the individual (personal) perspective needs to be explicitly included.

Finally, we are among a group of clinicians and researchers in North America who have proposed a person-centred framework for use with those who have aphasia. In this framework, called the Life Participation Approach to Aphasia (LPAA), consumer involvement is central because life participation is the explicit goal of treatment and the key area to evaluate (see Table 10.1). To use LPAA effectively, consumers must be actively involved in goal selection and must be regarded as the experts in evaluation of their own progress.

Judgements about therapy successes for individuals are based on whether the consumer perceives positive changes in "living with aphasia". Consumers therefore are the ones who are in the best position to judge therapy success. This framework requires authentic consumer involvement in order to ensure that the therapy has been relevant and that it has had a positive effect on their everyday lives.

In summary, the conceptual frameworks used by clinicians and administrators vary in the degree to which they incorporate consumer input. The medical model, one that casts the professional as sole expert and that aims towards the elimination of disease, affords little room for consumer input. Its accompanying experimental scientific approach relies on well-controlled instruments selected by the researcher. Similarly, the psycholinguistic model, requiring detailed knowledge of the linguistic system and its processing, allows for only cursory consumer input from consumers who are naive in these matters. The psycholinguistic model also favours objective experimental indicators when gathering evidence for therapy success.

The two frameworks that afford more room for consumer input are the ICF framework of the World Health Organization and the LPAA framework offered by a group of American and Canadian speech-language pathologists (LPAA Project Group, 2000, 2001). The ICF does not go as far as the LPAA framework in terms of necessitating consumer input on the evaluation of life participation. However, both models take into account the importance of treatment and evaluation related to coping with a disability rather than solely on curing it. In doing so, both require a focus on the lives of consumers.

CONSUMER-BASED INSTRUMENTS FOR EVALUATING THERAPY SUCCESS

Perhaps the most commonly used type of instrument for involving consumers in the evaluation of therapy success is the *consumer satisfaction survey*. These surveys usually involve a list of items in which consumers rate the quality of the service provided to them. The listed items usually have to do with aspects of service delivery and their own improvement. For example, a survey developed by the American Speech-Language-Hearing Association (1989), framed within a functional model, has 21 items grouped under seven themes. The themes are (1) the timeliness of the service, (2) the improvement made by the consumer, (3) the demeanour and courtesy of the clinician and support staff, (4) the knowledge and organizational skills of the clinician, (5) the quality of the physical facility, (6) the management of clinical service programme, and (7) an overall rating of the service. The consumer is asked to circle the best answer along a 5-point rating scale ranging from strongly agree to strongly disagree. They also have the option of circling NA (not applicable).

In the ASHA Consumer Satisfaction measure, there is a strong emphasis on the nature of the services provided. Of the 21 items across all of the seven themes, all but six have to do with the delivery of services, including timeliness, courteousness, management of schedule and referrals, expertise of the clinicians, and the environment. Three of the six remaining items require an overall evaluation of the service (overall satisfaction, whether they would come back, and whether they would recommend the service to others). The last three items concern the specific progress made by the client—one having to do with whether they are better, another about whether they have benefited from the service, and a third whether the newly acquired skills are retained after the programme ended.

A second type of consumer-based instrument is exemplified by the Communicative Effectiveness Index (CETI) developed by Lomas et al. in 1987. Like the ASHA FACS (Frattali et al., 1995), the CETI was designed within a functional frame. In the CETI, the consumers are the spouses or another person closely affiliated with the person with aphasia. The consumer rates the person's interactive skills (from "not at all able to" to "as able before the stroke"). The items range from functional goals such as "Getting someone's attention" and "Giving yes and no answers appropriately" to "Having a one-to-one conversation with you" and "Describing or discussing something in depth". The CETI is unusual in that consumers were directly involved in its creation.

A third type of consumer instrument is one that focuses on quality of life issues. For example, the Short Form 36 Health Survey (Ware, Snow, Kosinski, & Gandek, 1993) has been developed to determine the health and quality of life of those with disabilities. This rating scale to be filled out by consumers is designed to measure eight dimensions of quality of life: physical functioning (10 items), role limitations due to physical health problems (4 items), bodily pain (2 items), social functioning (2 items), general mental health (5 items), role limitations due to emotional problems (3 items), vitality, energy, or fatigue (4 items), and perception of general health (5 items).

Each of the above examples of consumer-based instruments has been used to evaluate aphasia therapy. They all involve standardized instruments in which consumers rate their progress along predetermined dimensions. The dimensions for most of the instruments have been determined by professionals and have to do with aspects of service delivery and improvements in various areas of communication or in overall health. Few have involved full consumer participation, in that the consumers have not been provided the opportunity to determine what dimensions of success are relevant for their particular circumstances. Nor have the instruments come to grips with how to surmount barriers for achieving consumer participation with consumers who have aphasia (but see Hilari, Byng, Lamping, & Smith, 2003 for a recent attempt to overcome this deficiency).

OVERCOMING BARRIERS TO CONSUMER PARTICIPATION

Clinicians who include consumer input in their practice typically do so by involving individual consumers in the process of setting their own goals or evaluating their own therapy. As a field, we have been less likely to pay attention to the expertise of the group of consumers who have been living with aphasia in the long term. This "attitudinal" barrier may be due in part to the influence of the medical model with its focus on curing rather than coping with long-term disability. It may also be due to the fact that most clinicians rarely come into contact with individuals who are no longer receiving aphasia therapy but are living with the consequences of aphasia. While these individuals with aphasia may hope to return to their former selves, they seldom can. They, as well as those with other types of chronic disabilities, often shift their hopes somewhere along the way, from full recovery of their communication abilities to being able to live satisfying lives, given their aphasia (Becker, 1997; Parr, Byng, & Gilpin, 1997; Pound, Chapter 3 this volume). By not paying sufficient attention to the views of consumers with chronic aphasia, our evaluation tools may be missing outcomes critical to success in living long term with aphasia.

A second barrier to full consumer consultation is inherent in the psycholinguistic framework that requires detailed technical knowledge of psycholinguistic processing. If psycholinguistics is taken to be the framework of evaluation, aphasia therapy success would be assessed by whether clients have improved in, say, their word-finding skills. To involve consumers fully in the design of a psycholinguistic instrument and in the evaluation of their own success would require that they too become familiar with the intricacies of psycholinguistic processing.

A third possible reason for the lack of widespread consumer consultation in the area of aphasia has to do with the issue of language barriers. It is especially difficult for consumers with aphasia to provide authentic, valid, and complex feedback about their therapies because of their language difficulties. Standardized consumer satisfaction surveys are not readily accessible to clients with language difficulties and consumer interviews involving the evaluation of therapies are difficult to conduct. (However, see Parr et al., 1997, for an outstanding example of how this has been done.)

We were interested in exploring methods for overcoming the barriers by (a) specifically targeting individuals who had at least a few years of experience in living with aphasia and who were therefore in a position to reflect back on their experience, thus acknowledging their unique contribution; (b) asking our questions within a life participation framework where they have knowledge and expertise because the subject matter was their own experience; and (c) providing support in order to get around the language barrier.

Targeting individuals who have experience in living with aphasia

The individuals who agreed to share their views with us have read what we have written about them and have chosen to use their own names. They have all received speech-language therapy and have had life experience in living with aphasia. They are currently regular participants in different activities at the Aphasia Institute in Toronto, Canada.

Prior to her stroke Pam Phillips worked as an office manager. She currently volunteers full-time at the Aphasia Institute. We were interested in Pam's views on dimensions of success for herself personally and for others with aphasia, as she has had extensive experience in living with aphasia. George Carter used to work in sales. He now participates as a member in conversation groups and recreational activities within the Aphasia Institute and also volunteers on an aphasia advocacy committee. Both Pam and George have mild to moderate aphasia. We spoke with them individually and together using a videotaped semi-structured interview format.

We also spent some time talking to other consumers at the Aphasia Institute in small groups. These consumers added to the ideas generated by Pam and George. Don Lingeman is a retired pharmacist who had a stroke in 1990. Like Pam, Oriana Quilici had a stroke in her twenties. At the time of the stroke in 1990, she was working as an accountant. Betty Wangenheim is a retired sociologist who had a stroke in 1999. Both Don and Oriana have moderate aphasia. The aphasia is obvious and does get in their way in some situations that are communicatively demanding. Betty has mild aphasia.

Discussion focusing on life experience of consumers

The project was framed for participants in terms of the following question: What makes therapy worthwhile? We conveyed this question in various ways, attempting to find out what they felt was worthwhile about therapy, given the investment of time, effort, and resources for all involved with aphasia (namely, consumers, speech-language pathologists, and funders). We explored the topic that we were investigating—why therapy was considered to be worthwhile—in light of the fact that many people will still have communication problems after therapies are over. Our specific aim was to find out whether consumers who have lived with aphasia for some time suggest different areas for evaluating success than those typically found in professionally designed instruments.

We interviewed our participants about what they felt they had achieved in their own therapies. Guiding questions and prompts were used to elicit their reflections. Pilot work helped us to create communicative prompts that were not too leading. We supported our consumers in thinking beyond their own particular life experiences so they could comment on potential indicators of success for others. The guiding questions about themselves included:

- Are there GOOD parts to your life right now?
- What are they?
- Are there FRUSTRATING things in your life right now?
- What are they?
- Why can't you do/enjoy X?
- What would help?
- What were stages of your success?
- How did you know things were getting better? (in the areas of success that ended up in the pie diagram described below).

Finally, in order to elicit more abstract thinking we asked our participants to relate their own experience to the dimensions of success that could be used when evaluating aphasia treatment in general. We did this by relating the specific aspects of their own experience to more general recommendations.

Getting around the language barrier and eliciting responses to a complex topic

As we learned through our pilot work, it is challenging to make our topic accessible to individuals with language problems. In addition, the notion of therapy success is abstract and difficult to talk about, even for those who do not have language difficulties. The language barrier made it especially difficult for our consumers to indicate the relative importance of different indicators of success that they had chosen.

In order to meet the challenge of the language barrier, we provided specifically designed support as indicated below:

• A written, abbreviated version of the large question: What was worthwhile about your therapy?
• Flashcards with a large written version of the individual question prompts listed above.
• A drawing of steps, used to support conversation about therapy progress over time.
• A pie diagram with flexible sections that allowed participants to attribute degree of importance to selected dimensions of success. When using the pie, we worked together with the participants to help them prioritize different areas of success. They placed a success domain in a particular segment of the pie and then indicated the size of the segment by moving the flexible "hands" or indicating the segment size as we moved the hands (see Figure 10.1 in results section for an illustration of the pie).
• Using Supported Conversation for Adults with Aphasia (SCA)™ as a framework (Kagan,1998a, 1998b), we checked with consumers throughout the interviews to make sure that they understood the topic and that we had understood what they had to say. We also provided them with alternative ways to respond. For example, we used gestures, rephrasing, simplified language, written key words, and drawings, within the context of natural conversation.

Analyzing the results of consumer participation

Our interpretative analysis was based on notes and observations of videotapes of the conversations. Using the notes and observations, we classified the responses of our participants into similar topics.

When interpreting our participants' comments, we asked ourselves "What is this comment about?". For example, several participants talked about their speech improving in the context of a conversation of what makes therapy worthwhile. We classified these comments together under the topic "talking better". Similarly, in the context of the prompt "Are there good parts to your life right now?" a participant talked about the importance of her being

Figure 10.1 Pie diagram showing relative degrees of therapy success for Pam.

able to drive again. This comment was classified under the topic of being independent.

When appropriate support was provided, the consumers we interviewed were able to converse in abstract, authentic ways. They reflected back on their experiences with aphasia therapies and responded to abstract questions such as the primary guiding question of "What makes it all worthwhile?". Although it was challenging, they were able to step out of their own life experience and reflect on the dimensions of success that they felt should be guiding therapy and evaluation of outcome. The consumers were also able to use the diagrammatic pies to portray the relative importance of different dimensions in terms of different allocation of resources. Some topics describing success that were put forward by the consumers were as follows:

Talking better

The speech pathologist put pressure on my larynx and I could talk and it was the weirdest thing and I thought I'm cured. Then I realized I can't talk and just work on it. The speech pathologist was encouraging. He motivated. Just go ahead and keep going... Try to phrase the words. Rochelle was encouraging me to speak

(Pam)

Getting out more, doing more

You have to get going. Doing, doing, doing

(Don)

Having hope

The hope is getting on in life. You have to have hope otherwise you're a nobody

(Don)

Having fun, enjoying life

Ask them to come in and watch the fashion show
(George talking about hope and ability to enjoy life)

Having satisfying relationships

You ask he, girl, the man, are you OK with all the different kids, your friends?
(Don talking about how to find out how people
with aphasia are doing)

Having self-esteem/confidence

You can do it because you are right in your heart

(Don)

You get the confidence to talk about aphasia

(Pam)

Feeling in control

Ten years ago, no. Now, ok.
(Oriana talking about changes in feelings of control over her life)

Being independent

My car . . . my baby
> (Oriana talking about the increase in her sense of
> independence resulting from her being able to drive a car)

Helping others

Help retirement, full of joy. Oh wow! Happy, ecstatic
> (Oriana talking about how important volunteering
> was in learning to live with aphasia)

Other dimensions included: improved communication skill of family members, feeling better (e.g., less anger) and improving academic skills (e.g., maths).

COMPARISON OF DIMENSIONS OF SUCCESS BETWEEN OUR CONSUMERS AND EXISTING CONSUMER-BASED INSTRUMENTS

Because of our particular line of questioning, the topics offered by the participants focused on engagement in life (e.g., getting out more, having fun) and psychological outlook (having hope, having self-esteem/confidence). These topics differ from those underlying many consumer satisfaction surveys in current use in aphasia treatment. For example, the ASHA Consumer Satisfaction survey focuses on service delivery features having to do with the clinician, the clinic environment, and the way services are rendered. These dimensions were not raised in the comments made by the veteran consumers.

The topics introduced by our consumers are also different from those included in published tools that compare past and present performance on specific communication tasks. Talking better, for example was only one of the topics covered by our participants. However, this increased breadth in areas covered should not be interpreted as a lack of emphasis or concern of our participants about communication.

A recent study conducted in South Africa (Band & Legg, 2001) supports our findings about the concern of people with aphasia about broad issues related to life engagement. Using Supported Conversation, the investigators interviewed ten consumers with aphasia as well as five caregivers on their perspectives on speech-language therapy. Four primary themes emerged from the data analysis related to areas that consumers felt were important: self-empowerment, the external environment, life participation, and emotional well-being.

CONCLUSIONS AND IMPLICATIONS

Our consumers were able to reflect on the impact the therapies had on their own success as well as to recommend what therapy outcomes might be of importance to others with aphasia. They offered indicators of success that were different from those found in existing instruments. Their recommendations and indicators were related to the life goals of the client rather than the quality of the services provided. Their topics fit well with the life participation models of aphasia. The consumers were pleased to have participated in the study and were enthusiastic about a role they might play in determining criteria for judging the success of their own therapies as well as therapies of others who are living with aphasia.

Our findings show that consumers who have had aphasia for a period of time can be valuable consultants to speech-language pathologists in the design of consumer input instruments for evaluating clinical outcomes. Current approaches to consumer involvement in aphasia service provision tend to be confined to having consumers evaluate the quality of the service. Our consumers focused more on life participation topics, such as whether the services resulted in people getting out and doing more, having more satisfying relationships, and being more independent.

Speech-language pathologists often focus strictly on the processing and delivery of the communicative messages when designing their indicators of improvement. For example, instruments showing communicative changes often include items evaluating changes in sentence structure, language comprehension, ability to exchange information, or abilities to maintain topics in a conversation. Our consumers treated communication in social terms, focusing on life participation dimensions.

Our results also show promise for increasing the involvement of consumers in the course of their own therapies. Supported conversation techniques, such as those used in this study, allow consumers to become authentically engaged in the setting of their own goals and tracking their own communicative progress.

Providing conversational supports, conducting semi-structured interviews, and working from the personal to the general are methods that show promise for involving consumers with communication disabilities in the evaluation of clinical services. In particular, the pie diagram has applications in many contexts where individuals who know more than they can say are asked to think about and prioritize items.

For many individuals and families affected by aphasia, the sole focus in the early stage of living with aphasia is on learning to talk again. Based on the views of our consumers who have the benefit of hindsight, we suggest that even in the early stages, therapy should occur within a broad participation-based framework that focuses on communication within a social context related to issues such as role, social relationships and life activities.

The purpose of our project was to broaden our views of therapy success by obtaining the perspective of a few consumers living with aphasia. The views of our participants and the use of this type of methodology should be kept in mind when developing instruments to evaluate the success of therapy, and when involving consumers in their own therapy planning and evaluation.

REFERENCES

American Speech-Language-Hearing Association (1989). *ASHA Consumer Satisfaction Measure*. Rockville, MD: ASHA.

Aten, J., Caliguiri, M., & Holland, A. (1982). The efficacy of functional communication therapy for chronic aphasic patients. *Journal of Speech and Hearing Disorders, 47*, 93–96.

Band, T., & Legg, C. (2001). *Insights into aphasia therapy: A study of client and caregiver perceptions*. Unpublished undergraduate thesis, Division of Communication Sciences and Disorders, University of Cape Town, South Africa.

Becker, G. (1997). *Disrupted lives: How people create meaning in a chaotic world*. Berkeley, CA: University of California Press.

Byock, I. (1999). Conceptual models and outcomes of caring. *Journal of Pain and Symptom Management, 17*, 83–92.

Duchan, J. (2004). *Frame work in language and literacy: How theory informs practice*. New York: Guilford Publications.

Duchan, J., & Black, M. (2001). Progressing toward life goals: A person-centered approach to evaluating therapy. *Topics in Language Disorders, 22*(1), 37–49.

Frank, A. (1997). *The wounded storyteller: Body, illness, and ethics*. Chicago, Il: University of Chicago Press.

Frattali, C., Thompson, C., Holland, A., Wohl., C., & Ferketic, M. (1995). *Functional assessment of communication skills for adults: ASHA FACS*. Rockville, MD: The American Speech-Language-Hearing Association.

Hilari, K., Byng, S., Lamping, D., & Smith, S. (2003). Stroke and Aphasia Quality of Life Scale-39 (SAQOL-39): Evaluation of acceptability, reliability, and validity. *Stroke, 34*, 1944–1950.

Holburn, S., & Vietze, P. (Eds.). (2002). *Person centered planning: Research, practice and future directions*. Baltimore, MD: Paul H. Brookes.

Holland, A., Frattali, C., & Fromm, D. (1999). *Communicative abilities in daily living* (CADL-2). Austin, TX: Pro-Ed.

Horton, S. (1999). Improving a service for dysphasia through consultation. *British Journal of Therapy and Rehabilitation, 6*, 424–429.

Kagan, A. (1998a). Supported conversation for adults with aphasia: Methods and resources for training conversation partners. *Aphasiology, 12*(9), 816–830.

Kagan, A. (1998b). Philosophical, practical and evaluative issues associated with "Supported Conversation for Adults with Aphasia": A reply. *Aphasiology, 12*(9), 851–864.

Lomas, J., Pickard, L., & Mohide, A. (1987). Patient versus clinician time generation for quality-of-life measures. *Medical Care, 25*(8), 764–768.

LPAA Project Group. (2000). Life participation approach to aphasia: A statement of values for the future. *ASHA Leader, 5*, 4–6. [Also on the ASHA website: http://

www.asha.org/aphasia-life-participation-approach-to-aphasia-a-statement-of-values-for-the-future.cfm]

LPAA Project Group. (2001). Life participation approach to aphasia. In R. Chapey (Ed.), *Language intervention strategies in aphasia and related neurogenic communication disorders* (4th ed.). Philadelphia, PA: Lippicott, Williams & Wilkins.

Mount, B. (2001). *Person-centered planning: Finding directions for change using personal futures planning*. Amenia, NY: Capacity Works.

Parr, S., Byng, S., & Gilpin, S. (1997). *Talking about aphasia*. Buckingham, UK: Open University Press.

Pound, C., Parr, S., & Duchan, J. (2001). Using partners' autobiographical reports to develop, deliver, and evaluate services in aphasia. *Aphasiology, 15*, 477–493.

Rao, P., Blosser, J., & Huffman, N. (1998). Measuring consumer satisfaction. In C. Frattali (Ed.), *Measuring outcomes in speech-language pathology* (pp. 89–112). New York: Thieme.

Robey, R. (1998). A meta-analysis of clinical outcomes in the treatment of aphasia. *Journal of Speech, Language and Hearing Research, 41*, 172–187.

Sanderson, H. (2000). Person Centered Planning: Key features and approaches. http://www.ibv.org.uk/helensandersonpaper.pdf

Sarno, M. T. (1969). *Functional communication profile: Manual of directions*. (Rehabilitation Monograph 42). New York: University Medical Center.

Simmons-Mackie, N., & Damico, J. (2001). Intervention outcomes: Clinical application of qualitative methods. *Topics in Language Disorders, 22*, 21–36.

Ware, J., Snow, K., Kosinski, M., & Gandek, B. (1993). *SF-36 health survey manual and interpretation guide*. Boston: Health Institute, New England Medical Center Hospitals.

WHO (2001). *World Health Organization, International Classification of Functioning, Disability and Health (ICF)*. www3.who.int/icf/icftemplate.cfm

Author index

Subject index